Woodbourne Lib
Washington-Centerville P
Centerville, Oh

D1169195

THE GHOST WORE BLACK

GHASTLY TALES FROM THE PAST

THE GHOSTS OF THE PAST SERIES

SELECTED AND EDITED BY

CHRIS WOODYARD

AUTHOR OF *THE GHOST OF THE PAST* SERIES
AND *THE HAUNTED OHIO* SERIES

Kestrel
Publications

ALSO BY CHRIS WOODYARD
Haunted Ohio: Ghostly Tales from the Buckeye State
Haunted Ohio II: More Ghostly Tales from the Buckeye State
Haunted Ohio III: Still More Ghostly Tales from the Buckeye State
Haunted Ohio IV: Restless Spirits
Haunted Ohio V: 200 Years of Ghosts
Spooky Ohio: 13 Traditional Tales
The Wright Stuff: A Guide to Life in the Dayton Area
A Spot of Bother: Four Macabre Tales (Fiction)
The Face in the Window: Haunting Ohio Tales
The Headless Horror: Strange and Ghostly Ohio Tales
The Ghost Wore Black: Ghastly Tales from the Past
When the Banshee Howls: Tales of the Uncanny
The Victorian Book of Death
See the last page of the book for how to order your own copy of this book or other books by Chris Woodyard

Copyright @ 2014 Chris Woodyard
All rights reserved. No part of this book may be reproduced or transmitted in any form or by any means, electronic or mechanical, including photocopying, recording, or by any informational storage or retrieval system—except by a reviewer who may quote brief passages in a review to be printed in a magazine, newspaper, or electronic media—without permission in writing from the publisher. For information contact Kestrel Publications, 1811 Stonewood Drive, Dayton, OH 45432-4002, (937) 426-5110. E-mail: chriswoodyard8@gmail.com

Several of these pieces appeared originally in the *Haunted Ohio* blog. The few stories included from the author's other books are marked in the text.

First Printing
Printed in the United States of America
Design and Typesetting by Rose Island Bookworks
Cover Art by Jessica Wiesel

Library of Congress Catalog Card Number: 91-75343

Woodyard, Chris
The Ghost Wore Black: Ghastly Tales from the Past / Chris Woodyard
SUMMARY: A compilation of 19th- and early 20th-century newspaper and journal articles on ghosts and hauntings from around the United States with commentary and annotations by Chris Woodyard.

ISBN 978-0-9881925-1-5

1. Ghosts
2. Ghost Stories
3. Ghosts—United States
4. Haunted Houses—United States
5. Ghost stories—American
BF1472.U6 W91 2014
398.25 W912H

Dedicated to Richard Crawford,
chronicler of Clermont County's history,
and everything an historian should be.

Acknowledgments

The Anomalist: Patrick Huyghe, Melanie Billings, and Chris Savia
www.anomalist.com

Dr Beachcombing http://www.strangehistory.net/

Bracken County [KY] Historical Society
http://brackencountyhistory.weebly.com/

Joseph A. Citro, Vermont Folklorist and Author of *Passing Strange, Vermont's Haunts, The Vermont Monster Guide*, etc.

Curt Dalton, http://www.daytonhistorybooks.com

Marsha Hamilton

Libby Hertenstein, Bowling Green State University Libraries

Killingworth Historical Society
http://www.killingworthhistorical.org/

The Killingworth Library http://www.killingworthlibrary.org/

The Lackawanna Historical Society http://www.lackawannahistory.org/

Susan Leonard, Rose Island Bookworks
http://www.roseislandbookworks.com/

Theo Paijmans

Susan Holloway Scott and Loretta Chase, the Two Nerdy History Girls
http://twonerdyhistorygirls.blogspot.com/

Paul Slade http://www.planetslade.com

Jessica Wiesel

Robert Wilhelm, http://www.murderbygaslight.com/

Table of Contents

Introduction

Resurrecting the Long-Lost Fortean Tale

"The stories continue to be told and our business is with the stories."

-Andrew Lang-

For many years I have spent days and nights excavating the morgues of old newspapers for the fresh corpse of a sensation. As a newsprint Resurrectionist, I try to rescue from obscurity the oddities, the ghosts, and the wonders that haunted our ancestors.

This is a book about those haunting obsessions. It is a sampling of paranormal preoccupations of the 19th and early 20th centuries.

Many of the narrators of these stories state: "I am not superstitious, but...." We find people wrestling over and over with the question of superstition vs. experience. "Superstition" is seen as the provenance of the poor, the uneducated and the unassimilated immigrant.

The 19th century lauded the self-educated and self-made man. Reason was paramount. Superstition equaled ignorance. While not wanting to be tarred with the ectoplasmic brush of the Spiritualists or the irrational, respectable people became baffled witnesses to the uncanny and inexplicable. It troubled them.

In these pages you will find anomalous and Fortean events of the past as reported by contemporaries. They are not documented as we would expect from, say, the late Dr. William Roll investigating a poltergeist case, but framed anecdotally, along the lines of letters to *Banner of Light* or other Spiritualist newspapers. The stories are presented as found in the file cabinets of 19th-century journalism—in their own historic voices. I may point out parallels or patterns, but, like people who see faces in clouds, I may be seeing patterns where there are none.

I have done what was possible to corroborate stories or to follow up, but sometimes the archive does not have a crucial newspaper edition or, a century ago, the story just ended. I've also tried to provide some context, annotation and backstories because the past really is a different country and topical references can be obscure. After each story you'll find a citation for that story, the state where the story took place, and notes or commentary.

I confess that I haven't tried to verify the truth of every single story. Some journalistic hoaxes are easy to spot. Other stories, often using names of real individuals are plausible enough to pass for truth. Newspapers also get the facts twisted. The raw material is here for a more thorough documentation by future historians. In this book, at this distance of time and space from the original events, we can trust nothing. But we can marvel at a hoard of Fortean treasures and historical oddities, resurrected for a new generation.

Soon it will be dusk. I have the dark lantern, the shovel, the hook, the sack. Let us go into the graveyard together.

✦•••——————•——•••✦

"Fortean" comes from Charles Fort, a researcher of all things strange. Fort, who lived from 1874 to 1932, spent many years researching scientific literature in the New York Public Library and the British Museum Library. He collected accounts of fish falls, phantom soldiers, and mystery airships, rains of blood and stones, poltergeist people and apparitions in *The Book of the Damned* (1919), *New Lands* (1923), *Lo!* (1931), and *Wild Talents* (1932). He was skeptical of conventional science, noting how often scientists ignored or suppressed inconvenient data.

Note on spelling and formatting.

I have kept most of the spelling as found in the original newspaper article except for obvious spelling errors. Punctuation varied greatly, depending on the newspaper. I have not tried to regularize this or make it conform to any standard. Period newspapers often inserted headlines into the text of an article for emphasis and these have been kept intact. I have divided some newspaper articles, which were often one long undivided column, into paragraphs for ease of reading. The language is as it came from the pencil of the reporter. It may include politically incorrect or bigoted remarks offensive to the modern reader. It should be understood that the sentiments expressed in these articles, no matter how odious or bigoted, are not my own, but those of the original journalist or newspaper in which they appeared.

The Ghost Wore Black:
Ghastly Tales from the Past

1.

The Ghost Who Wanted Her Hand Back

The Demanding Dead

> Ghosts seem harder to please than we are; it is as though they haunted for haunting's
> sake—much as we relive, brood and smoulder over our pasts.
>
> -Elizabeth Bowen-

Death does not put an end to desire. Ghosts appear with wants, demands, commands, and wish lists. These are the classic ghosts: the ones with a mission. We might think that the grave would offer scant scope for complaint, but even the entombed dead grumble that their crypt is too wet, their shroud pins are pricking, or—incredibly—that they can't breathe. The dead may come back to moan of a missing body part, denounce a murderer, reveal a will's hiding place, or to ensure that surviving children are being well cared-for. And some ghosts return simply to have the last word.

From the *Grand Rapids Enquirer*
A TALE OF HORROR AND FACTS
A NEW PHASE OF SPIRITUALISM

We have received the following letter from Dr. John Morton, a gentleman of veracity and professional standing, formerly from Cleveland, Ohio, and an old schoolmate of ours. We think its perusal will convince our readers of the entire truth of all that is said about modern Spiritualism:

GRAND TRAVERSE, Mich., Dec. 23, 1856.

EDITORS REGISTER:—I send you the following account of a most extraordinary event or transaction—or what you will— because in my opinion it ought not to be suppressed; but, on the contrary, thoroughly investigated. In the midst of the excitement here, such a thing as calm and unbiased examination is altogether out of the question; nor would it be safe to attempt it, inasmuch as the determination of the people is strongly to "hush it up." As I myself am one of the chief characters concerned in the affair, I dare not attempt, if I possessed the ability, to determine the character of what I am about to relate.

I left Cleveland to establish myself here, as you will remember, sometime last July—a young and inexperienced physician. Almost the first patient I was called to see was a Mrs. Hayden—a woman thirty-five years of age, a strong constitution, and a well-balanced mind (apparently), and (apparently) with little or no imagination. She was, however, a "Spiritualist," with the reputation of being a superior "medium." Her usual physician, Dr. J. N. Williams, was absent—hence her application to me. I found her laboring under a severe attack of typhus fever, which threatened to prove fatal. Having prescribed for her, I left, promising to send Dr. W. as soon as he returned. This was on Saturday morning. At night Dr. W. took the patient off my hands, and I did not see her again until Friday evening of the ensuing week. I then found her dying, and remained with her until her decease, which took place precisely at midnight. She was, or appeared to be, rational during the whole of my visit, though I was informed that she had been delirious the greater part of the week. There was nothing remarkable about her symptoms; I should say the disease had taken its natural course.

At the time of her decease there were in the room besides myself, her husband, Mrs. Green (her sister), and Mrs. Miles (a neighbor). Her husband, whom I particularly noticed, was very thin and weak, then suffering from a quick consumption, already beyond recovery. He bore the character of a clear-minded, very firm, illiterate, but courteous man, and a most strenuous unbeliever in Spiritualism.

There had been some subdued conversation, such as is natural in such scenes, the patient taking no part in it except to signify, in a faint and gradually diminishing voice, her wants, until about an hour before her death, when a sudden and indescribable change came over her features, voice and whole appearance—a change which her husband noticed by saying with, as I thought, wholly unwarranted bitterness:

"There go those cursed spirits again."

The patient hereupon unclosed her eyes, and fixed a look of unutterable emotion on her husband—a look so direct, searching and unwavering that I was not a little startled by it. Mr. Hayden met it with something like an unhappy defiance, and finally asked of his wife what she wanted. She immediately replied, in a voice of perfect health, "You know."

I was literally astonished at the words and the voice in which they were uttered. I had often read and heard of a return of volume and power of voice just preceding dissolution; but the voice of the patient had none of the natural intonation of such—it was, as I have said, perfectly healthy. In a few moments she continued in the same voice, and with her eyes still fixed upon her husband;

"William, in your secret soul, you *do* believe."

"Wife," was the imploring reply, "that is the devil which has stood between us and Heaven for so many months. We are both at the very verge of the grave, and in God's name let him be buried first."

Apparently without hearing or heeding him she repeated her words: "You dare not *disbelieve*."

"I do," he replied, excited by her manner, "while you are dying—nay, if you were dead, and should speak to me, I dare not believe."

"Then," she said, "I will speak to you when I am dead! I will come to you at your latest moment, and with a voice from the grave I will warn you of your time to follow me!"

"But I shall not believe a spirit."

"I will come in the BODY, and SPEAK to you. REMEMBER!" She then closed her eyes, and straightway sank into her former state.

In a few moments—as soon as we had somewhat recovered from the shock of this most extraordinary scene—her two children were brought into the room to receive her dying blessing. She partially aroused herself, and placing a hand on the head of each, she put up a faint prayer to the throne of grace—faint in voice, indeed, but a prayer in which all the strength of her great unpolished soul, heart and mind was exerted to its utmost dying limit—such a prayer as a seraph might attempt, but none but a dying wife and mother could accomplish. From that moment her breathing grew rapidly weaker and more difficult; and at twelve o'clock she expired, apparently without a struggle.

I closed her eyes, straightened and composed her limbs, and was about to leave the house, when Mrs. Green requested me to send over two young ladies from my boarding-house to watch with the dead. All this occupied some ten minutes.

Suddenly Mrs. Miles screamed, and Mr. Hayden started up from the bedside, where he had been sitting.

The supposed corpse was sitting erect in the bed, and struggling to speak! Her eyes were still closed; and, save her open mouth and quivering tongue, there were all the looks of death in her face. With a great heave of the chest, at last the single word came forth: "REMEMBER!"

Her jaw fell back to its place, and she again lay down, as before. I now examined her minutely. That she was dead there could be no further possible shadow of doubt; and so I left the house.

On the following day Dr. Williams made a post mortem examination of the body. I was prevented, by business, from attending; but I was, and am, informed by the Doctor, that he found her brain but slightly affected (an unusual fact in persons dying of typhus fever:) but that her lungs were torn and rent extensively, as if by a sudden, single and powerful effort, and suffused, partially, with coagulated blood. These were all the noticeable features of the case. She was buried on the afternoon of the same day.

About two weeks after the death of his wife I was called to visit Mr. Hayden. On my way I met Dr. Williams and told him my errand, expressing some surprise at the preference of the family for myself, as I knew him to be a safe and experienced practitioner. He replied that nothing could hire him to enter that house. He "had seen things that—well, I would find out when I got there."

I was considerably amused by the Doctor's manner and warmth; and beguiled my way by fancying what had alarmed him—a physician—from his duty.

On my arrival I found no person present with the patient except Mrs. Green, who informed me that the spirits had been playing such pranks that not a soul, Dr. W. included, could be induced to remain. The children had been gone some time. They were at her house.

I found the patient very low, and with no prospect of surviving the attack. He was, however, quite free from pain, though very weak.

While I was in the house, I noticed many manifestations of the presence of that power called spiritualism. Tables and chairs were moved and re-moved; billets of wood thrown upon the fire, and doors opened and shut, without any apparent agency. I heard struggles and unaccountable noises, too; and felt an unusual sensation, caused, no doubt, by the mysteries which surrounded and mocked me. Noticing my manner, the patient observed:

"It is nothing. You must get used to it, Doctor,"

"I should not be content unless I could explain them, as well as become indifferent to them," I replied.

This opened the way to a long conversation, during which I probed my patient's mind to the bottom, but without detecting a shadow of belief. Speaking of his wife, he said:

"You heard Ellen promise to warn me of my time to die?"

"I did—but did you believe her?"

"No. If it is possible, she will keep her word, in spite of heaven or hell. But it is simply impossible. She promised to come in the body and speak to me. I shall accept no other warning from her, save the literal meaning of her words."

"And what then?"

"How much of the body is there left, even now, Doctor?— and she has not come yet. She promised to come from the grave. Can she do it? No; it is all a humbug-—a delusion. Poor Ellen! Thank God, Doctor, the devil, which so haunted her life, and stood between her soul and mine, cannot reach her now."

"But if she should come; you may be deceived."

"I cannot. Others must see her, too, and hear her. I shall believe no spectre, if there are such things. Her body as it is, or will be—let *that* speak if it can!"

From that day up to the hour of his death I was with him almost constantly; and was daily introduced to some new and startling phenomenon. The neighbors had learned to shun the house, and even the vicinity, as they would the plague, and strange stories traveled from gossip to gossip, acquiring more of the marvelous at every repetition. Nevertheless, my practice increased.

On the morning of November 30th I called earlier than usual. During this visit, the manifestations of a supernatural presence were more frequent, wild and violent than ever before. I was informed that they had been exceedingly violent during the preceding night. Their character, too, had been greatly changed. Beside the moving of all moveable articles, the tinkling of glasses, and the rattle of tin-ware, there were frequent and startling sounds, as of whispered conversation, singing and subdued laughter—all perfect imitations of the human voice, but too low to enable me to detect the words used, if words they were. Still, however, none of these unusual sounds had entered the sick room. They followed the footsteps of Mrs. Green like a demon echo; but paused upon the threshold of that room as if debarred by a superior power from entering there.

I found Mr. Hayden much worse and sinking very fast. He had passed a bad night. Doubtful whether he would survive to see another morning, I left him, promising to call at evening, and spend the night with him, resolved, in my secret thoughts, to be "in at the death." If there was to be a ghostly warning, I meant to hear it, and, if possible, solve the strange enigma.

The day had been exceedingly cold and stormy, and the night had already set in, dark and dismal, with a fierce gale and a driving storm of rain and hail, when I again stood beside my patient. The moment I looked at him, I perceived unmistakable indications of the near approach of death upon his features. He was free from pain, his mind perfectly clear; but his life was ebbing away, with every breath, like the slow burning-out of an exhausted lamp.

Meanwhile the storm rose to a tempest and the gloom grew black as death in the wild night without. The wind swept in tremendous gusts through the adjoining forest, rattling the icy branches of the trees, and came wailing and shrieking through every crack and cranny of the building.

Within there was yet wilder commotion. All that had been said or sung, written or dreamed of ghostly visitations was then and there enacted. There was the ringing of bells, moving of furniture, crash of dishes, whispers, howls, crying, laughter, whistling, groaning, heavy and light footsteps, and wild music, as if in very mockery of the infernal regions. All these sounds grew wilder with the rising gale, until towards midnight they were almost insufferable.

As for us three—the patient, Mrs. Green and myself—we were as silent as death itself. Not a word passed our lips after nine o'clock. As for the state of our minds, God only knows. Mine, in the wild whirl of thought and event which followed, forgot all the past, save what I have recalled and penned, bit by bit, above. I remember only looking for the final catastrophe, which grew rapidly nearer, with a constant endeavor to concentrate all my faculties of mind and sense upon the phenomenon which I, at least, had begun to believe would herald the loss of my patient.

As it grew closer upon twelve o'clock (for upon the striking of that hour had my thoughts fixed themselves for the expected demonstration,) my agitation became so great that it was with extreme difficulty I could control myself.

Nearer and nearer grew the fatal moment—for fatal I perceived it would be, to the patient at least; and, at last, the seconds trembled on the brink of midnight; the clock began to strike. One—two—three! I counted the strokes of the hammer, which seemed as though they never would have done—ten—eleven—twelve! I drew my breath again. The last lingering echo of the final stroke had died fairly away; and, as yet there was no token of any presence save our own.

All was silent. The wind had lulled for a moment, and not a sound stirred the air within the house. The ghosts had fled. I arose, and approached the bedside. The patient was alive—drawing his breath very slowly—dying. The intervals between his gasps grew longer; then he ceased to breathe altogether—he was dead!

Mrs. Green was sitting in her place, her elbows resting on her knees, her face buried in her hands. I closed the open mouth and pressed down the eyelids of the dead. Then I touched her on the shoulder.

"It is over," I whispered.

"Thank God!" was her fervent reply.

Then we both started. There was a rustling of the bed clothes! Mr. Hayden was sitting erect, his eyes wide open, his chest heaving with a mighty effort for one more inspiration of the blessed air. Before I could reach him he spoke: "My God! She is coming!"

At the same instant, the wind came back with a sudden and appalling gust, and a wild shriek as it swept through the crevices of the building. Then there was a crash of the outer door! then a staggering and uncertain step in the outer room! It approached the sick room! the latch lifted! the door swung open! and then, my God what a spectacle!

I wonder, even now, that I dare describe it—think of it— remember it. I wonder I believed it then, or do now; that I did not go mad or drop down dead.

Through the open door there stepped a figure—a figure not of Mrs. Hayden, nor of her corpse, nor of death—but, a thousand times more horrible, a thing of corruption and decay, of worms and rottenness.

The features were nearly all gone, and the skull, in places, gleamed through, white and terrible. Her breast, abdomen and neck had been eaten away; her limbs were putrid, green, and inexpressibly loathsome, the cavities of her shoulders, chest, abdomen, neck and thighs, were a living mass of great and ugly grave worms, which, as she stepped, dropped away to the floor, together with gouts and clots of putrid flesh! Her trail, over the threshold and into the outer darkness, was marked by these loathsome tokens, a luminous line of corruption and crawling worms, the effluvia of which was most horrible!

And yet to those putrescent jaws there was born a voice—smothered, indeed, and strange, but distinct:

"Come! William! They wait for you—I wait!"

I dared not turn my eyes from the intruder—I could not if I dared— though I heard a groan behind me and a fall.

Then it—the thing before me—sank down upon the floor, in a heap, dark and loathsome—a heap of putrescence and dismembered fragments.

I remember that I did not faint, that I did not cry out. How long I stood transfixed, fascinated, I knew not; but, at last, with an effort and a prayer, I turned to the bed. Mr. Hayden had fallen upon the floor, face downward, stone dead. I raised and replaced him; I composed his limbs; I closed his eyes; I bound up his chin; I crossed his hands upon his breast, and tied them there. Then I bore out the body of his sister, insensible but not dead, into the pure air—out of that horror and stench into the storm and darkness—out of death into life again!

County of Grand Traverse, Michigan, ss:

Mrs. Josepha H. Green, being duly sworn, deposes and says, that the letter of Dr. John Morton, hereto appended, which she has read, is strictly true, so far as it goes, though much of the history of what occurred at her brother's (the late Mr. Hayden) house is omitted, and this she deposes of her own knowledge. JOSEPHA H. GREEN.

Sworn and subscribed before me, a notary public, in and for the county of Grand Traverse and State of Michigan, on the 20th day of December, A. D. 1856.

JAMES TAYLOR, Notary Public. County of Grand Traverse, Michigan, ss:

James Hudson, being duly sworn, deposes and says, that he, in company with Geo. Green, Albert J. Bailey and Henry K. Smead, on the 1st day of Dec. last past, in the afternoon of said day, did go to the house of William H. Hayden, then deceased, for the purpose of burying the body of said Hayden, deceased; and that they found upon the floor of the room in which the body of the said deceased lay, and near the door of the said room, the putrid remains of a human corpse, a female, as the deponent verily believes and avers; and that they carried away and buried the body of the said Hayden, deceased; and found the grave of the wife of said Hayden, deceased in the month of August last, open at the head of said grave, and that said grave was empty of the body of said wife of said Hayden, deceased, being gone from said grave; and that they returned to said house wherein said Hayden died; and, after removing the furniture from said house, the deponent did, at the request of Mrs. Green, sister of said Hayden, deceased, set fire to said house, and that said house was entirely consumed, with all that remained in said house, and burned to ashes. This I aver of my own knowledge. JAMES HUDSON.

We aver and solemnly swear that the above affidavit is strictly and entirely true, of our own knowledge.

GEO. GREEN,
ALBERT J. BAILEY
HENRY K. SMEAD,

Sworn and subscribed before me, a notary public, in and for the county of Grand Traverse and State of Michigan, on this 20th day of December, A. D. 1856.

JAMES TAYLOR, Notary Public.

Plain Dealer [Cleveland, OH] 17 January 1857: p. 2 MICHIGAN

NOTE: There are several versions of this story, including one that is set in March instead of December. Despite the official-looking affidavits, I can find no evidence for the existence of any of the people involved. If it is not a fictional story, Mrs. Hayden's grave being opened at the head suggests that body snatchers had been at work in their usual efficient manner: breaking open the head of the coffin and dragging the corpse out by the neck. However it is unlikely that the grave stood open from August to December with no one noticing and a badly decomposed corpse was worthless to a body snatcher's customers. It seems far-fetched, but could someone have dug up Mrs. Hayden and used her corpse to play a horrid joke on the Doctor?

But it is a cracking yarn, probably based on a combination of two stories by Edgar Allan Poe: "The Facts in the Case of M. Valdemar," (1845) with its loathsome descriptions of the instant putrefaction of a corpse and "The Fall of the House of Usher," (1839) where Madeline Usher returns from being buried alive. "The Facts in the Case" was originally published, not as fiction, but as a factual account, although Poe eventually admitted the hoax.

The question of fiction or exaggeration aside, the idea of the dead returning to convey some message was widely believed both in and out of the Spiritualist fold. And despite the tale's sensationalism, the portrayal of the conflict between husband and wife over Spiritualism adds a realistic note. The Hydesville Rappings heralded the beginning of Victorian Spiritualism in 1848, less than a decade before this story. We may look at Spiritualism with an indulgent eye, as a harmless, if eccentric pursuit, yet it was taken very seriously as a new revelation. Just as religious differences could destroy relationships, conflicts between believers and non-believers in Spiritualism began tearing marriages apart. Some women fell under the spell of Spiritualist mediums; some men were bewitched by "spirit brides" or young lady mediums. Both wives and husbands were sent to the insane asylum for their beliefs. For a critical, contemporary look at the damage done by Spiritualist belief, see *Spirit-Rapping Unveiled! An Expose of the Origin, History, Theology, and Philosophy of Certain Alleged Communications From the Spirit World,* Rev. H. Mattison, A.M. (New York: Mason Brothers) 1853. While the book has its own agenda, it contains a shocking toll of broken marriages, insanity, and suicide.

Other ghosts worried about very mundane concerns.

His Sister's Ghost.

A ghost that stalks about in the daytime is worrying Ambrose Laperle of 27 Whitcomb Street. The apparition is the form of a sister who died about a month ago. She appears to him, he tells neighbors, at his home, on the street, and as he does his work at a loom in the South Village mill. She wears a shawl over her head and carries her hands hanging stiffly by her side. She talks to him, but he cannot muster up courage enough to reply or else he is stricken dumb when she is around.

On several occasions while at work weaving in the mill he missed his reed hook and scissors. Usually he has them attached to his trousers waistband, and when he reaches for them they are gone. Search as much as he will he cannot find them anywhere, but after a few moments they return, but he sees no hand replace them nor any fingers loosen them from their accustomed place.

His sister confines her conversation with him to a small bill for rent she owed him previous to her death, and if he could talk he would tell the ghost to never mind payment of the bill. The apparition has been appearing to the man for about a week. In life his sister, when on the street and often about the house was in the habit of wearing a shawl thrown over her head and shoulders, and her spiritual visits to this earth are made in this customary wearing apparel. Frequently he has encountered the ghost in the hall of his home. Webster Mass. Correspondent, Chicago *Inter Ocean*.

Salt Lake [UT] Tribune 29 March 1903: p. 23 MASSACHUSETTS

NOTE: Laperle was a weaver in a Webster woolen mill. The reed hook was used to pull warp threads through the comb-like "reed," which pushes the weft threads together. Its handle usually has a small hole for hanging on a belt.

This next distressing tale hinges on the age-old dilemma of the step-mother. The nineteenth-century division of labor was such that few men could cope with household chores and childcare without help. A man with children who lost his wife needed to find a replacement quickly. And if that replacement was not kind to the children, there would be hell to pay when a ghost came to call.

DRIVEN From Home By a Spirit.
The Ghost of a First Wife Returns to Haunt Her Successor.

The locality in which this motherly ghost appears is what is known as Baltimore No. 2, a settlement of Irish and Welsh miners, who work in the Baltimore vein. The houses are red company structures, and in one of them lives Cornelius Boyle, a young man who is quite prominent in politics, having often been chosen as delegate from his ward to Democratic conventions.

Mr. Boyle's wife died about two months ago, leaving four small children. Two weeks ago he married again. Mrs. Boyle No. 2 spent a very happy week with her husband while on their wedding tour. But since their return she has led a most unhappy existence. She has been haunted, she says, by the first Mrs. Boyle, who during the last week visited her almost every day. After these visits Mrs. Boyle has remained unconscious for several hours.

I went to the place to-day and found Mrs. Boyle in the house of a neighbor, the visit she received from the spirit of the first Mrs. Boyle last Saturday having caused such a serious shock to her nerves that she says she will never enter the house again. Her husband, an intelligent young man, 28 years old, was with her and two children were playing about the room.

SHE IS A YOUNG WIFE

Mrs. Boyle is very young for a wife, being hardly 17 years old. She is a pretty girl. She was Miss Sarah Cullings before she was married two weeks ago, and lived in Ashley, near here. She met her husband last St. Patrick's Day, and not quite a month afterward they were married in Phillipsburg, N.J., by Rev. Father Burke. The week following they spent in New York and last week arrived at Boyle's home in Baltimore No. 2.

"I was washing some clothes in the kitchen Monday afternoon when I experienced a most singular feeling, as though somebody were in the room with me. I looked around but could see nobody. Then I went into the parlor, but no one was there. When I returned to the kitchen all the chairs and tables were upset and my washing spilled on the floor. I set them right again. Immediately they were thrown down. At that instant there swept by me a figure of no particular shape, except the head, and that I saw distinctly. The face was a woman's and had such a peculiar look about it that I cannot forget it. It was gone in an instant and I fainted. The children called in the neighbors, and after some time I was revived. When my husband returned home I told him the story. He called it a joke and said I had imagined it all. I tried to think no more about it.

"The next day," continued Mrs. Boyle, "I was alone in the kitchen making some bread when I again felt the dreadful sensation of the peculiar presence. It gradually grew in shape, until the head was fully visible. Then I could see the face. It was the same as on the day previous. Then it gradually faded away, and again I fainted from fright.

"Fearing to be alone the next day, I sent for my sister. That night I again told my husband about the ghostly visitor. My nerves were unstrung and I was very much excited. Mr. Boyle got some books to quiet me, and we began looking them over. Among the books was a photograph album. He was turning over the leaves and explaining who the persons were. Finally he turned a page, and there before me was

THE FACE OF THE GHOST

I had seen. So suddenly was the face presented before me that I shrieked with horror. My husband sprang to his feet, and asked me what was the matter. All I could do was to point to the album, which had fallen to the floor, and say, "That face, that face." "What about it," cried my husband. "It is the same as the ghost's I saw." He was very much horrified at this, and exclaimed, "It is the face of my first wife." Then he believed what I had said regarding the apparition, for he knew I have never seen her nor any photograph of her, until he showed me the one in the album.

"On Thursday my sister and I were in the kitchen, cutting carpet rags. Among the old clothing was a jacket of 'Jamesey's,' who is my husband's oldest boy. I took it out of the bag to give to Annie, my sister. I leaned over to hand it to her. As I did so it was pulled from my hands and thrown on the floor. At the same instant I felt the presence of the ghost, although I could see nothing. My sister then picked the jacket from the floor. As she did so the jacket was torn from her hands, and the ghost stood before us, the eyes glaring as though in anger. My sister shrieked with terror and fell into my arms. I managed to retain consciousness and the apparition vanished. Both Annie and I then went outside and would not go in until my husband returned home. Then Annie went out to Ashley. She was afraid to stay with me.

"The next day was Friday and my husband remained at home all day. In the evening he went down to the store and I began undressing 'Jamesey,' who is older than the others and had been allowed to stay up. He was very naughty and I had to scold him. Then I put him to bed, and returned to the sitting room.

"As I entered the room, the

GHOST STOOD BEFORE ME

"I was becoming less afraid of it, and, although greatly frightened, I managed to say: 'what do you want?' The ghost pointed one of its hands at me, and, although I could not see the mouth move, it spoke and said: 'Treat my children well,' three times, and very slowly.

"When my husband returned a few minutes later I was in a fainting fit. We agreed to leave the house as soon as we could find another. I did not want to stay another day, but my husband persuaded me to stay in order to pack up some of the goods.

"Yesterday afternoon 'Jamesey' was a naughty boy again. I caught his arm and began to shake him. Immediately the ghost appeared. It seemed to come from behind the kitchen stove. One hand caught the boy and pulled him from me, while with the other hand she struck me on the head.

"It was all over in a few seconds, and as the ghost disappeared I snatched up the boy and ran out of the house. I went to Mrs. McLaughlin's across the street. 'You look ill, Mrs. Boyle,' she said. 'What is the matter? Why, your head is all covered with ashes.' I put my hand on my head and there was ashes there. They must have come from the ghost's hands."

The boy "Jamesey" was then called. He is a bright little fellow, about 5 years of age. He was asked what had happened yesterday afternoon. "Me was bad boy," he said. "She shake me," pointing to Mrs. Boyle. "Then my mamma—not my new mamma, my old one—come out from behind stove and pull me away. I haven't seen my old mamma for a long time."

Mr. Boyle said he did not believe in ghosts, but he believes what his wife says, and will not allow her to go into the house again.

Cincinnati [OH] Enquirer 3 May 1894: p. 10 PENNSYLVANIA

So far, merely a standard visitation from the dead mother as a warning. But things quickly took a more sinister turn.

BABY BURNED BY A GHOST
Mrs. Boyle Declares That the Jealous Spirit is That of Her Husband's First Wife.
FOUR INCENDIARY VISITATIONS

Wilkesbarre, Pa., May 11, 1894. Mrs. Cornelius Boyle, wife of a well-known young miner of this city, was visited about two weeks ago by a supernatural being, whom she said was Boyle's first wife.

As told in the *Herald* at the time, Mrs. Boyle the second was married about two months after the first wife's death, and the ghost, according to her, had appeared to warn her to take good care of the four children.

The appearance of the ghost so affected Mrs. Boyle that her husband took another house. In this new place they lived happily until Tuesday, when Mrs. Boyle had another visit from the ghost. This time she said that it threatened her with horrible tortures if the children were not properly cared for.

Matters reached a climax yesterday morning when a bed on the second floor was found to be on fire. An alarm was rung, the Fire Department responded, and the flames were extinguished, but scarcely had the firemen left when the same bed was again discovered on fire.

The firemen returned and extinguished the blaze a second time. Later in the day the house was found to be on fire again, and the Fire Department was called out a third time.

BLAMES IT ALL ON THE GHOST.

An oil can and some kerosene were found on the floor and bed clothing.

When the firemen arrived Mrs. Boyle put the blame on the ghost and said she could give no explanation as to the origin of the fire.

The house was found to be again on fire this morning. When the firemen reached the house it was found locked and full of smoke. The blaze was located in a bed on the second floor.

"Sam" Bartleson, foreman of No. 8 Hose Company, upon smashing a window and entering the house found a little child lying unconscious in the blazing bed. The child was little Johnnie Boyle, the four-year-old son of Boyle by his first wife.

AGAIN IT WAS THE GHOST

The little fellow was carried across the street to the house of Thomas Manley. His burns were dressed and he is expected to recover. The flames were soon extinguished.

Mrs. Boyle was out when the blaze was discovered, but was found in one of the neighbor's houses. She blamed this fire also on the ghost, who, she says, is jealous of her and wants to drive her from her children and husband.

Mrs. Boyle is under police surveillance and the house is watched.

Mrs. Boyle is about eighteen years old, bright appearing and pretty.

New York Herald 12 May 1894: p. 11 PENNSYLVANIA

NOTE: I have not found the end to this story of what seems to be a very wicked stepmother. One does feel a certain sympathy for a 17-year-old bride married after a mere month's courtship and thrust into the role of mother to four very young children. I cannot discover what happened to the first Mrs. Boyle. The second Mrs. Boyle's spells of unconsciousness might possibly have been epilepsy or caused by stress, but what do we make of the young son saying that his mother came out of the stove? Had he heard his stepmother tell the story?

A concern about clothing and appearance did not, apparently, end with death. Some ghosts came back to complain about their burial costume before they were buried. Too much ostentation was as bad as too little for the Baltimore "old maid," who haunted her old boarding house when she was not buried in the shroud she had chosen.

A Baltimore Ghost

An Old Maid's Ghost has been sitting on a bridal bed in West Baltimore, and worrying all the lodgers in a boarding house. The old lady's spirit was exercised over the grave-clothes. A short time before her death, she asked the lady with whom she was boarding not to bury her in any costly dress, but in a plain shroud, and threatened to haunt the house if her direction was not heeded. Her friends thought that it was only an old maid's notion, and when she died, buried her in an elegant silk and adorned the casket with beautiful flowers. About two weeks ago, a bridal couple engaged board at the house. Enter the ghost. The young wife awakened her husband, one night, with a startled exclamation. There was somebody in the room, she said; somebody was sitting on the bed. He heard a noise. Somebody was moving softly across the room, he said; somebody had been sitting on the bed. Whereupon he struck a light; the shade was not in sight. The next night a gentleman in the next room was visited by the ghost, during the next fortnight, she paid visits to every sleeping-room in the house. All the boarders have left the house, and the landlady is talking of having the body exhumed, the silk dress taken off, and the plain shroud put on. It is just as well to let an old maid have her own way in matters of dress.

St Alban's [VT] Daily Messenger 12 October 1876: p. 2 MARYLAND

Other ghosts waited until they were buried to carp about their attire. Pins and knots were forbidden on burial clothing or shrouds, at least according to Irish tradition. If they were left in place, the ghost would come back to haunt the careless person until matters were remedied.

A STRANGE PROCEEDING
A Grave Exhumed in a Catholic Cemetery and the Shroud Carefully Unpinned.

Ansonia, Conn., Feb. 18. Yesterday morning four women, respectable in appearance and advanced in years, entered the side gate of the Roman Catholic cemetery, proceeded along one of the avenues and halted at a new made grave. Presently two men made their appearance and with shovels opened the grave. The women stood with bated breath, tears running down their faces. Presently the box which enclosed the casket and remains of a young girl was reached. One of the women gave a low scream. The strong arms of the men raised the box and placed it above ground. The lid was taken off the box and the casket opened. The features of a young, handsome, and beloved daughter of one of the women was exposed to view. The men looked on as if in wonder at what followed. None but the women understood it. Busy fingers went through the dead girl's hair and shroud and all the pins that could be found were removed. The string which was placed around the feet after death was removed. A needle and thread were brought into use to supply the place of the pins in the hair and shroud. The lid was then placed on the casket and the remains lowered into the grave, which was filled once more.

This strange proceeding gave rise to many inquiries. Only a few could answer them.

It was learned that there is a strong superstition among the Irish people that if a corpse is buried tied or with pins or with even a knot at the end of a thread that sews the shroud the soul will be confined to the grave for all eternity, and that the persons guilty of the blunder will be disturbed by the restrained spirits while on earth. Thus it was, according to the testimony of the one of the women, who said she had been bothered for two nights previous by the ghost of the girl, now all were happy. This is not the first time that an incident of the kind has occurred in the same cemetery.

New Haven [CT] Register 18 February 1886: p. 1 CONNECTICUT

In this next bizarre story, the ghost complained that she could not breathe in her coffin because of a misplaced cloth.

Genuine Ghost Story

The Monongahela (Pa.) *Republican* says: Not very long ago, the young and beautiful wife of one of our citizens was called to her final account, leaving her husband disconsolate, sad and bereft. She was buried in the adjacent cemetery, and the husband returned to his desolate home, but not to forget the loved one. She was present with him by day in spirit, and in his dreams at night. One peculiarity of his dreams, and one that haunted him, being repeated night after night, was this, that the spirit of his wife came to his bedside and told him that the undertaker had not removed from her face the square piece of muslin or napkin which had been used to cover her face after death, but had screwed down her coffin lid with it upon her; that she could not breathe in her grave, but was at unrest on account of the napkin. He tried to drive the dream away, but it bided with him by night and troubled him by day.

In despair he sought the undertaker Mr. Dickey, who told him that the napkin had not been removed, but urged him to forget the circumstances, as it could not be any possible annoyance to inanimate clay. While the gentleman frankly acknowledged this, he could not avoid the apparition, and continual stress upon his mind began to tell upon his health. At length he determined to have the body disinterred, and visited the undertaker for that purpose. Here he was met with the same advice and persuasion, and, convinced once more of his folly, the haunted man returned to his home. That night, more vivid than ever, more terribly real than before, she came to his bedside and upbraided him for his want of affection, and would not leave him until he promised to remove the cause of all her suffering. The next night with a friend, he repaired to the sexton, who was prevailed upon to accompany them, and there, by the light of the moon, the body was lifted from its narrow bed, the coffin lid unscrewed, and the napkin removed from the face of the corpse. That night she came to his bedside once more, but for the last time. Thanking him for his kindness, she pressed her cold lips to his cheek, and came again no more.

Canton [OH] Repository 13 November 1867: p. 6 PENNSYLVANIA

The folktale "The Golden Arm," is a classic ghost story long told at sleepovers and around the campfire. It is paralleled in this story linked with an Ohio River steamship disaster. Steam packets *United States* and *America* collided in the Ohio River December 4, 1868, two miles above Warsaw, Kentucky. The estimated death toll has ranged from 40 to 170—the passenger lists were destroyed in the ensuing fires. At the time it was the worst steamboat disaster in the country's history. There were several wedding parties on board the *United States* and a number of the victims were women, like the mutilated apparition in the following story.

WOMAN GHOST
Who Had Been Drowned in Ohio River
Came Back to Earth
To Reclaim a Lost Hand That Was Severed
At the Time of Death, When Steamboat *United States* Was Sunk.

Dillsboro, Ind., June 4. From time to time there have been many incidents published relative to the sinking of the large steamboat *United States* which occurred many years ago in the Ohio River about one mile above Warsaw, Ky., on the Indiana side of the river. Terrible, and even uncanny stories have been told about the wreck. A man of the name of Garret gives the following account of the tragedies:

"It was in the summer of 1881, and the Ohio River was low. My father was working in one of the wrecks near shore for some valuable relics. He was digging in the sand about four feet from the hull, which at that stage of the river was but half buried in the sand and water. He had not dug long when he unearthed something, apparently a lump of tallow. After handling it very carefully and washing the sand off, it proved to be a human hand—that of a young lady, presumably not more than 20 years of age. The member had been severed at the wrist.

"The fingers were slender, the finger nails being pink as a sea shell and perfect as in life. The joints and cords were very plain and even the veins were easily traced. The hand itself was of pearly whiteness, but cold and firm. The hand became my property and for a long time I kept it locked in a walnut box. Some months later a startling phenomenon took place, which for family reasons has thus far been withheld. At the time of the peculiar event my mother was away for a month's visit and my father and myself were left alone to "batch" it. I retired as usual about 9 o'clock leaving my father in an adjoining room reading. The light from his room showed in my bedroom, lighting up the corner in which my bed stood. About 10 o'clock my father concluded to retire, and as he was preparing to do so happened to look toward me, and to his surprise he saw standing by my bedside a fair young woman in a purple robe. She was leaning over my couch, with the palm of her right hand resting lightly upon my forehead. While my father stood gazing at the apparition it glided behind the door and disappeared. At the time of this strange visitation all the outer doors and windows of the house were securely fastened.

"Shortly after that, at about the same time of night, the apparition again appeared and this time my father crept stealthily toward it. The ghost, spirit, or whatever it may be termed, knelt beside the bed and raised up its arms as if in supplication to me, I being asleep at the time. To his horror my father saw that the right hand of the supplicant was missing, and that blood gleamed at the lacerated place. After a few seconds the phantom arose and disappeared as before.

"The next morning at breakfast my father seemed gloomy and troubled. I was in the same mood, for I had seen in a dream the same sight witnessed by my father. I began to tell him of the dream and the vision. When half through the story my father stopped the recital and with a pale face, asked me if it was not the right hand that was missing. I told him it was, and then he asked me if the hand in the box was a right or a left member. I could not remember, so we unlocked the box to find that it was a right hand.

"'Then we will bury that ghostly relic immediately,' said he, and without further ado the interment took place. My father at that little burial in the garden invoked eternal peace of the troubled spirit to whom it had belonged in life and we agreed to say nothing about the incident, fearing people might think us partially demented. I no longer fear such a verdict and have given the facts in the case.

"The apparition never visited us again."

Cincinnati [OH] Enquirer 3 June 1901: p. 1 INDIANA

NOTE: Assuming that the hand was, in fact, from a victim of the steamship crash, could a severed hand survive thirteen years buried in a sandbar? The answer is yes, if the hand turned to adipocere, also known as "corpse wax," a substance produced when a body is buried in a damp area with no oxygen— such as in a river sandbar. I kept waiting for the ghost to demand, "Give me back my hand!"

While the grave may be a fine and private place, apparently it is not so secluded that a ghost cannot do a little shopping.

GHOST ORDERS A HAT
Returns to Earth and Leaves Order at Millinery Shop.
Strange Customer Shows Rare Taste in Selection of a Bonnet Which Has, Thus Far, Not Been Called For.

That spirits do return from the grave and appear to mortals is a proposition that for ages has had its believers and disbelievers, but in the little town of Dublin, Ind., there is now only one opinion, and that is that spirits do walk the earth at times in mortal form. The reason for this pronounced belief at Dublin is an occurrence which has recently taken place there and which is so well vouched for that there is not a skeptic in the town.

Dublin, says the Chicago *Inter Ocean*, is occupied by a well-to-do and intelligent class of people, shrewd, hard-headed specimens of the Hoosier type, a class that is not led away by its emotions, and is intensely practical. Among the residents is a Mrs. Sallie Smith, who has lived there many years and who conducts a millinery store.

One day last May a nice-looking old lady came into Mrs. Smith's store. She appeared to be about 70 years old, and was tastefully dressed in black. She introduced herself to Mrs. Smith as Mrs. M___, and said that she had only recently come to Dublin and wanted to order a bonnet. The selection of this and the determination of its trimmings proved to be a long operation, for old ladies are quite as fastidious as the young ones when it comes to the selection of a bonnet.

During the work of choosing the bonnet Mrs. Smith and her customer got quite well acquainted. In the course of their conversation Mrs. Smith learned that her customer was the sister of Mrs. Rhoda Scotton, of Brownsville, Ind., who is well known to her, and that Mrs. M___ was well acquainted with many of Mrs. Smith's people. When the customer left she said she felt as if she had always known Mrs. Smith because she knew her family so well and had heard her sister, Mrs. Scotton, speak of Mrs.

Smith so often. The last seen of Mrs. M___ she was standing underneath a shade tree in front of Mrs. Smith's house.

A few weeks later another lady called at Mrs. Smith's store to order a bonnet. She, too, gave her name as Mrs. M___, and said that she had only recently moved to Dublin. There was a decided resemblance between the former customer of that name and the last, and yet the last had something about her that puzzled Mrs. Smith and made her doubtful of the identity. Finally Mrs. Smith became satisfied that it was the same woman, and remarked that the bonnet ordered some weeks preceding was ready for her.

The customer was greatly surprised.

"You must be mistaken," she remarked to Mrs. Smith. "I am a stranger in the town and have not only not ordered any bonnet of you, but have never been in your place before."

Mrs. Smith looked at the woman and was puzzled. She looked like her former customer, and yet there was a something about her that did not appear the same. Mrs. Smith finally became convinced that she had made a mistake, and this led her to tell her customer all about her previous visitor. Mrs. M___ appeared greatly interested in the narrative and asked Mrs. Smith to describe her former customer. When the latter had done so Mrs. M___ said:

"You have described my dead sister. She was older than I, and we married twin brothers."

Mrs. M___ then told Mrs. Smith that her sister had died at Indianapolis in September, 1900, and was buried in the cemetery in the west part of Dublin. Mrs. M___ is 68 years old, while her sister, had she lived, would have been 70. She is not a spiritualist, but is satisfied that it was her sister that called on Mrs. Smith and ordered a hat. The bonnet that was ordered, a small black Tuscan straw, prettily trimmed with black chiffon, is still in Mrs. Smith's possession, and she does not expect it to be called for.

"And I'm not going to sell it, either," she says. "It's the first bonnet I ever had ordered by a spirit, or that I ever heard of one ordering, and I'm going to keep it just as a specimen of the taste of spirits in millinery."

Daily Herald [Biloxi, MS] 14 September 1901: p. 16 INDIANA

NOTE: A neat and satisfying tale. Could it possibly be true? Those discreet dashes and that infernal surname "Smith," would seem to baffle attempts at verification. However, a Rhoda Scotton, age 50, is found in the Brownsville, Indiana Census report for 1880, with a 17-year old son, who was described as a farmer. A Sallie Smith, age 34, is found in Dublin, Indiana, occupation, "milliner," in that same census and again, in 1900, where she is called Sarah.

In my book *The Face at the Window*, a chapter called "The Death-Bed Promise," told of the ghost of Simon Fisher who returned to haunt his wife who had broken her promise to Fisher not to marry her lover. Death-bed promises, whether of a serious or trivial nature, had an almost sacred force and there are hundreds of stories of ghosts returning to reproach or take revenge when their last wishes were flouted.

COURTS HIS WIFE'S SPOOK
An Iowa Man's Appreciation of the Presence of his Wife's Ghost.

A refusal of a husband to cremate the remains of his wife has, according to his story, entailed upon him a haunt by her disappointed spirit. Mrs. V. was a vivacious brunette and an aesthetic woman, always abreast of the times. The idea of cremation won her most enthusiastic support in a moment, and being a society lady, with little else to do but gratify her whims, she allowed the new scheme for disposing of the dead to enthuse her.

It took so much of her attention from her devoted husband that he grew jealous, as it were, of the innovation. He grew to hate it more on the ground of its divorcing his wife's devotion from him than aught else. Suddenly she died, and on her deathbed made him promise to cremate her corpse. She talked until the last moment of how her spirit would delight in watching the urn containing her ashes on her husband's mantel, but vowed that she would haunt Mr. V., if he was untrue to his promise. It is even said that her longing to become a subject for the furnace actually hastened her death. The husband, however, spurned the thought of giving all that was mortal of his adored wife to the cause that he believed had robbed him of his darling, and, placing the remains in a costly casket, he had her quietly buried.

He kept their chamber, where the urn was to have been, sacred to her memory and his own use. Two negro servants were employed to live in the basement and take care of the house. After a few nights the colored man's wife awakened him with the exclamation: "Mrs. V's upstairs." He laughed at it at first, but after listening a little while, was convinced she was right. Mrs. V. seemed pouring out a torrent of invective and reproach against him, which was varied by a smart controversy. In the morning he appeared with a haunted look in his eyes and face pallid. The spook kept getting worse every night, until finally they heard a struggle and a sound as of glass breaking. They rushed up and, breaking into the room, found him struggling with an imaginary foe. The debris of a lot of vases that had stood on the mantel were strewn about the floor. The next day he complained to a friend of his trouble, stating that his wife haunted him every night. He was advised to have her remains taken up and cremated, but says he would rather have the company of her spirit than none if the phantom would only desist from pulling hair and breaking furniture.

Plain Dealer [Cleveland, OH] 30 December 1888: p. 11 IOWA

NOTE: Cremation, promoted by burial reformers for health reasons, was regarded with suspicion and distaste at the time of this story. Its enthusiasts were widely seen as irreligious, eccentric, or crankish. Perhaps we think that this is a trivial reason for a haunting, but this is not the only story I have seen of a ghost returning to complain about its wish for cremation being disregarded.

In this most unusual story about ghostly desire, a fiancé returns to claim his living bride. Was it the delusion of a woman unhinged by grief? Or a ghost determined to marry, despite the poet's assertion that "the grave's a fine and private place, But none I think do there embrace."

GIRL WEDS A GHOST
WOMAN IN OKLAHOMA MARRIES THE SPIRIT OF HER DEAD FIANCE
Bride Keeps House—Midnight Ceremony in Graveyard Shocks Village Gossips

Witchita, Kan., Oct. 10. Bessie Brown, of Cameron, Okla., is married to a ghost. Furthermore, she and her spectral husband are living together in a five-room cottage. The wedding took place one week ago, and the bride and groom moved at once into their new house, which Miss Brown had furnished with her own money. They are as happy as any young married couple could be, and persons who pass the house can hear them talking and laughing just as if they were both in human form.

This is the strangest romance ever known. Bessie Brown, of wealthy parents, high social standing, and possessed of many natural charms that make her one of the most beautiful girls in Oklahoma, married the ghost of the man she loved. She is not demented. Her mind has been tested, her brain has been examined by specialists, and her actions have been watched carefully, but no trace of insanity can be discovered. Therefore her parents agree that she must be wedded to an apparition, something which she imagines she can see and know, but which no other human being can recognize. This is what her father says about his daughter's queer actions:

"Bessie had been brooding continually over the death of John Allen, to whom she was engaged to be married when he was killed. We tried to console her in her grief, but she wanted us to leave her alone. We feared she would lose her mind if she did not stop grieving so intensely. I had a doctor visit her several times and he said her mind was all right, but that she was failing in health on account of constant worry. That was a year ago. About six weeks ago Bessie brightened up so much that we feared she was under the influence of some drug. Then one day she made the statement that she had seen the ghost of Mr. Allen, and that hereafter she would not be sorrowful any more, for she was going to marry the ghost. She said she had given her promise to her sweetheart that if ever he died she would marry his ghost, and that now, since his spirit had appeared to her, she must keep her promise.

"Mrs. Brown and I feared the poor girl had lost her mind surely by this time, so we sent to Dallas for a specialist to make another examination of her brain. He pronounced her mental condition perfectly normal, and said that she was not under the influence of any drug. He said her case was a strange one, and that she must surely see the ghost she talked about so much. I asked her to introduce me to the ghost, and she said I could not see it, but that it was with her always. She talked reasonably about it. She seemed to know that we thought her insane because of her strange declarations, but insisted that she was actually going to marry the specter. She called upon our minister and asked him to perform the ceremony. He tried to persuade her that it was sinful that she should marry a mere apparition, but she insisted.

"The minister went with Bessie last week into the graveyard where her lover was buried and at midnight the ceremony was performed which united her to the ghost of the man whom she had promised to marry two years ago, but who was killed in a railroad wreck just a few weeks previous to the wedding. I believe after close study of the girl's actions that she truly thinks she is wedded to the ghost, and that the apparition appears to her as naturally as if the spirit were still in the body. We are trying to do everything we can to make her forget her ghost, but it seems as if we are going to fail."

Before the graveyard wedding Miss Brown rented a cottage and furnished it for two. She is now living in it with her ghost husband. She can be seen sitting on the back porch conversing with an invisible companion, and often walks along the street talking aloud to some person whom no one else can see. The town people are much excited over the matter. They all know Miss Brown to be a Christian young woman, and one who would not deceive anyone for the world. Most of them actually believe she is married to the ghost of her dead lover.

Jackson [MI] Citizen Patriot 10 October 1900: p. 2 OKLAHOMA

NOTE: One of the versions of this story tells of the young Mrs. Allen setting the table for two and sitting down to eat with her ghostly husband. I wonder if one day she looked across the table and realized with a sudden shock that the chair was empty. Did she ever fall in love with another, living man and, if so, how would she get a divorce from a ghost?

2.

Death Angels and Banshees
Tokens of Death

We stand upon the dust of ages. Everywhere there are around us the tokens of
death, and the emblems of mourning. We must die, and we know not when we
may be summoned into an unseen world.

-The Rev. James Spence, 1858-

In a world defined by Christian traditions, the medieval notion of *memento
mori* and of making a "good death" lingered on in the scrupulous spiritual
accounting of the 19th-century Christian. While we may find the idea of preparing for death distasteful, it was not an abstract sentiment to the people
of the 19th and early 20th centuries to whom Death came swiftly and in all
manner of guises: A runaway horse, cholera, an exploding lamp, a bottle of
carbolic acid in the dark. "Ye know not what hour your Lord doth come," was
no idle threat.

As Victorian death rituals grew more elaborate, the idea of dying well
shifted to an anomalous and obsessive interest in harbingers, portents, and
tokens of death. The Civil War, with its unprecedented scale of casualties and a
certain fatalism—the minie ball with one's name on it—may have encouraged
this necrological attentiveness. Omens of death could be anything from a
prophetic dream, a vision of a phantom funeral, the sound of a spectral coffin-
maker, the apparition of a Woman in White, a disembodied voice calling one's
name, a crown of feathers in a pillow, mysterious lights, or the banshee's wail
or knock.

That keening spirit of doom, the banshee, was common in the British Isles. Yet,
curiously, few immigrants brought their family banshee to the New World
with them. Accounts of "real" banshees are much more common in the European papers and many of the articles in the United States press mention these
entities only in connection with folklore or superstition in articles with titles
like "The Banshee: An Irish Legend." I have collected only a handful of "true"
banshee accounts within the United States, far fewer than expected, given the
large number of 19th-century English and Irish immigrants to this country.

While we may believe that banshees only wail, they were also known for
"the Death Knock," such as that which sounded for Mr. Thomas Feast in the
following story.

THE BANSHEE APPEARS
How It Has Summoned all the Members of an Evansville Family to Prepare for the End.

Evansville has a sensation in the appearance of the Banshee or wraith in the announcement of the death of one of its citizens. A local account of it is as follows:

The death of Mr. Thomas Feast last Sunday afternoon, at 4 o'clock, has developed a singular circumstance in the history of his family, which illustrates dramatically the old Highland tradition of the "Benshie" or "Banshee." The "Banshee," as it is commonly called, is an embodied spirit or ghost, which gives warning to persons whose death is approaching by a peculiar scream or wail in the night, by appearing to the vision of the doomed person, or in various ways. It is a tradition among the Highlanders, and, at one time, was wide-spread in portions of England, Wales and Ireland. Those who have read "Waverly" or, in fact, any of the Scotch romances, will be familiar with the superstition, if it may be called such. *The Journal* does not pretend to take issue with the question in the light of recent developments, but with this explanatory preface, will relate the story as heard yesterday.

Mr. Feast was born on the Isle of Ely, Cambridgeshire, England, forty-seven years ago, and came to this country when he was young and has been living in Evansville about twenty-three years. He was a shoe-maker, a good citizen, a man of quiet unobtrusive demeanor and universally respected by all who enjoyed his acquaintance. He was, moreover, a very intelligent man, it appears of good education, and devoted a portion of his time to the study of the philosophy and religion of life. It does not appear that he was a Spiritualist, but that he had a leaning that way, or at least had investigated the beliefs of that sect. His wife, who was an Englishwoman, it seems, held to spiritualistic belief more strongly than her husband.

Since Mr. Feast came to Evansville with his family there have been five deaths in the home circle, the last of which was the father himself, which occurred last Sunday afternoon at 4 o'clock. Each one of these deaths has been preceded at

MIDNIGHT OF THE PREVIOUS NIGHT

By the warning of the "Banshee," or the death knock on the door, which forms the warning assumed in this case. Of the first two deaths we have no interesting information, but Mrs. Feast's death which occurred last summer, was preceded at midnight by a heavy, sudden knock on the front door which aroused the entire family. Upon search being made nobody was at the door and in accordance with the warning from the other world Mrs. Feast died next day.

Three weeks afterward her infant child died, and the same terrible warning was repeated at the same hour of the night.

The death of his wife seemed to prey upon the heart of her husband, and he appears to have lost all desire or hope since then he has been feeble and ill, but thought he would live through this winter. He was able to be about the house and preserve control of the household. Last Saturday afternoon he had a sudden spell or spasm and came through it much weakened but safely. When the family retired that night he was apparently as well as usual.

Suddenly, in the middle of the night, there came a

LOUD, HOLLOW KNOCK

Upon the street door, which aroused all of the family. His son George, a young man aged about twenty-three, was awakened by the sound, and rising from his bed sought his father's room, thinking he had been seized with another spell and desired assistance. When he entered the room he found his father awake, and inquired if he called.

"No," replied the old gentleman, "It was somebody knocking at the front door."

George descended the stairs and opened the door, but nobody was without and further examination revealed the fact that no one was passing in the streets. He went upstairs and told his father of this. A sudden change passed over the face of the doomed man, as he softly said:

"Go to bed, George—it is the same knock."

George went upstairs and returned to bed, observing that it was a few minutes past 12 o'clock. The singular warning occurring in the other cases in the family had been observed by all the family, and after lying down the son remembered the fact, but, dismissing it as a coincidence, went to sleep. Next morning the father called him up in his usual voice, apparently losing no strength. George went down to take his order for breakfast, but he said:

"I want no breakfast; nothing but a quiet room to-day."

A second application met with the same response, and accordingly the younger children were sent away to the house of a friend and George remained with him. During the morning he was very quiet, and then he was discovered asleep. This continued during the afternoon, and at 4 o'clock it was discovered that he had glided quietly from life to death— had fallen into the last sleep that knows no waking.

His funeral occurred yesterday afternoon from the family residence,

313 Locust Street, and was largely attended. He was a member of good standing of Morning Star Lodge No. 7, I.O.O.F., who took charge of the funeral.
Cincinnati [OH] Enquirer 5 January 1877: p. 2 INDIANA

One well-known token of death was the apparition of a ghostly hand reaching out from the Other Side.

GHOSTLY HAND BECKONED
A West Virginia Man Claims He Was Warned of His Child's Death

Uniontown, W.V., April 6. The death of Omie, the 3-year-old daughter of Mr. and Mrs. Marion C. Ballard, occurred at their home, near Linside, this county, after an illness of several weeks. Mr. Ballard declares that he was warned of the death of his little daughter in a very peculiar manner.

At a late hour last night, he says, he was sitting in a room where she lay. His wife and the rest of the household were asleep, and he alone was awake when suddenly the door opened and two great white hands appeared and beckoned toward his little daughter, who was lying on the bed. He got up and closed the door. Presently it opened again, and a second time the beckoning hands appeared.

He then went out into the hall, and from thence out of doors, but could hear or see nothing more. At exactly the same hour to-night the little one's death occurred.
Wilkes-Barre [PA] Times 6 April 1896: p. 2 WEST VIRGINIA

William Martin, a Chattanooga iron worker, was lying in bed when what at first seemed to be a shadow formed into the shape of a woman's hand. On one of the fingers was a ring which he recognized as having given to his mother some years ago. When he arose the next morning he received a telegram stating that his mother, who he had not known was sick, had died the night previously, and her last words had been the mention of his name.
Juniata Sentinel and Republican [Mifflintown, PA] 20 March 1889: p. 2 TENNESSEE

A recurring theme in death omens is a loved one coming in ghostly form to "fetch away" the dying. In this touching case, the ghost was seen literally "carrying off" his wife.

A Danbury Ghost Story
Woman Saw Dead Father Carry Her Mother Away – The Mother
Found to Have Died at the Same Time.

Danbury, Conn., March 19. As Mrs. C. W. Lee of 55 Jefferson Avenue, this city, lay on a bed of sickness, it is declared that she saw the apparition of her father, Oliver B. Pettit, formerly of Brooklyn, who died sixteen years ago, enter the room across the hall, where her mother was, and carry her out in his arms.

Mrs. Lee avers that she distinctly saw her father walk through the hall, and heard him call his wife by name, and ask her to go away with him, pleading with her until she consented. At first, the wife, Mrs. Margaret Pettit of 39 Grove Street, Brooklyn, refused, but her love for her husband evidently overcame her fear, and the daughter saw the stalwart form of her father emerge from the room and disappear with his wife in his arms.

Mrs. Pettit had been visiting her daughter, and, although not ill, was in the habit of spending the morning hours in bed. Yesterday she remained in her bed later than usual, and it was at noon that her daughter saw the vision. Calling for her husband, Mrs. Lee told him what she had seen, and Mr. Lee, hurrying to the room of his wife's mother, found her dead. Her death must have occurred at exactly the moment when Mrs. Lee saw her father enter the room. A physician later said that Mrs. Pettit died from heart failure.

The New York Times 20 March 1900: p. 1 CONNECTICUT

Some fatalists knew for a long time that a certain type of death was inevitable, like this woman with an unorthodox method of reading the future.

READS THE FUTURE ON ICE
Barberton Woman Who Feared Husband's Death Gets Tip from Frozen Design

Akron, O., Jan. 8. Mrs. Richard Calvert of Barberton told her husband 13 years ago that he would meet death in a violent manner. [This past] New Year's Eve she placed a bucket of water on the front porch of their hut in which the couple lived on the canal, her purpose being to see what would form on the ice. The next morning she found there the outline of a coffin and a lone woman.

"I know that the coffin stood for my husband and that the woman meant me, and I knew my husband would be brought home dead within two months. I warned him against the trains because he walked so often on the track." Two nights ago Calvert was on his way to his daughter's when a B & O passenger train killed him.

The Evening Telegram [Elyria, OH] 8 January 1910: p. 4 OHIO

Others had only scant warning, by dream or a premonition, that their doom was imminent.

WARNED IN DREAM OF DEATH HE MET
Railroad Conductor's Tragic End Foretold by Vision Week Before.

Chicago, July 31. Robert Moore, 106 North Maplewood Avenue, the conductor of a Northwestern freight train who was killed at Rochelle, Ill., Sunday, was warned in a dream of his fate just one week previous. So unnerved was he that he tried in vain to get a "sub" to take his place on the run which proved a fatal one for him.

Moore awoke suddenly a week ago Sunday night and arose from his bed ghastly pale. His wife, startled from her sleep, asked him what the trouble was.

"Oh, I have had an awful dream," he said, "and I can't sleep any longer. It seemed to me that I was being cut to pieces and that I was dying."

The dream was so vivid that it preyed upon his mind. His next run on the Northwestern was scheduled for Saturday night last, but he did not want to take it for fear of an accident. The train was held twenty minutes for him while he made a last effort to get a substitute. It being Saturday night, he was unable to find an available man, so he took charge of the train himself. At Rochelle he stepped off the caboose and started across the tracks to the depot, when he was struck by another train and killed.

The Minneapolis [MN] Journal 31 July 1906: p. 9 ILLINOIS

And still others made certain that their premonitions came true.

Suicide by a Spiritualist. A short time since it was stated in the newspapers that a young lady, Miss Hattie A. Eager, of Boston, had died under peculiar circumstance—being a spiritual medium, she had predicted her own death at a certain time, being at the time of the prediction in good health. She was buried with ceremonies peculiar to the spiritualists, and since the event, her case has been mentioned by spiritualists as a clear and convincing proof of the truth of their theory. It has come out now that she committed suicide. The examining physicians say that 20 grains of antimony was found in her stomach after death.

Lowell [MA] Daily Citizen 15 December 1856: p. 2 MASSACHUSETTS

NOTE: The day after she died, Miss Eager was said to have appeared at a Spiritualist circle and proclaimed, "It is all true!" According to a caustic letter from psychic investigator and one-time Spiritualist La Roy Sunderland, printed in the *Daily Democratic State Journal* [Sacramento, CA] 20 January 1857: p. 1, "one of her friends, fearing, 'all was not true,' obtained the assistance of two physicians, who, unknown to the 'circle' aforesaid, took the stomach and a portion of the bowels for future examination," which is how the poison came to be discovered. Some Spiritualists said that Miss Eager was too fine a soul to have killed herself merely to prove the Truth of their religion; others said she killed herself under the influence of evil spirits or had ingested the poison while in trance; still others insisted she had earthly troubles that had led to her suicide. There were a startling number of stories in the newspapers about Spiritualists committing suicide. The subject would make a fascinating study.

I expected to find more stories in the 19th-century press about the Grim Reaper or the Angel of Death, but those terms are rarely used outside obituaries or in a non-metaphorical sense. This is a chilling exception.

Death Angel Visible

In the summer of 1899, after my second term in medical school, I secured a position in the Lakeland Insane Asylum at Lakeland, Ky. I was day warden for a couple of months then was changed to night warden on ward No. 56. The ward had 54 patients, most of whom were epileptics. But there was one by the name of Frank who was not only insane, but through paralysis, was so helpless he had to be fed and carried around from place to place. This made him a great care. We had another patient by the name of Ellis, who was so full of devilment that he would often go down along the foot of the beds along the ward and jerk the covers off. Then he was very quarrelsome also.

Frank had taken sick and did a great deal of groaning, which seemed to annoy Ellis more than a little: and we had to watch him to keep from jumping on Frank. I came on the ward at 9 p.m. At that time all patients were supposed to be in bed. The dining room was at one end of the ward, divided from it by a heavy iron netting. I made a trip through the ward about thirty or forty minutes to see if all were in bed, as we had several who had tried to hang themselves. Of course, I was to keep a close watch on the ward at all times. The ward was about eighty feet long and we always kept a sixteen candle power electric light burning at the opposite end from the dining room, where I sat by a table when not busy going over the ward.

On one side of the ward were a couple of rooms with the side end opening into the ward with no partition between.

On this particular night we had Frank lying on the floor in one of these rooms. And as he was going on and groaning considerable, the day warden said to me when I came on duty that night: "You must watch Ellis close, for he has been wanting to get at Frank all day."

Everything went well and I had made several rounds making them more often. I had just been on a round and stopped a minute before Frank's room and I noticed he was breathing very hard. As I walked back to the table and sat down, just inside the dining room in front of the gate, which was open, I looked at my watch and it was twenty minutes of twelve.

Earlier in the evening I had started a letter and for the time being I turned my attention to it again.

All of a sudden there was a low rustle something like a lady's skirt will make when walking by, but there was no sound of footsteps. I looked up at once and as Frank's room was near the lower end of the ward close to the light a glance was sufficient to see anyone in that end of the ward. When I glanced up a figure in a night robe was nearly in the middle of the ward and went directly into Frank's room. As the form had come from the direction of Ellis' bed and seemed to be about his size, I concluded, of course, it was him. I ran down there as quick as I could on tiptoe, hoping to get there before Ellis would have time to jump on Frank.

But when I got there you can imagine my surprise when Ellis was not to be seen. In fact, no one was there. And Frank had quit breathing.

I instantly glanced at Ellis' bed and to more of my surprise, he was in bed seemingly sound asleep. I then made an examination of all the beds and found every patient in bed sound asleep.

I have pondered over this many times, and to this day I can't make out how anyone could have gotten in there and out, and in their bed all still without having been caught, as I only had about sixty feet to go and I ran with my eyes in that direction. Then why was I so sure that it was someone, and then it was not? After I had gone over the ward thoroughly and walked back to the table I looked at my watch again and it was five minutes after twelve. I have to believe my own eyes and believe it was a death angel who came for Frank that night. L.R.E. [From a 1914 ghost story contest held by the *Dayton [OH] Daily News*.] KENTUCKY

Birds, as a symbol of the soul, were perhaps the most common omen of death. I was told as a child that a bird flying into a window means that someone is about to die. It was also believed that a bird flying into the house was equally ominous.

While George Robb of Paw Paw was sick in bed a bird flew into the house when a door was opened and sat on the pillow of Robb's bed. Twice the bird was put out of the house, but both times it returned to the pillow. Shortly after Robb died and the bird disappeared.
Grand Traverse Herald [Traverse City, MI] 6 April 1893: p. 3 MICHIGAN

A MESSENGER OF DEATH?
A Buzzard's Visit Regarded As An Omen of Death.

In connection with the death of Mr. Elias V. Albaugh, which occurred at his home, near Woodsboro, Frederick County, Friday night, the following story is related by the *Frederick Daily News*.

"Not many days before Mr. Albaugh's death two buzzards flew to his home and alighted at one of the doors. The day was warm and the door was open. One of the birds walked into the house, while the other remained outside. Mrs. Albaugh found the strange intruder in the house and drove it out. Instead of flying away immediately it lingered about and remained for some time perched on a bell post near the door.

"Mr. Albaugh's sister, Mrs. Etzler, who also lived near Woodsboro, was ill at the time. His daughter-in-law, widow of William Albaugh, lives on the same farm on which Mr. Elias Albaugh resided, but in another house. In telling a neighbor of the buzzard's visit she expressed a fear that it was an omen of death—that either her father-in-law or his sister would die before long.

"Mrs. Etzler died on Thursday night last. Mr. Albaugh died on the following afternoon."
Sun [Baltimore, MD] 13 April 1905: p. 10 MARYLAND

In many Native American traditions, the owl is a symbol of death and evil.

OWL HOOTED; SISTER DIED
Ghostly Bird Was True Death Harbinger for Woman in Minnesota

Orwell, Vt., Jan 8. Whenever Henry Sherman, a farmer of this place, hears a barn owl hoot he is just as sure that a near relative has died as though he had received a letter containing the news. Mr. Sherman is not a spiritualist nor a believer in signs, yet he has absolute faith in the owl. Seemingly he has good reason.

Two years ago the farmer was awakened in the night by a loud hooting and was rather surprised, as, while saw-whet owls are not at all uncommon hereabout, the barn variety of bird is rare and in late years they have not been heard. Being curious to get a look at the nocturnal disturber he arose and peered out of the window. There, sitting on a stump close to an apple tree, was the owl hooting at intervals.

Next day Mr. Sherman received a telegram from St. Paul, Minn. announcing that his sister had died the night before at 12 o'clock. It was 12:15 when he was awakened by the owl. The two incidents were not connected until three months later, when the bird again appeared on the night that Mr. Sherman's uncle, John H. Dodge, of Water Mill, L.I. passed away. When it was found that his death had taken place at the very hour the owl set up his cries the farmer began to feel queer.

Last March a cousin in Scranton, Pa., was killed by a trolley car at 4 o'clock in the afternoon. About 4:30 the owl showed up, blindly flapping about over the house and emitting long and discordant cries. This was almost too much for Mr. Sherman and he shot at the bird. He missed and away went the owl.

The feathered messenger of death did not appear again until last week, when for an hour one night he sat silently on his old perch. That day Mr. Sherman had received word that Mr. Dodge's son was seriously ill of pneumonia, and he feared the worst. At 6 o'clock in the morning the owl hooted and the farmer was certain that his nephew was dead. In fact, he had died at that hour.

Oakland [OH] Tribune 8 January 1907: p. 3 VERMONT

Phantom funerals are a particularly well-known motif in European ghost lore. These mysterious visionary processions either can be seen or heard, but not both simultaneously. Invariably, the real funeral is identical to the preview. They are a relatively rare phenomenon in the United States, but here is a strangely technicolored phantom funeral from Georgia.

A DEATH FORETOLD
A gentleman from Georgia relates the following curious story:

Some years ago, when I was a school boy, attending school at Calvary, Ga., I, in company with one of my cousins, witnessed one of the most wonderful of spirit processions.

'Twas on a Friday afternoon, in the spring of the year, and we were on our way from school. We came down the road, laughing and talking together. We were just opposite the grave yard, at the Primitive Baptist Church (Piedmont), where we witnessed one of the grandest burials imaginable. Just in front of us, as silent as moonlight, came the burial procession. On, on, it came. First the corpse in a blue wagon drawn by two white mules. Then the mourners in black. Then the rest of the procession in all the colors of the rainbow, moving with silent tread to the grove which surrounds the yard.

Coming to the grave they halted, lifted the coffin from the wagon, lowered it into the grave and filled it. Then re-entering their wagons and buggies, all of them moved off, passing over graves, trees and everything else in the way. The whole procession then disappeared like a mist. We knew all of the people, and knew whom they buried. When it disappeared we went home in a hurry and told my mother about it. She would not let us tell Uncle J. and his wife, because it was their little girl that we saw buried. She was at the time, to my certain knowledge, well and hearty. Before Saturday night she was a corpse, and she was carried to the grave in exact accordance with the scene we had witnessed.

Logansport [IN] Pharos Tribune 2 April 1889: p. 3 GEORGIA

In the next story, a vision of a hearse panicked the conductor—for good reason.

A Spectral Procession

On the evening of the 21st of August the passengers on one of the cars of the Mount Penn Gravity road were startled by a sudden outcry from a man who had been gazing fixedly up the mountain. "There is a hearse," he cried, "and a coffin!" Then in awestruck tones he added, "It is a ghostly funeral and means—death!" Within twenty-four hours the same train, in charge of the same conductor, was hurled from the track and a number of the passengers were killed.

As a matter of fact what seems at first to be a pronounced ghost story has a most substantial basis of truth, and a number of people who were on the train on the night preceding the accident are willing to make affidavits that they saw the ghostly procession. Nothing was said of the matter at the time. Conductor Rettew, who was on both trains, and who was killed on the second night, seemed to think that there was something in the so-termed warning, as he particularly requested a

number of those who witnessed the incident to say nothing about it. Now it is the talk of the town. *Philadelphia Times.*
Jackson [MI] Citizen Patriot 28 October 1890: p. 1 PENNSYLVANIA

NOTE: The Mount Penn Gravity Railroad, in Reading, Pennsylvania was an excursion train which encircled Mount Penn and dropped passengers off at the summit to enjoy the views and picnic grounds. On August 22, 1890, at the top of the route, a passenger car became detached from the engine, rushed down the track at 80 mph, then jumped the track and rolled down a 50-foot embankment, the crushed car landing upside down. Six people, including Conductor Rettew, were killed. [Source: "A Swift Swirl Down to Death," *Watertown [NY] Daily Times* 22 August 1890: p. 8]

Perhaps because of the extreme danger of their work, miners believed in a variety of death tokens: rappings and knockings made by the spirits known as "kobolds" or "knockers," and mysterious lights. For example, in *The Face in the Window*, there is a story of a star-shaped spook light that warned of a mine cave-in in Belmont County, Ohio.) The black apparition in this story is not typical; usually the warning signs were the more abstract lights and sounds.

BLACK SPECTER IN MINE
Two Men After Warning of Subterranean Apparition Are Speedily Killed

Eveleth, Minn. Superstition has been aroused among the miners at Eveleth and its surrounding locations by statements said to have been made by Walter Koki and Rjalmar Linna, mining partners, who were killed in the Adams Mine recently.

According to report, Linna said that when he and his partner were at work in No. 4 shaft on Friday, April 6, they were met by what seemed to be a black man. The apparition is said to have put its hands on the men and to have commanded them to go away. Linna told his friends that he was so impressed by the vision that he had determined to work in the shaft no longer.

Koki, however, laughed at his partner's awe, and, refusing to leave the drift, joined the timber gang. The same day Koki wandered into a deserted shaft that was filled with deadly gases and met his death. He was not missed until the following Sunday, when searchers found the body. So overpowering were the fumes that it was necessary to raise the body to the surface with a hook and tackle.

Linna was deeply impressed by the fate of his partner and talked with several countrymen about his experience with the "black man." He was told that he was the victim of a practical joker, but nevertheless he adhered to his resolution not to work in the shaft again. Linna secured a position as an ore sampler and a week later he was thrown from an ore car and so badly injured that he died.

His death caused his fellow countrymen to recall the "black wraith" which is alleged to have warned the men, and although there are many skeptics some of the miners firmly believe that the spirit will again make its appearance and if it does the persons approached will meet a certain doom.

Elkhart [IN] Weekly Truth 7 June 1906: p. 9 MINNESOTA

NOTE: While the male black wraith was not a typical omen, in the mining communities of 19th and early-20th-century Pennsylvania the apparition of the "Woman in Black," was a harbinger of death by disease or mining disaster. These apparitions (see Chapter 12) became linked with the black-robed banshee.

As we began this chapter with a banshee, let us finish with one more. In this case, there is a knock, a keening spirit, and a far-away death.

A TOKEN OF DEATH
The Strange Tapping On the Window
And the Low, Mournful Moan, Like the Cry of a Woman
in Distress.
How a Mother's Demise Affected Her
Daughter's Family Many Miles Away.

"Something that has always appealed largely to my credulity and that I never could explain occurred to me, or rather to my wife, some twenty years back," said J. F. Davis, who is stopping at the Laclede [Hotel], to a *Globe-Democrat* reporter yesterday. "It is a case of genuine spiritual telegraphy, as I deem it. I'll make a story of it.

"In 1855 I was married in Dayton, Ohio. My wife was the daughter of a well-to-do farmer who resided in that vicinity, where I was buying wool at that time. My wife was one of three children, and the only daughter. I will say here, and you will see how it figures in my story later on, that my wife was a very attentive and hard-working girl, and I knew that her parents loved her the best of all. After we were married we moved to Terre Haute,

Ind., and I took charge of a very large woolen mill as manager. My wife's parents, Mr. and Mrs. Schauab, removed to Western Pennsylvania, very close to Red Bank. We did very well in Terre Haute. I bought an interest in a woolen mill there myself, built a good home and raised a large family.

"After about five years of absence my wife desired to revisit her parents and nothing would do but that we must go. Traveling eastward or westward in 1861 was not what it is to-day, I assure you. It meant that I must forsake my business for many weeks; that all the family must be taken along for the sake of safety, and that cost a large outlay of money. We paid the visit and I the bills, and finally returned home. At the time of parting from her mother my wife said that she felt just as though she should never see her again. The whole parting scene was rather sad, now that I recall it.

"Well, we returned to Terre Haute, and for eight or nine years my wife corresponded regularly with her parents. Along about 1877 a letter came from home saying that her mother was ill, but not seriously so. Still it worried my wife a great deal and set her to thinking seriously of going home again. The weight of business and family affairs had grown by this time to such an extent that it required constant attention. My family was a large one, ten children in all, and my wife was an excellent manager, so that in view of the constant need of her I was seriously opposed to her going. Any how she wrote a letter saying that she would come home if they needed her, but that she hoped all would be well without.

"A few days after I mailed this letter—it was in the winter time and snowing—I came home from the mill and prepared to enjoy myself as I usually did of a winter evening. We had supper and my wife straightened things. She put the children to bed, that is, the little ones, and we sat alone in the sitting room. I was reading my paper and she was knitting, as she always did, before the fire. About 10 o'clock she stirred in her chair and said:

"'Did you hear some one walking?'

"I said, 'No,' for I didn't. I felt at once that that was a queer question for her to ask, for it was snowing outside rather heavily. It was one of those soft, wet snow-storms, and it would take a rather heavy walker to be heard on a gravel walk. I said, 'Why, it's snowing out. You certainly did not hear anyone walk.' Just then she said:

"'Listen; some one's tapping on the window.'

"'Bah,' I said, half nettled at what I deemed her odd fancies, 'I don't hear anyone.' I arose from my chair, just to satisfy myself and her, and opened the side door to which the gravel path led. I looked, but no one was there. It was simply snowing heavily, and no boot marks were visible.

I turned back, fully assured that it was all her imagination. For a little while nothing happened. I got interested in some newspaper tale, and she again rocked to and fro in her chair, when all at once I heard a tapping on the window pane. My wife heard it too. She stopped and looked at me with that triumphant glance of 'there, now, I told you so,' coupled with wild-eyed surprise.

"We listened. It came again—once, twice, three times. I dropped my paper and opened the door. My wife came and looked over my shoulder out into the darkness. There was not a sign of anyone, although I had reached the door quickly, and no footprints were in the snow. I remember saying, 'Well that's queer.' And shutting the door. Then we sat down to discuss the matter. It was rather a serious discussion, I assure you, although I was not, and am not now seriously given to a belief in the supernatural. We talked of the matter, I dare say, ten minutes, when all at once my wife said:

"'There it is again.'

"Before I could realize what it was, a low, mournful sound came from without; not from the ground, I thought, but from the lower branches of a tree that stood a little distance from the door. It was just like a woman crying in most woeful bitterness. Oh, that cry was simply awful. It was just a long, low human wail that seemed to contain the bitterest sorrow. I was almost dumbfounded. I thought my wife would faint, but she only sat still, very pale and looked at me. Finally I got up and went to the door. It was the same story as before. There was not a sign of anyone's presence.

"My wife took it at once for what it was—a token. She said that she knew something must have happened at home, that mother was worse or dead, but she could hardly think of that. Four days later a letter came to my office for her. It was not black bound, for they couldn't buy mourning paper that far out in the country, and maybe they didn't care to. But it was from home, and I felt that it must bring news of death. I opened it, and sure enough it told her mother's end, how at 9 o'clock on the night that the omen came her mother had died from a sudden inflammation and that her dying exclamation was, 'Oh! I want to see Sarah' – that is my wife's first name. I withheld the letter for ten days, or until I thought her nervousness had passed away and that she had strength enough to bear the news. Then I broke the tidings to her and gave her the letter. It was a cruel blow, and it seemed cruel on my part to withhold the news so long; but I still think it was best.

"Not long after, to appease her anger and satisfy her longings, I took her home again, where she visited her father and the grave of her mother. But, aside from all that, I firmly believe in tokens now. I have had some other queer, unexplainable things to happen since then, all of which have convinced me in the belief that there is something that passes between those who have strong bonds of affection between them, that in moments of extreme joy or sorrow flies like an arrow with the news, and we call them tokens."

Cincinnati [OH] Enquirer 3 December 1892: p. 13 INDIANA

FURTHER READING: There is a chapter on spook lights and another with a section on death omens in *The Face in the Window*. On spook lights and corpse candles as omens, see http://hauntedohiobooks.com/news/spook-lights-and-corpse-candles-lethal-lights/.

For primarily European stories of phantom funerals see http://hauntedohio books.com/news/phantom-funerals/.

For information on phantom coffin-makers see http://hauntedohiobooks. com/news/the-phantom-coffin-maker-a-death-omen/.

British Goblins by Wirt Sikes (Boston: James R. Osgood and Company) 1881 has much useful information on the many varieties of phantom funeral portents. Paul Devereux also has written extensively on earth/spook lights and the so-called corpse roads, the paths of the phantom funerals.

3.

A Bowl of Bloody Water

Traces of Terror

But O for the touch of a vanished hand,
And the sound of a voice that is still!

-Alfred, Lord Tennyson-

Sometimes it is not enough that the dead return in spirit; we long for a physical sign. We want the dead to fetch an asphodel from the Underworld, leave the print of their hand on a wall or their image fixed in a window pane.

The Spiritualists' séance rooms were littered with the detritus of Summerland, or "apports," as they were known: fruit, live birds, fake jewels, a seven-foot lily in a pot, all of which materialized out of thin air or the capacious pockets of the medium. With such an embarrassment of riches showered on the living by the spirits, it is no wonder that stories of ghosts who left proofs of their visits—a scorched handprint or a smear of blood—were so popular.

A Telegraph Hill Ghostess—The Woman in Black

Allusion was recently made in the *Bulletin* to a Telegraph Hill ghost story, and as there really is something remarkable about the matter, we now present the whole story as received from an intelligent disbeliever in "spirits." Said he:

It's a week ago last Monday when the first visitation came to a house on Kearny Street, between Greenwich and Lombard. George—something—he's an Englishman by birth and a stevedore by occupation—lived there. Long ago he married a widow who already had a daughter. The widow died, and George ___ (he's got a curious name that I can't recollect, so I always call him by his Christian name) married again; this time to a servant girl in my house. By the last wife George has two children; so the first girl has a step-father and step-mother, you see.

Well, on Monday week, George and his wife had gone out to a neighbor's nearby, leaving the children at home. The little ones after a while saw a lady dressed in black, walk into the house and through the rooms to the bed-chamber of their parents. There was nothing ghost-like about the woman in black—she looked natural enough, and it was not until she entered their parents' bedroom that the children became curious and followed her. They saw her go in and lie down on the bed. Then they were frightened and ran to find their parents. The father came in with the little ones, but as he could see no one he supposed the visitant was simply one of the neighbors, looking perhaps for his wife.

On Tuesday the mysterious visitant again appeared. The father and mother couldn't see her, but the little ones (4 and 5 years of age) could. She again walked to the same bed chamber. "There; don't you see her? She's going to the bed again!" cried the children. The parents saw nothing. "Her face is all bloody!" whispered one of the frightened children. "She's lying down on the bed, and now her face is on the pillow!" As the little one spoke, sure enough, the parents saw a great blotch of wet blood appear on the white pillow; but they could see nothing else. It was very singular.

From that time until last Saturday dishes and furniture were capsized and broken, and there was the old Harry to pay generally. The eldest girl (the step-daughter) seemed to be most affected. George's wife, too, who didn't believe at all in spirits, was also attacked. She was sitting in a chair, when she suddenly felt and heard a rap up under it. Looking under it, she could see nothing. She had heard how Spiritualists converse with spirits; so she asked: "Are there any spirits present?" when a loud voice close to her ear exclaimed "Yes!" Yet she was alone.

"Do you want me?" she queried.

"Yes," said the voice.

"Then you can go to the old fish," she relied; whereupon her chair seemed to be seized by hands on either side and carried all round the room as she sat in it.

The eldest girl, too, had frequently been slapped on the face by the woman in black, and blood always appeared upon her cheek on such occasions. It was found best to leave the house, so annoying had this come to be; so the family moved to a house on Montgomery Street, near Green, still on Telegraph Hill. But the singular woman in black also appeared here. On Saturday the older girl went to the house of Mr. S. It was broad daylight, and, attracted by the mysterious rumor, some thirty or forty persons also went to the house to talk with the girl. While they were there she suddenly declared that the woman in black was approaching her with her bloody hand. Then she was struck again, and bloody marks of fingers suddenly appeared upon her face. The blood even ran down upon her neck.

Mrs. S. with a damp towel removed the blood from the girl's face and was standing beside her, talking, when all at once Mrs. S. was herself struck in the face, and blood appeared all over it! That's about the whole story, but it may be well to add that Mrs. S. and the oldest girl believe to a certain extent in "spiritual manifestations."

San Francisco [CA] Bulletin 10 July 1862: p. 3 CALIFORNIA

The Telegraph Hill Ghostess again.

A communication that goes over much of the same ground as was covered in our yesterday's account of the "Woman in black, or the ghostess of Telegraph Hill," and tells how this mysterious visitant left not the blood alone, but the marks of her gory fingers upon the girl's cheeks, proceeds as follows:

The blood discolored all the water in a basin at Mr. S.'s house, so it is believed to be genuine blood—blood of the body. Some clots of it that dried on the pillow and bedclothes have been preserved for analysis, so as to be sure that no one has been squirting blood-colored liquid at the supposed victims of spiritual assaults.

Very many persons supposed to be rational disbelievers in spiritual manifestations, assert most positively that this occurred, and it is rather perplexing to account for it. The father was a firm disbeliever, but now says he can doubt no longer. He hates to talk about it. The mother firmly disbelieved and won't believe now, although she was carried round a room, heard strange voices and so on. The eldest girl was perhaps a believer before this happened. The two children knew nothing about such things. Mrs. S. believes in it a little, but not much.

Part of it is accounted for in this manner: Medical books say that where the skin of the face has been diseased, then from a spasm of fear or pain it sometimes happens that the vicarious blood rushes through the skin just as though it had been brought out by a blow. And it so happens that the girl's face *was* affected by poison oak sometime since. But this would hardly apply to Mrs. S.—happening at the same time, too. Nor would that account for the blood on the pillowcase, which had no diseased face nor vicarious blood; nor for the carrying a person round a room, nor the smashing of dishes and furniture, nor the voices, nor the figure of a woman in black visible to the two little children who first saw it.

The whole matter affords a fine field for investigation, particularly as many of those who have seen these things persist in disbelieving that they arose from any spiritual visitation, although they cannot at present account for the material agency. S.S.S.

San Francisco [CA] Bulletin 11 July 1862: p. 3 CALIFORNIA

While the following tale has a very literary tone and wraps up more neatly than "true" ghost stories usually do, it still Grips. It is very realistic in at least one detail: the newspapers were full of stories as horrible as this one: of train wrecks, ensuing fires, and trapped, doomed passengers who begged for a merciful death.

A STRANGE STORY

Some years ago I was riding along this road on my return from a trip into Virginia, where I had a business mission. On the way, and in fact just after we left Pittsburg, I fell in with a young fellow who was on his way to the Rocky Mountains—I think Denver was his objective point. He was a young Virginia lawyer who had been educated at the University of Pennsylvania.

During one of our chats the boy—for he was scarcely more than a boy, being probably 23 years of age—took me into his confidence considerably and showed me a photograph of a beautiful girl of whom he seemed exceedingly proud and told me she was his sweetheart, to whom he was engaged and whom he expected to marry as soon as he could become established in practice.

Along about five miles back, where you noticed that old mill down by the creek, is a smooth piece of track for nearly two miles and upon reaching that little stretch the engineer usually pulls his throttle open a little wider and lets the train run at a very lively rate. It is a very level piece of track, and there is not much danger in fast running there.

Suddenly, however, and without any warning, the engine left the rails and the long train of coaches followed. There was no embankment, only a flat piece of country, and so it was not so disastrous as it otherwise would have been. I was so bruised and stunned that I scarcely realized what had occurred. It was after 9 o'clock in the evening and I had scarcely more than extricated myself from the car, which was literally torn to pieces, when the wreck caught on fire. Most of the passengers, however, had been rescued, but a few of them were still in the wreck, and so we started at once to assist the trainmen in doing what we could. I lost sight of my companion as soon as the car went over, but after I got out of the car I wondered where he was.

Just then the flames shot into the air and we heard a shriek. Rushing to the other side of the car I beheld my young friend underneath a heavy beam—in fact, the lower half of his body was under the debris of the wreck, and he was jammed in so tight that we could not possibly remove him without more assistance. We had nothing to work with, only one ax having been taken out of the cars, and that was broken and of little use. The flames had already reached his feet, and his cries for help were heartrending, I can assure you. There was absolutely nothing we could do to help him—not a thing in which we could get any water and if there had been there was not a drop nearer than a mile, for the creek at that point was at least that far away. I pulled at the debris until I burned my left hand so severely that I have used it but very little since, and, as you see, it is badly scarred.

We worked trying to save him until the fire drove us back. His appeals were something terrible to hear, and he begged us again and again to shoot him. This, of course, no one would do, although it would have been the thing to put him out of his misery.

But just then help came to him.

From the side of the track in the darkness—for it was an inky night— appeared a slender figure in white. It came up without a sound. I stood where I could see her very plainly, for the figure was that of a young woman. Her face was ashen, her features perfect, and I recognized at once in her features the photograph my young friend had shown me on the train. She glided up to where the victim lay. We heard the sharp report of a pistol, and the apparition vanished instantly. I just had time to see the poor fellow before the flames closed over him, and there was a bullet hole in his forehead. He was dead. The flames rushed over him, and I turned away.

The next day from out of the ruins we took his remains. The skull was badly charred, but in it was a hole like that made by a ball, and inside of the remains of the skull was a small piece of molten lead. I went to the telegraph office only a few miles down the track and telegraphed to the girl, whose name and address he had fortunately given me. An answer came from the girl's father stating that steps would at once be taken for the proper care of the remains, and that they would be taken back to the Old Dominion.

From there I went home. Only a short while after that, I was compelled to make another trip to Virginia. While in the state I chanced to pass through the town where the prospective father-in-law of the young man resided, and so I took the liberty of calling at his home, knowing that they would no doubt like to hear about the accident in which the young man met so untimely an end.

The old gentleman was at home and very glad to see me. I told him all the circumstances of the strange event that had taken place. When I was through he went into another room and brought out a small pistol and said he had no doubt that was the weapon that put Harry as he called him, out of misery. He said that the night before the accident occurred his daughter, the lady to whom my young acquaintance was engaged, was taken suddenly ill, and died before morning. On the table in her room was this small ivory handled pistol which her fiancé had presented to her before he left. It was loaded.

The morning after the accident one cartridge was found to have been exploded and no one could possibly account for the curious happening, as the pistol had not been touched by any one after the young lady's death. I had the little lump of lead which I found in the unfortunate young man's skull and we weighed it and also one of the pistol balls, and after careful examination they were found to be of exactly the same calibre. I am firmly of the belief that the spirit of that young woman came that dark and awful night to the relief of her intended husband. *Philadelphia Times.*
Marion [OH] Star 6 March 1895: p. 6 VIRGINIA and PENNSYLVANIA

There is a folklore motif about a condemned person asserting their innocence and proclaiming that either grass will not grow upon their grave, the stain of their blood will never be washed away, or, as in this case, a handprint will never be obliterated. Alexander Campbell was a tavern keeper accused of being a member of the Mollie Maguires, a controversial organization of Irish immigrants that was either a pro-union movement courageously fighting for workers' rights, a terrorist organization fomenting violence against the mine owners, or non-existent, depending on your point of view. Campbell apparently admitted an accessory role in the killing of two mine operatives, but vehemently denied that he was actually anywhere near the scene of the murder.

A GHOSTLY HAND
Imprint Made by a Mollie Maguire That Cannot Be Obliterated.

A Mauch Chunk correspondent vouches for the story that upon the wall of cell No. 7 in the Carbon County jail at that place, appears to be the imprint of a ghastly hand. The strange story connected with its appearance is vouched for by many of the leading citizens of Mauch Chunk and the surrounding towns.

In 1877 Alexander Campbell, one of the convicted Mollie Maguires, was confined in this cell. He stoutly protested his innocence, but was convicted through the confessions of several of his comrades in crime. On the night before he expiated his crimes upon the gallows he stood upon his narrow cot, and, placing his left hand upon the wall, is alleged to have said that if he was innocent the impression of his hand would remain upon the wall forever.

No one paid any attention to the remark at the time, but it has been brought before the public in a vivid manner many times since that memorable night. Although 19 years have passed, the imprint still remains upon the wall just as clearly as though it was placed there yesterday, although many attempts have been made to obliterate the marks.

The walls have been whitewashed many times, but the lime is hardly dry until the hand's impression can be plainly seen, although all other defects upon the wall may be covered by the application of lime. The strange phenomenon has been viewed by throngs of curious people, but no reasonable theory has been advanced by anyone.

Morning Herald [Lexington, KY] 18 March 1896: p. 2 PENNSYLVANIA

Stories of victims murdered by ghosts are uncommon outside the pages of fiction. We might call this tale a rare exception, if we take it at face value.

A BONY HAND
Strangled Him To Death
Strange Apparition That Visited a Railroad Man.
He Dared Not Open His Eyes When the Thing Was Near.

Kansas City, Mo., March 26. A most remarkable story is being told around the train dispatcher's offices of the roads which center in Kansas City, regarding the supernatural appearance, which visited one of the men employed in the offices and the strange outcome of the same. Among the men employed at the offices was William Freyer, who was accredited as being one of the steadiest and most reliable operators in the service. Freyer was of a retiring disposition and made few confidants among his fellowmen and was always looked upon as being "queer." About a month ago it was noticed that he was careworn and haggard, and his general appearance was that of a man who dissipated, but his habits were known to be so regular that there was much comment about Freyer's looks. At last he was asked by the dispatcher what made him look so bad, and he told a most remarkable story.

He said that he was

PURSUED BY A DEMON

Or spirit which was worrying the life out of him. He said that it might sound like insane talk, but he was perfectly sane and knew how his statement would be looked upon and consequently he had been very careful never to say a word to anyone about his strange visitor.

He said that every night when he went alone to his room he saw a terrible apparition approach him from the corner of the room. It walked solemnly and slowly toward him, and as long as he kept his eyes on it, it would continue to approach until it got very close to him and then it would stretch out its arm toward him. At that moment he would have an irresistible desire to close his eyes, and when he opened them the spirit would be gone. He said he had tried time and again to keep his eyes open to see what would be the outcome if he continued

TO LOOK AT THE GHOST

But his fear at the close approach of the horrid object completely unnerved him and he was compelled to close his eyes and thus send the spirit away. He had on several occasions tried to get a courage by drinking, but when it came to the point he could not keep his eyes open, and the visitor would go away.

The train dispatcher was disposed to laugh at the story, but Freyer was terribly in earnest and begged that nothing be said to the other men about what he told them, as they would look upon him as being insane and make his life a burden to him. Freyer was asked why he did not go away and thus get rid of the spirit, but he said it was no use, he had tried it. He firmly believed that if he could keep his eyes open until the spirit got to him it would grasp him by the throat and choke the life out of him, and that his deadly fear served to prolong his life.

CHOKED TO DEATH.

Now comes the remarkable part of the story. About a week ago Freyer was found dead in his bed at Lenexa, Kan., where he had been sent on temporary duty, and the indications were that he had been strangled to death. His eyes were protruding and his every feature showed every sign of fear. Around his throat were the marks as if made by a bony hand, while no other indication of violent death was there. The Coroner's jury brought in a verdict that he had died at the hands of some person or persons unknown, as every indication of foul play was present.

When the story of his death and appearance after it came to this city the train dispatcher told his story, and the general belief among the men at the offices here is that he kept his eyes open and died from excess of fright at the supposed approach of the spirit which he thought was haunting him.

Cincinnati [OH] Enquirer 27 March 1892: p. 9 MISSOURI & KANSAS

NOTE: I do not find the unfortunate and perhaps unbalanced Freyer in the census or grave records. While there are not many "true" stories of ghosts murdering, there are plenty of stories of victims dying of fright in a ghost scare. A printing of the identical story (*New York [NY] Herald* 4 April, 1892: p. 10) is titled "Choked by a Demon: Strange Story of a Railroad Man's Hallucination and Death." If not merely a yarn, Freyer's death might have been a case of the "Old Hag," where victims feel a horrifying presence which either sits on their chest or chokes them. But I have never read of the "Old Hag" leaving marks.

This story has some interesting technical detail from the Golden Age of hand-set type, when every letter, space, and comma of a densely packed newspaper page had to be arranged by hand—human, or not...

SET UP BY GHOSTLY FINGERS
A Typesetter's Story of News Getting That Beat the Telegraph

"In the summer of 1881," said a compositor, "I was running a paper in a little backwoods town in Pennsylvania. The paper was not so metropolitan in its makeup but that I was able to do all the work myself with the exception of the printing. Publication days I called in the services of a half-witted fellow, who, under my instruction, had developed into an expert roller. I was the only man within a radius of twenty miles who knew how to set type, and if I had fallen sick the paper would not have come out until I was well again. Naturally I am not a superstitious man, but an incident occurred while I had charge of that paper which I cannot explain, and until it is explained I shall believe that anything is possible in the way of ghosts, spooks, wraiths, etc.

"It was the morning of June 10. I had locked up my forms the night before so that I could begin printing early in the morning. I was pulling the old lever promptly at 7, and at 9 the local list was in the post office. Soon after the delivery had begun one of the merchants of the hamlet—a very intimate friend—came into the office.

"How did you come to hear of the death of your brother so soon?" said he. (There was no telegraph station within fifteen miles.)

"'What do you mean?' said I.

"'Mean?' said he. 'You ought to know what is in your own paper. Have you forgotten that you heard this morning that your brother is dead? Have you forgotten that you set up a notice of it an hour or two ago?'

"'Are you crazy?' said I. 'I swear that I do not know what you are driving at.'

"At this juncture he opened the damp sheet that I had so recently printed and folded, and pointed me to the following item at the bottom of the third column of the local page:

"'John Jones, brother of William Jones, was killed at Peoria, Ills., at 5 o'clock this morning.'

"My breath was fairly taken away from me. The merchant was right. There was the notice of my brother's death in my own paper, and I had not set it up nor heard of it.

"'You are right,' said I, 'but this is the first that I have known of it. If there ever was a mystery this is it.'

"I went over to the 'form.' There was the three-line item. The moment I saw the type I was more amazed than ever. It was the type setting of my brother, who, like me, had been bred to the printer's trade. I could tell his work from that of a thousand. He was a marvelously even spacer, and he carried his taste so far that he always put less space after a comma.

"But how were the lines put into the locked form? No item had been taken out. I examined the form closely. Yes, there was some more of my brother's work. To gain the space, leads had been taken from here and there just as he used to take them. He was a great stickler for good looks in a page, and was very fastidious as to where he pulled his leads. It struck me right away that the notice of the death would not have been so short, would have gone into details more, but for the fact that my brother did not wish to remove any of my matter nor any lead which could not be spared as well as not.

"Though utterly skeptical about supernatural visitations, from that moment I believed that my brother's disembodied soul had made its way hundreds of miles, had entered my office in the early dawn, had set up the notice of his death and put it in the 'form.'

"Late that afternoon a dispatch came to the effect that John Jones was killed at Peoria, Ills., at 5 o'clock that morning." *Cleveland World*. *Bismarck [ND] Tribune* 25 June 1891: p. 4 PENNSYLVANIA

NOTE: The narrator gives the obligatory "I'm not superstitious, but..." introduction to his story. This particular compositor was setting up his newspaper entirely by hand, unlike a bigger newspaper, which would have used a linotype machine. Individual type elements like letters and punctuation or perhaps engraved plates were placed into a "form," which was locked into a "chase" or frame to make up a page. The "leads" were strips of metal used to make blank space between lines. I was particularly entertained by the compositor's claim that he could tell his brother's careful spacing. I recall a similar tale about a man receiving a telegraphic message from the dead where he claimed to be able to identify the sender's "fist," or telegraphic style.

THE BLOODY HAND
Family Driven From a Haunted House.
Dishes Broken, Bells Kept Ringing and the Dog's Neck Broken.
Shrieks and Wails, Horrible Beyond Description, Fill the Air.

[Woodville, Texas] Special Cor. *St. Louis Globe-Democrat*]
On the outskirts of this town is an old house which has stood untenanted for years, but was recently repaired and once more rendered inhabitable. A Mr. Z., who is a recent arrival in Woodville, though well known in the county as an honorable gentleman, moved into this house about six weeks ago with his family, which consists of his wife, a grown daughter, and a little boy of 7. One night about a week after they got settled the child came running in from the hall, which was unlighted, into his mother's room, crying out:

"Oh, mamma, somebody with their hands all wet caught hold of me."

His mother commenced to soothe his fright, when, to her horror, she perceived that the sleeve of the child's little jacket of white linen bore the marks of

A BLOODY HAND

She called to her husband who was sitting on the porch, and told him what the child said, showing at the same time the crimson marks. The two proceeded to search the house, but found only the usual occupants. Mr. Z. was certain that no one could have passed him and the servants, on being questioned, declared that they had been sitting on the back porch and had seen no one come in. The whole occurrence was dismissed as a mystery that would in due course explain itself in some natural way, for both Mr. Z and his wife were people of strong religious convictions, besides being possessed of cool, practical common sense.

Scarcely a week, however, had elapsed when, one night about 10 o'clock, shrieks were heard issuing from the room of the young lady daughter, who had just retired. When reached the girl was found to be nearly insensible from fright, and it was several minutes before she was restored sufficiently to be able to tell the cause of her alarm. She had been standing before her toilet mirror in her night-dress braiding her hair when, happening to cast her glance on the reflection in the glass, she perceived a man's hand all dripping with blood lying familiarly on her shoulder. Seeing this frightful sight and knowing that there was no living creature in the room beside herself, the terrified girl attempted to run from it, but was mysteriously held fast by that bloody hand.

HER NIGHT-DRESS

Was plainly impressed with the print of a large hand outlined in fresh blood. Mr. and Mrs. Z. were now thoroughly alarmed, for these things were wholly inexplicable from any but a supernatural stand-point. However, with a courageous determination to accept none but a purely natural explanation, they resolved to remain in the house a while longer, but sent away their children. Mr. Z. went to the owner of the house and inquired if anything in its history could account for the strange appearances that had been witnessed in it. Mr. O., to whom the house belonged at that time, informed him that he had bought it from a family who had left the place suddenly—for what reason no one ever knew—about eight years before. No tragic event had ever been known to have occurred within its walls.

For a time nothing further was seen or heard of the bloody hand and the Z.'s were beginning to congratulate themselves that it would trouble them no longer, when it began

A COURSE OF PERSECUTION

That finally ended in driving them from the house. Mrs. Z. would be awakened by the touch of clammy fingers playing over her face, her husband found himself struck violently over the head whenever he entered a room unlighted, the servants left complaining that their work was interfered with constantly, for the dishes were thrown to the floor, freshly laundered clothes sprinkled with blood and gory marks defaced the white, plastered walls. The door-bell kept up a perpetual ringing day and night and occasionally there would be a fearful crash as if the very roof had fallen. Mr. Z. procured a dog, which was kept in the house all the time, but one morning, after an unusually disturbed night, the animal was found dead with a broken neck, and a look of almost human terror in its wide-open eyes. One day Mrs. Z. in broad daylight was seized by her back hair and dragged violently from room to room until she repeated the Lord's Prayer aloud, when her invisible enemy relaxed its hold and a pitiful moaning or lamentation filled the air, as if some lost spirit

BEWAILED ITS DOOM

The climax, however, was reached one magnificent moonlit night when Mr. and Mrs. Z. were sitting on their porch quietly conversing. And at once the husband without speaking directed his wife's attention to the floor. There was a hand, severed at the wrist, and with a faint blue light playing about it, writing with the index finger on the white plank flooring of the porch. When the hand finished its writing, it seemed to wring itself in the air in speechless despair and disappeared and the pair read the sentence traced by the hand in blood.

"The wicked cry rest, rest, and there is no rest."

Scarcely had they finished reading it when the lamp was snatched from the hand of Mr. Z. and flung violently to the floor, shrieks and wails, sad and terrible beyond describing, filling the air and the husband and wife, conquered at last, rushed from the accursed house and sought refuge at a neighbor's. In a short while the alarm of fire was given and the house just deserted by the Z.'s was found enveloped in flames. The lamp in its fall had set it on fire, and it was completely consumed. As to the truth of the story told by Mr. and Mrs. Z., no doubt of its genuineness is entertained by our citizens for the veracity of either is not to be questioned.
Cincinnati [OH] Enquirer 8 September 1889: p. 15 TEXAS

NOTE: The sentence traced by the hand is probably inspired by Isaiah 57:20: "But the wicked are like the troubled sea, when it cannot rest, whose waters cast up mire and dirt." Assuming that this is not a work of journalistic fancy, the blood is a truly nasty detail, as is the slain dog. There are some common poltergeist features: the crash as if the roof had fallen in, the dishes and the lamps flung about and a young lady in the house. The ringing bells and the bloody writing suggest the much later haunting of Borley Rectory during the residence of the Foysters, and the fictional *Haunting of Hill House* where Eleanor finds her name written on the wall in what looks like blood.

Borley Rectory was famous for its ghostly nun, as were many English hauntspots. However, very few ghostly nuns are found in the United States outside of college legends and other internet-driven tales.

GHOST OF A NUN WAS HIS STRANGE PASSENGER. A NEWSPAPER SAVES A LIFE AND GIVES A WOULD-BE SUICIDE A FORTUNE.

I was a driver of a bob-tail car right here in New York. There were two passengers in the car at the time—a saintly-looking Sister of Charity and a man who looked a tramp in the last stage.

There was only one nickel in the box, and, after knocking repeatedly on the door, I stopped the car and went inside. The tramp protested that he had paid his fare, and I turned to the nun. By a gesture she signified that I should hand to the man a paper that was lying on the seat. I did so, and when I turned again the nun was gone. The tramp declared that he had not seen her—that he had been alone.

Utterly mystified I went back and started the car. A little later the tramp got my name and address and left the car. That night I went to my doctor and told him my story.

"Now, doctor," I said, "if I am loony out with it!"

"No, no, Jim," said he: "very sane men have optical illusions now and then."

"I don't want any more of 'em," said I. "Collecting fares of optical illusions don't pay."

"I should say not," said the doctor. "But my opinion is that you turned your back a minute and that the woman got off without paying her fare. Probably she was not a real Sister of Charity. The city is full of frauds. She made you take the paper to the man to give herself a chance. See now?"

I didn't see; but what can you do when folks are so sensible they can't believe anything?

"Twasn't like that—there she was and there she wasn't," said I. "That's how it was."

"If it happens again come to me and I'll write you a prescription and make you a present of it," said the doctor.

So I thanked him kindly and went away, and it didn't happen again. Weeks went along, and it was winter, and as cold as Greenland, and passengers more bothersome than I ever knew 'em, when one day, standing in the stables, talking to Mike Gallagher, the old fellow that watered the horses and always had a joke for everybody, I heard my named called.

"You're wanted, Jim," said someone, and I went out into the street, and the man that had called me pointed to a gentleman—about as fine a looking one as I ever knew—and he, the gentleman, walked up to me.

"It's your dinner time, isn't it?" said he.

"Yes, sir," said I. "I've got a few minutes left."

"Come along, then," said he. He walked me into a restaurant close by the stables, and said: "Call for what you want," and I named it. Then said he: "You don't remember me, Jim Brown?"

"You gave me a paper about six months ago," said he. "A newspaper. I asked your name."

"Oh, oh!" said I. "No, sir: I didn't know you. I begin to see the likeness, but you—you—"

"I know," said he. "I was pretty well down on my luck then. See here?" He unbuttoned his coat, a sealskin, bless you, and took out of the breast pocket a newspaper—"read that," he said, pointing to where it was folded.

I read it. This is what it said:

"If Ferdinand Melrose will return home all will be forgiven by his dying father." And after that where he was to inquire for "further particulars."

"Well, I am Ferdinand Melrose," says the gentleman. "The black sheep of my family. Long ago my stepmother made mischief between my father and myself. He forbade me his house, and I rather went to the bad. No matter for my story. Beside the fare you inquired about I had only a bottle of laudanum in my pocket. I was going to Central Park to take it. I should have slept myself out of life into eternity, and the city would have seen to my funeral if you had not given me that paper. I went to the place mentioned, and found, as I expected, that money had been left in a lawyer's hands to take me home. When I got there I found that my stepmother had been dead three years and that my father had been attacked by a disease that must be fatal. We were reconciled and when he died I found myself a rich man. I had kept Jim Brown's address, and I felt that I owed him something."

"Nothing at all," says I. "The lady—the sister—told me to give it to you."

"What lady?" asked he.

"I'd like to know, myself," said I, and then I told him my story.

"It is strange," says he. "I could swear that I was the only passenger at the time. I felt so miserable and so shabby that I purposely waited for an empty car. And another thing that is strange, Jim Brown," said he. "We had a ghost in our family. A nun is said to appear now and then, always to do good. And my father declared that while he was ill she appeared to him three times, always pointing to my portrait, which hung in his bedroom, and always conveying to him in some way that it was his duty to search for me. In fact, she was the cause of our reconciliation." I couldn't say anything. Neither of us spoke about the thing again; but when he insisted on starting me in the eating house line I wasn't fool enough to refuse, and, as you see, I'm not a bob-tail car driver any longer.

"No, I haven't seen anything queer since that time, and I can't say I'm anxious; but whether the lady was what the doctor called an optical delusion, it's certain that she only did good to all concerned. Bless her for coming!"

Cincinnati [OH] Enquirer 4 March 1894: p. 24 NEW YORK

NOTE: As you can tell, many of the stories of physical traces have a literary tone and tidy or convenient endings, as well as heroes with generic names like Jim Brown. A bob-tail car was a horse-drawn trolley. The Sister of Charity would have been one of the religious order founded by St. Elizabeth Ann Seton, whose members ministered to the poor in the spirit of St. Vincent de Paul. They wore black bonnets, rather than the large starched white winged cornets of the French Sisters of Charity.

Once we move beyond the quasi-fictional ghost stories, there remain a few tales of physical manifestations without easy explanations.

There is witchcraft, or cutaneous disorder, or epileptic fits, or downright lying in Washington Borough near Columbia, Pennsylvania. A woman living in a small frame house is pursued by uncanny spirits of the air and also by cats. A mysterious hand grasps her and throws her to the floor. The hand is as cold as ice at first and then it is burning hot and leaves a red mark on her body. Sometimes the hand chokes her until she is black in the face, and again the clutch is so terrible that the imprint of finger-nails are left in her flesh. Soon after she took to her bed she saw a fiery hand before her face, and after that two balls of fire at the window. One night a black cat jumped against the window trying to force an entrance. Noises as if sticks being rattled together and of horses trampling on the porch were heard every night. All the neighbors have flocked to her cottage, and there are many simple souls who insist that the woman is bewitched.
Territorial Enterprise [Virginia City, NV] 15 February 1878: p. 2
PENNSYLVANIA

NOTE: The author may have gotten it in one with "cutaneous disorder," because this affliction sounds like an instance of dermographism, or possibly hysterical "stigmata." In 1935 Dr. Edward Hartung theorized that the stigmata of St. Francis of Assisi was caused by a complication of quartan malaria called purpura, a subdermal hemorrhage. Could this unfortunate woman have suffered from something similar? [Source: http://www.time.com/time/magazine/article/0,9171,883261,00.html]

While mysterious lights and fires are part of the standard paranormal canon, there is an entire genre of "fiery hand" stories typically found in Catholic literature. These tell of Poor Souls in Purgatory returning to ask for prayers and scorching textiles or wood to prove to the witness that they were not dreaming. In fact there is a Museum of Poor Souls in Purgatory, in Rome, Italy, which houses scores of these relics. (See the note after this next story.)

HAND OF GHOST SEARS PILLOW
Woman Near Collapse After Apparition's Visit

Erie, March. 1. The home of Mrs. Mary Giaconia, 133 Huron Street, was besieged today by an excited and curious throng of men and women who had heard that an apparition had appeared to her.

Mrs. Giaconia's husband was killed in France. According to her story, she was awakened in the night by the specter of her husband at the bedside. The apparition asked what had been done with his insurance, and then warned the woman that anything it touched would be burned.

The specter laid a bony hand upon her pillow and then disappeared, the woman says. She screamed and others in the house came to her. The impression of a hand was found burned black through the pillow casing and into the pillow beneath.

Welfare nurses who visited the house saw the burned pillow and are at a loss to explain the mystery.

Mrs. Giaconia is in a state of nervous collapse.

Plain Dealer [Cleveland, OH] 2 March 1919: p. 1 PENNSYLVANIA

NOTE: The linen-scorching apparition goes back to visions of souls in Purgatory from the medieval era. This notion survived the longest in the Mediterranean countries so it is not surprising to find a fiery-handed ghost in an Italian household. The usual scenario would have had the ghost asking his widow to spend the insurance money on Masses for the repose of his soul. For more such relics in the Museum of Poor Souls, see these links: http://www.traditioninaction.org/religious/e048-Museum_1.htm and http://www.traditioninaction.org/religious/e049-Museum_2.htm

In this next story we find a ghost with a burning hand, who emerges from his grave with a mission. This tale comes from Maryland, founded as a haven for Catholics, but while there is some suggestion that the dead man is in purgatory, his words are ambiguous.

In the dim past a rich old man of Talbot, whose home still stands, left his fortune to his three sons in equal shares; but the eldest, in the absence of his younger brothers, so changed the will that he was to get the lion's share, and also to hold the estate in his keeping. His plan went well with him until one night, a year after his father's death to the day, he was returning on foot with some friends from a long hunt after birds, and, to save time, being tired, decided to cut across a field and over a fence where his father had lost his life. The old man had died from the effects of a fall in getting over a fence, which the party of hunters would have to scale at the fatal spot.

The family burying ground was right at this very place, and the son did not care to pass where his father lay buried, after his act against his brothers. But with friends to accompany him he pushed on, and the three were suddenly brought to a halt when within a rod of the fence and old burying-ground. And no wonder, for there stood in their path a shrouded, misty form. The face was indistinctly visible, but the erring son knew it and stood in horror, trembling violently. Suddenly a voice was heard, cold, sepulchral, yet distinct: "My son, do not wrong your brothers, but do right by them as you hope for mercy when you die!" Then the white form turned, placed one hand upon the top rail of the fence and leaped over—a flash of fire and sulphurous smoke bursting forth from where the fingers touched it.

Another moment and the form leaped the wall of the burying ground and disappeared among the trees that surrounded the old man's grave. The three men had seen the form, as also the flash of the burning rail, though the latter felt sure that the ghost of the old man had come from a very hot place, and from the advice he gave his son about hoping for mercy could realize how it was himself. Whether it was a real ghost or one of the brothers, the next day the imprint of a hand was found burned on the rail. The ghost served its purpose, too, for the eldest brother hastened to the county Courthouse the next day and "did the right thing by his brothers," so that he might "hope surely for mercy when he came to die."
Land of legendary lore: sketches of romance and reality on the eastern shore, Prentiss Ingraham, (Easton, MD: The Gazette Publishing House) 1898, p. 89
MARYLAND

This next story of a fiery hand searing the wallpaper during a wake, which comes from *The Headless Horror: Strange and Ghostly Ohio Tales*, is quite an unusual one. Was the wallpaper glue spontaneous combusting? If so, that does not explain the hand of fire witnesses saw. Was it some form of ball lightning perhaps tracking metals in the ink of the wallpaper? In its appearance at a wake, it suggests the burning hand of a soul in Purgatory, but we know nothing about the religious beliefs of this family.

SAW A FIERY HAND
WATCHERS IN A CHAMBER OF DEATH VERY
MUCH FRIGHTENED

Midway between Mechanicsburg, Ohio, and the neighboring village, Catawba, a something ghostly has been creating a stir. The house is upon the Springfield Pike, and is a neat appearing two-story frame house of modern architecture. It is in the interior of this house that the ghostly scenes are enacted. The last person who occupied the house with his family was a gentleman of the name of Prentiss, but himself and family remained no longer than they could help. A little child of Mr. Prentiss died, and several of the intimate friends of the family were sitting up with the remains. The occasion afforded the first intimation of a ghostly vision about the premises.

It was about 12 o'clock at night, and the occupants of the room sat dozing from their vigil, when with a muffled exclamation, one of the ladies arose from the chair, and, with a trembling hand, pointed toward one of the walls of the room. Seemingly a hand of fire had suddenly appeared upon the wall. The hand first appeared near the ceiling, but did not remain motionless. With the index finger again pressed against the papered wall the hand moved downward until the floor was reached. It then returned to the ceiling and back again, making six perpendicular visits downward and upward, after which it disappeared and was seen no more that night.

What it meant no one could tell or conjecture. Upon examining the wall where the hand had traveled another strange sight was disclosed. Lines, the width of an average adult finger, were upon the wall in the track the fiery finger had pursued, and along each line the wall paper appeared as though seared with a red hot iron. It is not ascertained whether any unaccountable noise occurred during the manoeuvres of the mysterious hand, as the living occupants of the room fled in terror. Although the house is not now occupied, it is supposed that the hand of fire is still at work, as visitors to the house during the day notice additional tracks where it is supposed the hand had traveled and the same seared appearance of the wall paper.

How long the mysterious proceedings will continue is, of course, unknown, but at the present time it appears as though the hand of fire is going to leave its mark upon every inch of paper on the wall.

Repository [Canton, OH] 23 January 1892: p. 11 OHIO

Perhaps the classic "physical trace" of a ghost was the spirit picture. Photographers such as William Mumler and William Hope were well-known for their photographs containing spirit "extras," although Mumler was taken to court for fraud and Hope was exposed by Harry Price. Most spirit photographs were taken in studios. The one in the next story, unusually, appeared on an innocent family snapshot.

SPIRIT PICTURE
Portrait of a Man Who Has Been in His Grave a Year
Appears in a Family Photograph
The Negative Taken by a Kodak During the Last Month—
A Mysterious Photograph Taken at a West Virginia Homestead.

Wheeling, W.Va., Nov. 22. The appearance of the "astral" or spirit encasement of a man who had been dead more than a year, in a photograph made with a Kodak was the cause of the almost total suspension of animation on the part of Mr. A. Allen Wheat of this city today. He had made a lot of photographs of people and things about the home of his wife near Danville, Va., and had sent them to the Kodak factory to be developed and received them back today. Among the lot was a group composed of his wife, his father-in-law, Capt. Haase, formerly of the Baltimore & Ohio railroad, Miss Maud Halcolm, and his brother-in-law Master Charles Haase.

The picture was taken at the home of Capt. Haase, about ten miles from Danville, and was made by the usual pressure of the button about three weeks ago. When it was taken the party were ranged about the veranda of Capt. Haases's residence, the sun was shining brightly and Mr. Wheat, who operated the camera, was stationed about forty feet away. Miss Halcolm, who lives near Capt. Haase's residence and who is a friend of Mrs. Wheat, called on the day in question, as it was the first time she and Mrs. Wheat had met since the death of Miss Halcolm's brother Charles, they naturally talked about him considerably. After dinner the party repaired to the veranda to make the picture. Nothing unusual was noticed by anyone and no further thought of the picture was given by Mr. Wheat till today when he opened a package from the Kodak factory, when to his amazement he found a perfect likeness of Charles Halcolm standing immediately back of his sister on the veranda. The figure of Mr. Halcolm and his head are four times as large as those of the other persons in the picture, although he is further away from the camera, being in the extreme background. He wears the clothing which he wore in life, a stiff hat, tilted back to show his forehead, as was his custom, a turnover collar, with a small, black bow, black coat and white shirt. He appears to be coming out of the double doors at the back of the veranda, although the picture shows the doors to be closed. He is smiling and appears to be in the best of humor. Mr. Halcolm died under ordinary circumstances of typhoid fever a little more than a year ago. He was not a spiritualistic believer, nor was he interested in such things. His family were not spiritualistic people, nor is

Mr. Wheat or others who were present at the time the picture was taken.

Mr. Halcolm was well known among a certain set in Wheeling, and nearly all of them have seen his picture today, and all recognized it. Hundreds of others have seen the wonderful picture, today and several photographers, who have been called in are unable to give any explanation of the phenomenon.

Mr. Wheat, who made the picture, is the head of the firm of Wheat & Hancher, the leading jewelers of the city, and a man of stability and merit. He is not a photographer and merely took the camera along on his recent visit to get some views of his wife's homestead. The negative plate is in his possession, having been sent back by the people who developed the pictures. It shows the same figures as the photograph.

The fact that the figure of the dead man is so much larger than the others is one of the mysteries.

Plain Dealer [Cleveland, OH] 22 November 1893: p. 1 VIRGINIA and WEST VIRGINIA

NOTE: Mr. Wheat and his jewelry firm were real enough, although I haven't found documentation on Charles Halcolm. At this time, amateur photographers sent their entire camera back to Kodak to be developed. The camera would then be returned with the photographs, reloaded with film.

Perhaps because their ticking echoes the heartbeat of a man, clocks have intimately been linked to death. Folk- and family lore is full of stories of clocks stopping at an owner's demise, and of stopped clocks restarting and chiming madly on the anniversary of a death. This next tale turns clock/death folklore on its head as the spirit of a young woman hovering between life and death influences a clock.

An Uncanny Clock Story.
Timepiece Wouldn't Stop and It Saved This Young Girl From a Terrible Death.

[New York Press]

The boarders were talking about how foolish it is to be superstitious. The landlady said every person was entitled to his or her opinion. As for herself she laughed at superstition until a few years ago. Then something happened that made her believe in things uncanny, and she was loath to-day to ridicule anything, no matter how absurd it might appear.

"Two women occupied the second-story front room of the house I used to keep down in Nineteenth Street," said the landlady. "The women were sisters. One was a widow named Mrs. Belden, the other was a Miss Carlton. Miss Carlton was engaged to a man who traveled for a big photographic concern. His business took him pretty much all over the world and the young women's room was cluttered up from floor to ceiling with mementoes he had sent them from the various countries he had visited. Among these curios was a very peculiar clock that he had picked up somewhere in Southern Europe. Miss Carlton was especially proud of that clock. She said she thought it the rarest treasure James had ever found anywhere, and I guess it must have been pretty valuable because I know for a fact that some dealer down in Fourth Avenue heard about it and offered her $150 for it. But, of course, Miss Carlton would not sell the clock, and the way things turned out afterward it was a mighty lucky thing for her that she didn't.

"Along in July of the year they were with me the two women planned a month's vacation, but before they could get away Miss Carlton was taken sick. She was sick four days. On the morning of the fifth day she died. It was just 10 minutes past 9 o'clock. I was in the room when the end came, and Mrs. Belden was there, and the doctor and two servants. The minute we saw it was all over Mrs. Belden made a dash for that clock.

"'I must stop the clock,' she said. She opened the door and caught hold of the hands of the clock, but it never stopped ticking. So long as she held the hands they could not move, but as soon as she let go they hurried on to mark the number of seconds that had been ticked off while they had stood still.

"Mrs. Belden got frightened. 'What in the world ails this clock?' she said. 'I can't stop it.'

"The doctor came and tried to stop it and I tried, and the girls tried, but no matter what we did the clock kept on ticking. We turned it upside down; we laid it on its face; we did everything, in fact except break it, but it ticked steadily away. When night came that clock developed another crazy freak. It was built to run only 24 hours without winding. Eleven o'clock at night had been Miss Carlton's time for winding it, and Mrs. Belden said that when that hour came around it would surely stop of its own accord, because the clock had never been known to run five minutes over the 24 hours. But that night it broke the record. It did not stop at 11 o'clock. It ran all night and all the next day. By that time Mrs. Belden was half crazy with grief and superstitious fear. The funeral had been set for 1 o'clock on Thursday, but when the time came Mrs. Belden would not allow the undertaker's men to take the body of her sister away.

"'The persistent ticking of that clock in the face of all natural laws means something,' she said, 'and I am not going to have Nannie buried till I find out what it is.'

"So all day Thursday and Friday we kept Miss Carlton in the second-story front room, and all the while that clock on the mantel beside her kept up its everlasting ticking. Saturday morning about 10 o'clock I happened to be passing through the second-story hall and I heard a hair-raising shriek let out by some one in the front room. I rushed in and found Mrs. Belden on the point of fainting, while Miss Carlton lay on the bed with her eyes wide open and her lips twitching as if she wanted to say something. I fainted, too, but before I did it I managed to scream loud enough to bring everybody up from the parlor floor and the kitchen, and they all set to work to revive Miss Carlton. Mrs. Belden and I were allowed to come to of our own accord, and by the time we were fully braced up the doctor had come and had taken Miss Carlton in hand. He was scared almost as badly as we were when he found that Miss Nannie was not dead, but he worked over her all that day, and by night she seemed so much improved that he had hopes of her recovery.

"At 11 o'clock that night the clock stopped. Miss Nannie was conscious, and she noticed when it stopped ticking. She asked her sister to wind the clock. She did wind it, but it wouldn't run. It never did run again. We did as many things to get it to go as we had previously done to get it to stop, but not all the winding and coddling we could give it would ever persuade that clock to start up again. Miss Nannie was very much disappointed about that, but when she got well enough to understand how the clock had behaved in her trance she didn't have the heart to feel very hard toward it for stopping as soon as she got well."

The landlady tilted her head back and closed her eyes as if her story were ended.

"But what made the clock keep on running all that time?" asked the young woman who had insisted upon hearing the story.

"I don't know," said the landlady. "Nobody ever found out. It is because the strange freak was never explained that I am superstitious now, at bottom, even though I always say I am not."

Cincinnati [OH] Enquirer 28 July 1906: p. 11 NEW YORK

We finish this chapter with something you don't see every day: a ghost who leaves footprints.

A Kansas Ghost Story

The Atchison *Globe* says the man in that town who had a strange experience recently with his deceased wife's empty chair, which rocked in a strange manner, is having another experience that is still more remarkable. Wherever he goes of late he hears a soft footfall keeping step beside him. Every step he takes he hears that mysterious step joining in with his own. Walking in the snow the other morning, side by side with his own footprints, there appeared the prints of a woman's feet. He is sure that the ghost of his wife is shadowing him, and that for some reason it distrusts him. He is much worried about it.

The Wichita [KS] Daily Eagle 15 April 1891: p. 7 KANSAS

4.

The Hoodoo Hat and Other Horrors

Cats, Hats, and Hangmen's Ropes

Black cat on my doorstep, black cat on my window-sill
Black cat on my doorstep, black cat on my window-sill
If one black cat don't cross me, another black cat will

-"Black Cat Hoot Owl Blues," Ma Rainey-

A popular story and sitcom theme in the 1950s and '60s was "the jinx." A character superstitiously fancied himself cursed or believed he was bringing bad luck to those around him. Naturally some clever rationalist would trick him into seeing the error of his ways, leading to a happy ending and a victory for scientific thinking.

Stories of such bad luck streaks (without the happy ending) were widely reported in the press throughout the late 19th and early 20th centuries. The Evil Eye, bad luck, Jonah, curse—and hoodoo—these were all names for negative conditions ranging from a bad run at the poker table to malign influences leading to death.

Nowhere is the 19th-century conflict between superstition and rational thought more visible than in these articles. On one hand, the papers solemnly disparaged ignorance and superstitious delusions. On the other, the stories very often told of a character who scoffed at superstition, only to fall victim to a hoodoo himself. If the message was that hoodoos were nonsense, it was a mixed one.

When I first started looking at some of the thousands of articles about hoodoos, I assumed that the more far-fetched stories were simply made up. Certainly some were invented on slow-news days, but I was surprised to find that, when I took the trouble to look for documentation about the people involved, many stories had a strong element of truth. Or, at the very least, they involved some singular coincidences.

Historically, what constituted a hoodoo? There are the usual suspects: black cats, the number thirteen, and broken mirrors. A hoodoo could be a person, place, or thing and the list was apparently endless. A sampling of objects I've seen labeled as "hoodoos" included hundred-dollar bills, mummies, chairs, clocks, a sack used to hood a lynching victim, the Hope Diamond, stray dogs, the country of Panama, opals, red-heads, people with crossed eyes, bicycles, ships, and trains. Soldiers, sailors, miners, and railroad men all had their own unique sets of hoodoos and remedies for the same. One well-known, if distasteful antidote for a hoodoo was to spit into one's hat. We might want to pocket a four-leaf clover for this look at the hoodoos of the past.

There were a good many jocular stories in the press about people who defied hoodoos, particularly those stalwart rationalists who started "Thirteen Clubs." Here is a typical specimen.

Hoodoo Gets Even
Member of Thirteen Club Cut in Breaking a Mirror.

From the New York American.

Three hundred and thirteen members and guests of the Thirteen Club, which exists to defy superstition, were not so sure after their banquet at the St. Regis Monday night, that it is—well, discreet, say, to go out of one's way to hoot at the old beliefs.

J.R. Abarbanell, one of the members, volunteered to break a mirror—provided by the club—which hung over a $15,000 piano in the banquet hall. He struck it with a skull, and it broke, all right, and he struck so hard that his hand became involved with a shower of glass fragments and was seriously cut. Abarbanell ran from the room, yelling with excitement. It took a doctor nearly an hour to extract the glass from his hand and dress the cuts.

That wasn't all. Several big fragments from the mirror fell upon the specially made woodwork of the $15,000 piano, cut and scratched the cover so badly that it will cost several hundred dollars to patch it up.

Apart from that disturbing incident, the dinner went off very well. The guests entered the banquet room through a door above which hung a thirteen foot ladder with thirteen rungs, on which was inscribed, 'Abandon all hope, ye who enter here.' Then they sat down, thirteen at a table, and raised umbrellas, spilled salt, and used little skulls for candelabra.

Thirteen of the members after coffee had been served left the room, which was darkened, and returned in shrouds chanting, "Quaff a cup to the dead already; hurrah for the next that dies." Then they groaned, laughed wild ghostly laughs, and carried out The Revelry of the Dying while little pans of alcohol gave blue tinged light to the proceedings.
The Washington [DC] Post 15 January 1909: p. 2 NEW YORK

Objects such as mirrors, rings, or hats formed the largest category of hoodoos. This story from Montana cites some very high tolls for a hoodoo mirror and a Native American game wheel. One suspects that state pride might have encouraged some exaggeration.

DEATH ABIDES IN IRON RING AND MIRROR
One "Hoodoo" Article Kills Nine Men and the Other's Record Is Two Score.

Montana is believed to have two of the most remarkable death dealing instruments extant. At least, they are popularly accredited as such, and if the stories related of their supposed "hoodooism" continue much longer the fact will be considered pretty well established. More or less superstition attaches to the articles at any rate, and the tales concerning them are worthy of repetition.

The first has to do with a "haunted" mirror at Glasgow, Valley County. According to the stories, the "hoodooed" glass has at various times been in the possession of nine men, all of whom have met violent deaths.

The chain of title to the property begins, according to the narrative, with a man named Dunn, who was a noted character in Valley County and who died with his boots on a number of years ago in consequence of a disagreement with a man who was bred in Texas.

From Dunn, the story goes, the mirror went into the possession of "Long Henry" Thompson, of Valley County who soon had no use for it, as he was put into a grave with leaden weights to assure his staying there.

To five other men, who met deaths by violence, the story current in Montana traces ownership of the wicked glass at various times, and the chain finally leads up to William A. Humphrey, who owned the mirror until five years ago, when he was shot and killed in a Glasgow saloon by H.R. Stephens, upon whom Humphrey had opened fire.

After Humphrey's death the stories about the mirror became current and many to whom it was offered refused to purchase it, freely admitting that they were afraid to have it in their possession.

Robert L. Conatser, town marshal of Glasgow, purchased the mirror and a week later while hunting Conatser was drowned in the Missouri River.

The custodian of Conatser's effects tried to sell the mirror, but could not find a purchaser.

The person who now has charge of the mirror has been urged to destroy it, but he declines to do so and will not even touch it, declaring that it may remain forever where it now is, as far as he is concerned.

The story goes that while "Long Henry" was the owner of the property, he had it stored away for a long time, and that while it was so hidden he refrained from the use of liquor, prospered and was living down his bad reputation, but that as soon as he had placed it in use he resumed his old career and his killing soon followed.

It is also related by those who discuss the history of the glass in awed tones that Humphrey, before he started out to look for Stephens, stood in front of the mirror, and, leveling a revolver at his image therein, demonstrated to a friend the aim that he would take if he found it necessary to kill a man.

There are many such stories concerning the mirror in circulation in Valley County, and the subject has been discussed so generally that the death of almost every man in the county who has not died a natural death has been attributed to the influence of the magic glass. It is known that it was owned by four of the men named, while rumor has greatly extended the number of dead possessors.

Wallace Coburn, of Helena, possesses the other freak. This is an Indian gambling contrivance—a "hoodoo ring," to which is ascribed the death of between 30 and 40 men. The history of the ring goes back many, many years into the shadowy land of legend, and this history is one long record of bloodshed, violent death and murder. Every owner of the article up to Mr. Coburn has died, either under the blow of a tomahawk, the barb of an arrow, or, in later days, from a bullet wound.

The "hoodoo ring" is a small iron ring, about three inches in diameter, covered with elaborately beaded buckskin. The beads are of different colors and different sizes, each color and each size indicating a different value. The hoop is intended to be rolled along the ground, and, while it is in motion, arrows are shot at it. Upon the position of the arrow with reference to the vari-colored and vari-sized beads when the hoop falls to the ground depends the outcome of the game. It is, in fact, a primitive roulette wheel.

An old squaw on the Fort Belknap Indian Reservation gave the hoop to Mr. Coburn. She was afraid to have it because of its history. Her husband had owned it, and he died a sudden death. His father had owned it, and he also had died a sudden death.

According to the legendary lore of the squaw the hoop had been made many years ago by a warrior of another tribe. He was poor, had no horses, no blankets, no chattels of any kind. Then he fashioned the ring, and spent many days on the job. When it was finished he began gambling with the other members of the tribe. His worldly possessions increased rapidly. Soon he owned horses, fine tepees, and wonderful bead work. He became influential. His affluence aroused the jealousy of the other members of the tribe. The medicine man whispered that there was an evil spirit in the hoop which would bring destruction on the tribe. Young braves sought to steal the hoop. Its owner was watchful and slew them—three of them.

Then war broke out with another tribe. The owner of the hoop went with the rest of the band. He was slain. The fame of the hoop had spread to the rival tribe and the slayer of the hoop owner took the ring. Then he gambled with it and had the same wonderful luck in winning the possessions of the rival players. He was killed in a dispute over a game. His son took the ring, and he soon met a similar fate. The hoop passed into other hands, but everyone who laid claim to it died a violent death, either in battle, or in a fight provoked over a game. Riches first, and death soon afterward, it brought to all.

It fell into the possession of the squaw after her husband's death. No Indian on the reservation would accept it from her as a gift. Then Mr. Coburn learned of it and the squaw gladly gave it to him. [*New York Tribune.*]

Springfield [MA] Union 7 January 1911: p. 9 MONTANA

NOTE: I am usually skeptical when seeing a long string of hoodoo victims. However, some of these back-stories check out. Here is a headline about "Long Henry" Thompson's death:

NOTED DESPERADO SHOT AND KILLED

"Long Henry" Thompson Is Filled Full of Lead by Ed Shufelt at Saco as Result of Trouble Which Is Supposed to Have Started About a Woman.

Anaconda [MT] Standard 16 February 1902: p. 1

And a note about William A. Humphrey's death:

Politics Causes Duel in Montana – Four Shot

Glasgow, Mont., Nov. 6. As a result of ill feeling engendered during the campaign, James R. Stevens, Untied States deputy collector of customs, instantly killed William Humphrey during a pistol duel in a saloon here last night...Stephens emptied his six-shooter and Humphrey three chambers of his revolver.

Denver [CO] Post 6 November 1902: p. 6

Opals, unless they were the wearer's birthstone, were considered extremely unlucky, as this luckless man found out.

STOLEN RING A HOODOO
Mother Warns Thief to Get Rid of Opal.
SAYS IT CURSED HER SON
Had All Sorts of Bad Luck Whenever He Wore It.
SAFE ONLY WHEN IN PAWN
Lost Money, Got Hurt by Cars and Finally Died When He Took It Out.

New York, Oct. 6. If an ex-soulmate or an ex-affinity of her son stole an opal ring from Mrs. Silas Smith of 372 Main Street, Paterson, N.J., she will do well to return it or hastily dispose of it—according to Mrs. Smith. It once belonged to the late George Burris, her son by a former marriage, who was prosperous when he didn't have it and had troubles when he did, and before that was the property of at least a dozen persons who have had tales of hard luck to tell. Burris died last February.

"My son was a good man so long as he didn't wear that ring," said Mrs. Smith yesterday to a reporter. "He prospered, never got into trouble and had a smile for everybody. Just let him begin wearing it, however, and street cars would run against him, he would fail in business and women would cross his path.

"If I mistake not, George bought the ring fifteen years ago." Stories vary, as to just how long the ring has been in Paterson. Some say it was made here, but it is certain that the stone is foreign.

"Some say it is a Persian stone that carries death and destruction. It certainly did as much for my son George.

"My son was shot in February 1898 and came near dying, but recovered. He then pawned the ring, and everything seemed to come his way. He got control of the best roadhouse on Stony Hill Road near Paterson, and everything was lovely until he was seized with a desire to have the ring again. He got it, and debt overcame him and he had to retire. Then he became a barber, and adversity caused him to pawn the jewel.

The Hoodoo Working Again.

"He did well at his new trade and in a remarkably short time was the proprietor of one of the biggest shops in Newark. One day he told me he was eager to have that ring on his ringer again. I told him that it had been redeemed and I had hung it on the statue of St. Ann in the chapel of St. Joseph's Hospital when he was ill there of typhoid fever. I am not a Roman Catholic, but somehow I thought maybe some good might come from that little act.

"It was 1899 when he was sick. When he got the ring back he began having trouble with his creditors and with street cars. Three years in succession he was injured by the cars. If he had been a drinking man I should have attributed the accidents to too much liquor, but he wasn't. He just couldn't overcome that hoodoo.

"During this run of bad luck, my son determined to pawn the ring and never redeem it. The money he realized brought no luck, but when it was spent we prospered once more.

"About two years ago George decided that he would get the opal out of pawn and try it once more. Then came the woman who claimed all he left and his death through a fall on the steps of the Elks' Club in Newark. I have always thought that but for the ring my son would have recovered in a few weeks. Instead the injury developed blood poisoning.

Not a Superstitious Woman.

"Then came several women who claimed to have been his friends or his companions. I turned them away without the tokens they asked for. I may be wrong, but I think that one of them came here last Thursday afternoon when I was away and stole the ring and about $300 worth of other jewels which I possessed. I can't call names, of course, but I have my suspicions. If my boy had only let that ring remain on the statue of St. Ann, I feel somehow that we should all be happy now—and yet I know I am not superstitious."

The Paterson police say this remarkable ring figured in Paterson long before it became the property of Burris. It was owned by a widely known business man, who failed shortly after he purchased it. He sold it to a man who had always been prosperous, but who had a series of misfortunes immediately after his purchase.

Evening Star [Washington DC] 6 October 1908: p. 12 NEW JERSEY

A FATAL HEADPIECE
Tale of a Hoodoo Hat and the Many Victims of Its Influence in the Civil War.

John Cooper, one of Dooly County's most prominent citizens, was lately in this city on his way to Augusta to attend the old veterans' reunion. When he got off the train he looked up Capt. Warren Moseley, one of the bravest of the boys who went out in the '60s, and they immediately began swapping reminiscences about their army life in Virginia. Finally Mr. Cooper asked Capt. Moseley if he remembered the Yankee hat. A reporter who was standing there heard the following story, which both men vouch for as being absolutely true:

On the first day of the battle of Winchester a Yankee was killed so near the line of battle that a soldier by the name of McLondon, Company I, Fourth Georgia, picked up the hat and put it on and wore it, says the Macon (Ga.) *News*. He had not had it on his head for more than two hours when he was shot through the head, the bullet piercing the hat in almost the same hole that the bullet had entered that killed the Yankee.

Another soldier by the name of Wooten, of Company H, Fourth Georgia, picked up the hat and put it on, and in less than an hour he, too, was killed, the bullet striking him in the head near the place where the two other bullets had entered.

The next day another soldier by the name of Kilpatrick, of Company H, Fourth Georgia, was wearing the hat, when he, too, was struck in the head and killed.

Although the hat was a fine one, it was left lying on the field, as there was no one who would wear it, as four men who had worn it were then cold and stiff, and each one had been shot through the hat in almost the same place.

Daily Herald [Biloxi, MS] 16 February 1901: p. 3 VIRGINIA and GEORGIA

NOTE: Initially I thought this was another too-good-to-be-true tale, which was borne out by the difficulty in finding any of the men mentioned. Finally I found an online history of the Doles-Cook Brigade by Henry W. Thomas, published in 1903. On the roster were John Cooper, Captain Moseley, and the late Wooten, all present and correct.

Anything associated with death could be a hoodoo. Lynching ropes were particularly potent charms.

A Veritable Hoodoo
Strange and Eventful History of a Piece of Hangman's Rope.

A couple of evenings ago a young man named Tollman, who lives near Ellenwood, dropped in at the police station and gave a reporter there about an inch of the white plow line with which the negro who poisoned the Burks family was lynched. Mr. Tollman was present at the inquest the preceding day and had there secured the relic.

The plow line was in three strands, and some hours later the reporter separated one of them and gave it to Call Officer Beavers. A negro who happened to be in the station at the time begged a strand for himself.

He said a piece of plow line with which a man has been hanged makes a formidable hoodoo, and if the plow line is white the efficacy of the hoodoo is doubled. The reporter accordingly gave him one of the two remaining strands and wrapping the other in tissue paper put it in his pocket.

Now for chapter 2. As Officer Beavers was going home yesterday he thought to attach the string to his watch guard for safe keeping, and in so doing dropped the watch and broke it so badly that is its doubtful if it will ever run again. He put the bit of plow line in his pocket and inside of two hours barked his shin on a chair, got a cinder in his eye, spilled a bottle of ink on his pants, and had a counterfeit dollar passed on him. He then threw the hoodoo on the back of a negro who was splitting wood in the yard, and before the man struck a dozen more blows he cut his little toe off.

The reporter's first misadventure was to break a pair of eyeglasses he prized highly and a little while later he tore up a lot of "copy" by mistake and had to write it all over again. This was Monday night. Yesterday he took the hoodoo string to the dining room of his hotel and quietly stuck it in the folds of the apron of the waiter who attended him. A few minutes later the darky fell down the kitchen stairs making an unearthly clatter and dropping the fatal talisman. He picked it up and instantly suspecting witchcraft put it down the back of another waiter.

This victim, all unsuspicious, loaded a tray with meals for six and went up to the dining room. At the head of the stairs he caught his foot and fell sprawling, breaking every dish on the tray and scattering beefsteaks, potatoes and miscellaneous eatables all over the apartment. Somebody informed him of the hoodoo, and he put it in the stove.

The possessor of the third strand has not yet been heard from, but if he gets run over, falls out of a window, breaks a leg or meets with some kindred adventure, it will occasion no surprise. *Atlanta Constitution. Daily Journal and Journal and Tribune* [Knoxville, TN] 21 November 1893: p. 7 GEORGIA

NOTE: Here is a brief summary of the fate of the man hung with the plow line.

Ned Jenkins, a negro, was lynched in Clayton County, Ga., Saturday night. He confessed that he poisoned William Burk's (his employer) family of seven a few days before. He had quarreled with his employer and put arsenic in the meal.

State [Columbia, SC] 23 October 1893: p. 1

The newspapers seemed to delight in lists of hoodoo victims and their dooms.

STAR IS HOODOOED
The Kokomo Police Fight Shy of Badge No. 3

Kokomo, Ind., Dec. 17. A strange superstition attached to the police force of this city has been intensified by the death of Officer Kirkman. By some singular fatality every "No. 3" policeman since the organization of the force nine years ago has died within a year after beginning duty. No deaths have occurred among the other numbers, but the death mark has been on every "No. 3," all extraordinarily active and efficient officers. The first to pin on the fatal number was A. M. Martin, who died of tuberculosis. The second, Edward Everett, succumbed to typhoid fever. The third, Thomas A. Seacrist, died from injuries received in jumping from a train. The fourth and last, who has just died from fever superinduced by injuries received in quelling a riot election day, was Jerry Kirkman. No other officer can be induced to don badge "No. 3" and the police board has abolished the fatal number.

Grand Rapids [MI] Press 17 December 1900: p. 2 INDIANA

Less than a year later, Badge No. 3 was back in service—and claimed another victim.

HOODOO BADGE Being Busily Side-Stepped By Police Officers in Kokomo

Kokomo, Ind., May 7. Police Badge No. 3, that has been held for years a hoodoo, may claim another victim. In all the history of the town no officer wore the fatal star and lived more than a few months. "No. 3" has five victims, whereas none of the wearers of the other six numbers have died. Two weeks ago in reorganizing the force under the metropolitan police system all of them asked to be excused from wearing "No. 3." It was finally agreed to draw cuts for numbers and the fatal "No. 3" was drawn by Marshal Edwards. The same day Edwards became ill and is still confined to his bed. The badge had not been worn since the death of Officer Kirkman six months ago. Previous victims of the evil star were A.N. Martin, Edward Everett, and T.J. Seacrist.

Cincinnati [OH] Enquirer 8 May 1901: p. 2 INDIANA

Perhaps abolishing the star in 1900 broke the hoodoo. Marshal Edwards apparently recovered and did not die until 1927.

Moving from the hoodooed object to the animal kingdom, black cats and owls were the top two hoodoo animals. Robins, doves, and howling dogs were also on the list.

As we saw in the previous chapter on tokens of death, owls have a long-standing evil reputation as a bird of ill-omen. Are they just the messengers of misfortune, or are they a hoodoo?

A WINGED HOODOO

A gray-and-white owl, which lurks in trees in the early morning and hoots in the twilight as trains of the New York, New Haven and Hartford Railroad go whizzing by, has come to be regarded as a hoodoo by the trainmen. Death and catastrophe have marked the system for weeks. Hardly a day has passed but a wreck has occurred or a trainman has gone to his death. In nearly every instance, engineers and firemen say, the hoodoo owl appeared by night or day a few hours before. Engineer Harry Chapman, of this city, whose wild engine ran into and wrecked a passenger train in Waterbury, March 31 last, saw the fateful bird the night before he went to his doom. The express train leaving this city at 8:10 o'clock in the morning for New York has within two days killed three persons. Thursday the train struck and killed a woman near Mamaroneck, and a man near New York City. The third was a woman killed by the same train at Bridgeport on Friday. The gray-and-white owl has appeared most frequently within the past week. George Rennie, a brakeman, fell from a freight train near Waterbury. His companions say he spoke of seeing the owl previous to his fall. He died in the hospital. Conductor George E. Whipple, of the Federal Express, was struck by a truck on the platform as his train pulled through Wickford Junction, Rhode Island, Friday night and was instantly killed. Mrs. Margaret Lakin, the only woman passenger agent in the employ of the road, was killed while on duty at Cohassett, Mass., Friday. Andrew Lang was found dead beside the track in Waterford Friday, and his body was taken to New London. So strong has grown the superstition concerning the hoodoo bird that attempts have been made to kill it, but though stray shots have been fired from trains in the suburbs, no one has reported having hit the owl. It was last seen this morning on the Naugatuck Division.

Cincinnati [OH] Enquirer 25 April 1903: p. 13 CONNECTICUT

THE BLACK CAT TRAIN.
Uncanny Apparition That Is Always Followed by a Mishap

The Madison branch of the P., C., C. & St. L. sports what is called by the railroad boys the "Black Cat" train, says the Louisville *Times*. Some time over a month ago the train, in charge of Conductor Wheedon, pulled out from Columbus, and just beyond that city the trainmen observed two black cats crossing the track ahead of the locomotive. It was jokingly remarked that this was a sign of ill-luck, and, sure enough, the train was wrecked a few moments after. Fortunately nobody was hurt. Since then the trainmen claim to have seen one or both black cats crossing the track ahead of the train several times, and some mishap always followed. Night before last the black cat crossed in front of the train again and sure enough the engine broke her "saddle" a few miles below Columbus. This is the last piece of ill-luck credited to the black cat. It is said that the trainmen are becoming nervous over the persistence of the ebon-hued feline, and next time they see it cross before the train will turn back for a fresh start at the risk of a discharge.

The belief in the evil influence of a black cat is as old as the hills, but is especially strong among railroad men.

Chicago [IL] Herald 28 February 1891: p. 12 KENTUCKY

NOTE: The P., C., C. & St. L. is the Pittsburgh, Cincinnati, Chicago & St. Louis Railroad. The "saddle" was a water tank mounted atop the boiler. The quantity of black cat / railroad hoodoo stories in the papers is quite staggering. As a side note, certain locomotives got the reputation as "hoodoo engines" or "man-killers." You'll find a good selection of hoodoos of the rails in *The Face in the Window: Haunting Ohio Tales.*

Properties described as hoodoos usually had a long history of financial misfortune, murder, and/or suicide for the occupants. The following farmer seems, like the rationalist members of the Thirteen Club, to have gone out of his way to tempt Fate.

BAD LUCK GOES WITH PURCHASE OF CEMETERY
Flower Converted Burial Ground Into a Farm, But Nothing Would Grow
HIS HOUSE HAUNTED
Lightning Strikes His Barn and Flames Destroy the Buildings

Vincennes, Ind., Aug. 15. George Flower, a prominent young farmer, bought a strip of land at Sand Ridge, near here, on which was located the oldest cemetery in this section. The cemetery was surrounded by a grove and contained three hundred headstones.

Flower removed the headstones, throwing some of them into the Embarras River, and with the rest built a foundation for his house. The cemetery he plowed up and planted it in melons and potatoes. Although similar crops on the rest of the farm grew in abundance, the cemetery crop has been eaten up by a strange bug.

His House Haunted

Flowers' house is now haunted, and for several nights past, the building was shaken violently. Flower, his wife and two children are distracted with fear and have fled from the place. People having relatives buried there have taken the matter up, and threatened to prosecute Flower for obliterating the graves without giving them notice, so that they could have reinterred the dead. The grand jury of Lawrence County is investigating the case and may indict Flower. Flower's brother and sister and two of his children lie buried in the devastated cemetery. Flower secured the money from his father, Frank Flower, in Colorado Springs, to buy the farm.

Family May Go Insane

The Flower family, it is feared, will go insane with fear. The neighbors dare not harbor them. The father seems to be impelled by an irresistible force to visit the haunted farm daily, only to flee again with increased fear.

To-day lightning struck the barn on the Flower place and burned the stock and buildings. The place is in an unfrequented portion of the county, and the little settlement of the vicinity is greatly excited over the mystery.

Philadelphia [PA] Inquirer 16 August 1902: p.2 INDIANA

If we can believe the newspapers, entire families were wiped out by hoodoos.

HOODOO IN HIS FAMILY
Nine Members of It Have Already Met With Violent Deaths.

Toledo. Nov. 19. A story of a badly hoodooed family comes from North Baltimore, a small town about forty miles south of this city. Will Archer of that place was last evening struck by a Baltimore and Ohio train and instantly killed, his head completely severed from his body, his legs cut off and his body horribly mangled. The man was intoxicated when he met his death.

Archer is the last of seven brothers, who with two brothers-in-law have met with violent deaths. The first fatality occurred fifteen years ago when a brother, John Archer, was killed at Fostoria by a Baltimore and Ohio train. He, too, was intoxicated at the time.

James Archer, the second unfortunate member of the family to meet his fate, was killed in the woods near North Baltimore by a falling tree. This was about ten years ago. Two years later Burt Archer was killed at Deshler by a C.H. and D. train. His body was ground to pieces and strewn along the track for a distance of half a mile.

Frank Archer met death from a pistol wound by Marshal Kratz of North Baltimore, who went to the Archer home to make an arrest. Frank attacked him and the marshal fired, the bullet killing Frank instantly. Kratz was arrested for murder, but was never tried.

About seven years ago Lute Archer was killed by a B. and O. train at North Baltimore. The story runs that he was murdered and his body laid upon the track, but the general impression is that he was under the influence of liquor. Dan Archer was killed several years ago on an excursion train coming from North Baltimore to Toledo. He fell between the cars and was instantly killed.

Jesse Baker, a son-in-law, was killed recently at North Baltimore. He was marshal of the town and was shot by Harry Davis, a notorious crook who later escaped from jail. Hunter McMurray, another son-in-law and a saloonkeeper at Bairdstown, was shot and killed in a quarrel with a railroad man who was tried and sent to the penitentiary, but is now out on parole.

The women members of the family have so far escaped violent deaths, but the body of a daughter who died of typhoid fever was taken from the grave by ghouls, cut to pieces, and deposited in a barrel in Bloomdale, Ohio. Joseph Archer is the only son of this remarkable family who has not died with his boots on, and the father, John Archer, still lives in North Baltimore.

Evening Post [Charleston, SC] 27 November 1897: p. 7 OHIO

NOTE: So many of these hoodooed family stories tip into a kind of parody of hyperbole. Yet independent documentation can be found on the individuals in this story, for example, this *Plain Dealer* article, which predates the above by five years:

Lute Archer of North Baltimore was killed by a Baltimore & Ohio freight train last night near the village. He was partially drunk and was walking home on the track. His body was cut in halves from the head down. Ar-

cher was thirty years old and unmarried. Two of his brothers have been killed in a similar manner, one brother was killed by a falling tree and one brother was killed in Bairdstown by Marshal Kratz who was trying to arrest him. These deaths happened in the period of ten years, and there are two more brothers of whom the neighbors predict similar fatalities.
Plain Dealer [Cleveland, OH] 20 July 1892: p 3

HOODOO GETS LAST OF UNLUCKY FAMILY

Hawesville, Ky., July 6. Hancock County's "trouble woman," Mrs. Nancy Newman, is dead here at the age of eighty-seven years. She was the last of thirteen brothers and sisters whose stepfather, Capt. John Sterett, was the first sheriff of the county. Tragedies came often into Mrs. Newman's life. Her youngest child was scalded to death in a tanning vat. The second was burned to death on the home hearth two weeks later. The third, a Confederate soldier, was murdered in a riot at Mobile, Ala. The fourth was killed two years ago when a house fell on him. The fifth met death in a runaway five years ago. A son-in-law and a grandson met violent deaths. Two weeks ago the aged woman herself, hobbling into the kitchen for a drink, fell and broke her leg which had not begun to mend when she died.
Grand Rapids [MI] Press 6 July 1912: p. 10 KENTUCKY

This last story presents another extraordinary saga of accidental death and domestic atrocities blamed on what the paper labeled a haunted district.

SHUN OHIO WOODS STEEPED IN CRIME
Napoleon People Fear District of Violent Deaths and Gory Deeds
Say Witches Revel Near Spot Where Man Kills Wife and Himself.

Napoleon, O., April 1. The funeral of Joseph Motter, who killed himself after shooting to death his wife, held at his farm four and a half miles northwest of here, has recalled to an old resident a series of crimes and suicides, tragedies and strange happenings within a mile and a half radius of the Motter homestead within two decades.

Eight years ago, Motter's brother, Emanuel, committed suicide by shooting himself in the forehead with a shotgun—the same weapon used in Wednesday's double tragedy. On an adjoining farm, William Badenhop, a prosperous German farmer, killed himself in a closet. A mile east, Badenhop's brother ended his life with carbolic acid. A half mile west Justus Morey killed himself with a rifle held to his ear. In a woods one and a half miles south, the body of D. Joost was found hanging from a limb. Later his son met a tragic death on his way to Iowa.

In the same neighborhood lived ex-Commissioner H.R. Rohrs. His sister was burned to death from a spark from a bonfire. His 14-year-old grandson, Carl Vajen, met the same fate there four weeks ago. Rohrs' daughter died from accidentally drinking a cup of lye. In a nearby saw mill three brothers were badly mangled, one dying when whirled on a shaft. Their grandmother soon afterward was burned to death. Later the saw mill was moved a short distance. A boiler exploded and Sam Willard was killed. The owner of the mill, George Rickenberg, recently dropped dead.

Fred Otte was found dead in a cornfield last year. An attempt was made on "Old Man" Hutch's life by poisoning with croton oil. A neighbor, John Hutchinson, was struck by lightning. He was found lying on his back, and by a strange freak of nature his cane lay balanced across his throat.

Some years ago a New Year's Eve barn dance was held in the neighborhood and a sleigh load of Napoleon young men were run down by a Wabash passenger train. Frank Lon and Fred Rohrs were killed. Several serious cutting affrays have occurred and six years ago a real duel was fought. Knives were the weapons and the bodies of the two men were hacked and slashed and the combat ended only when the duelists fainted from loss of blood.

Weird and creepy legends abounding with witches, ghosts and mysteries were woven about the locality. Between the Motter farm and Peter Lettick's, one half mile east, lay a patch of woods, commonly called the Woods of Witches. Lettick's home, eighty rods away, burned. Terrifying noises and brilliant lights soon were reported about the ruins. A flaming, headless infant nightly dived into the cellar of the ruins. Balls of fire darted here and there and lamp-bearing witches hovered in the woods.

A wandering peddler had mysteriously disappeared in the forest. The country folk watched the phantasm for several months, but fear precluded an investigation. Ed Rhodda finally drove his old gray mare down the abutting pike. It scared at the phantom infant and Rhodda's leg was ripped from hip to ankle when thrown against a fence. A few weeks later a search with picks and spades was made for the peddler, but to this day his disappearance remains unsolved.

Joe Motter's nephew, Walter, had his head crushed recently while moving the house in which Morey suicided. Joe shot his wife and then himself while despondent.

Plain Dealer [Cleveland, OH] 2 April 1911: p. 1 OHIO

NOTE: This impressive necrology of Napoleon, Ohio sounds too incredible to be true and the date made it suspect. However, I have located nearly all of the people named in the census reports and local directories, as well as the graves of some of the unfortunates. Some I also found in other articles about their dire ends. For example, Joseph Motter shot his wife in the back on the first anniversary of their wedding, then shot himself in the heart. His step-son came to the house to congratulate them and found the bodies in the parlor. The day before Motter had gone to his step-son's to retrieve the shotgun—the same shotgun Motter's brother had used to kill himself. [Source: *Plain Dealer* (Cleveland, OH) 30 March, 1911: p. 3] The Motters died 29 March, 1911, so the April date is only a coincidence.

It is interesting that no names are mentioned for the "cutting affrays" or the "real duel." Dueling was, of course, illegal.

Croton oil is a caustic oil made from the seeds of an Asian shrub. It was used as a purgative and a counterirritant—in the same class as mustard plasters—but was dangerous in high doses.

I have not yet discovered anything more about the sinister "Woods of Witches." Napoleon stands in on the banks of the Maumee River in the former Great Black Swamp of Ohio, and is about 20 miles from Richfield Center, site of a "witchcraft scare," in 1897 where many families in the village went mad, claiming their houses were infested with demonic black cats.

Now, just to be on the safe side, go spit in your hat...

FURTHER READING: There are chapters called "A House in Which Nothing Will Thrive: Haunted and Hoodoo Houses" and "The Malice of Inanimate Objects: A Haunted Telegraph, the Murderer's Clock, and a Hoodoo Chair" in *The Headless Horror*. In the same book there is also a lengthy story on the many suicides in the hoodoo Cell Thirteen at the Ohio State Penitentiary and articles on the Richfield Center witchcraft scare.

5.

The Men in Black

Unearthly Entities

The Prince of Darkness is a gentleman.

-The Goblins' Song, Sir John Suckling-

The next three chapters include a mix of atypical apparitions, from Men in Black to giant ghosts and fiery phantom devils. Also included are a few gnome-like entities and other Fortean creatures to show the great variety of unearthly entities being reported. Most seem to claim descent from panic-inducing apparitions like Spring-heeled Jack, the fleet-footed boogieman who terrorized Victorian England with his uncanny appearances and unnaturally high leaps—the most prominent in a series of 19th-century Phantom Attackers.

Spring-heeled Jack's finest chronicler is historian Mike Dash. In his definitive work on the entity that appeared in *Fortean Studies 3* in 1996, Dash has collected what appear to be all the known contemporary sources, references, and reports on the unearthly creature known for his inhuman ability to leap over tall walls and roofs and for his terrifying, diabolic appearance: he was sometimes seen with horns, claws, and eyes like "red balls of fire." He also vomited flame and seemed impervious to gunshots. He made his stunning Satanic debut in London in 1837 and isolated reports of similar entities continue until today.

I have run across some stories of mysterious beings that echo some of the features of a "Jack:" 1) extreme height/ ability to leap high in the air, 2) a gliding motion, 3) imperviousness to bullets, 4) an ability to disappear quickly, 5) aggressiveness, and 6) dressed in a cape (Spring-heeled Jack was said to wear a cloak over a tight, oil-cloth suit.) Few of these entities have the fiery eyes or fire-breathing ability of the original Spring-heeled Jack. Yet, the creatures in the stories that follow, if not precisely "Jacks," are from the same family of phantom attackers, cut from the same oilcloth, if you will...

Although we may think of the Men in Black as late-20th-century figures associated with the UFO age—think John Keel and *The Mothman Prophecies*—their roots go back to the 16th and 17th centuries where a visit from "The Black Man:" that dark-visaged man dressed in black, meant an encounter with the Devil. They appear here both as standard, black-clad ghosts or as attacking entities. There are so many of these phantom aggressors that one wonders if the choice of a black costume was merely for nefarious convenience. I make no judgment about whether these Men in Black were "real" ghosts, living malefactors, or pranksters.

THOUSAND PEOPLE
Gather To See Lafayette's Ghostly "Man in Black" Walk Out.

Lafayette, Ind., March 19. Last evening fully 1,000 persons gathered on the South Fifth Street crossing of the Wabash Railroad to see the apparition in black that now haunts that locality. Every night for the last week a mysterious man, dressed in black, bareheaded and with his dark hair waving in the wind, glides spectrally down from the hill east of South Fifth Street and south of the Wabash tracks, and thence to the hominy mills in that locality.

The apparition has created more talk in the south side of the city than anything in years, and the neighborhood is terrified. Details of police have visited the scene, and the spectre has been seen by Detective Weinhardt and Policeman Cole. They are as completely baffled as others who have seen the apparition.

It is declared that after coming down the lonely path of the hillside and crossing the Wabash tracks the man flickers into invisibility. Residents of the neighborhood whose integrity cannot be questioned claim to have seen the apparition.

The police arrested 15 men in the crowd that gathered to-night awaiting the appearance of the "man in black." The trouble grew out of the police ordering a number of boys home after the curfew hour, when several toughs of the neighborhood interfered and a battle took place.
Cincinnati [OH] Enquirer 20 March 1903: p. 3 INDIANA

NOTE: A puzzling feature of many of these cases is the large numbers of people reported as turning out to witness them. How could a hoaxer count on being undetected under those circumstances?

THE FACTORYVILLE MAN IN BLACK

Most every town in existence has had a "Woman in Black" but it has remained these years for Factoryville to produce a genuine "Man in Black." Such seems to be the case here at present. This mysterious apparition is reported to be about six feet six inches in height, with a very long jet black beard and hair and wears a black suit of clothes, and a slouch hat pulled well down over his eyes. This walking "Hoodoo" it seems, mysteriously and suddenly appears in the remotest parts of town, and on dimly lighted streets, frightening women and children nearly into convulsions, although he has made no attacks on anyone yet so far as learned. There are all sorts of rumors about town as to who it might be, and what his object is, but no one seems to have had the courage yet to approach him and investigate his nationality. The story is going the rounds that it is one of our young married men, and that if he catches the object of his search his mission in disguise will soon be ended.

The Scranton [PA] Tribune 12 January 1897: p. 8 PENNSYLVANIA

NOTE: See Chapter 12 for Women in Black cases.

This story of an Ohio ghost-in-black was previously published in *The Face in the Window*. Note the cloak and the gliding motion, which are found in subsequent stories.

LEGLESS GHOST IS WALKING
Residents of Spruce Street Describe Strange Apparition Which Haunts Locality

There is a real ghost in this city although the presence of the weird thing has been kept a secret for two or three days in order that a delegation of local sleuths could unearth the mysterious rendezvous of the unwelcome visitor.

Spruce Street, which heretofore has had the reputation of being one of the most quiet and peaceful thoroughfares in the city, threatens to share honors with Sleepy Hollow where the famous headless horseman was wont to chase poor Ichabod Crane up and down the hills near Tarrytown.

But the comparison stops here, for instead of the headless phantom which infested the Sleepy Hollow district, the good neighbors on the street say it is a legless man that dashes out of the yards and jumps across the road only to disappear in an orchard across the street.

Mrs. John Gehrke of 108 Spruce Street was the first of many residents to discover the "awful thing" last Thursday night about ten thirty o'clock and she flushed the ghost in the yard and was terrified when the thing which looks like a man dressed in a long black cape, skimmed over the ground across the road and disappeared in an old orchard which has the reputation of being spooky on account of a suicide which occurred there one winter's night.

Mrs. Eva Collier of 110 Spruce Street was the second party to witness the aeroplane antics of the specter, and although the story told by Mrs Gehrke was laughed at, the smiles from the lips of the doubting Thomases changed to looks of grave concern when Mrs. Collier described the unnatural flight which she witnessed.

Mrs. Ella Danforth of 120 Spruce Street was the third resident of the street to run across the night flyer and when her story was told among the neighbors, the cold chills began to creep along the spines of her listeners, and to add to her description of the ghostly thing, a young lad burst into the room and said he had seen the gruesome object the night before and had pursued it until it was lost in an old grape arbor near Woodford Avenue.

Needless to say there are few windows remaining open on Spruce Street these nights, and it is confidentially reported that several men on the street have failed to spend their evenings over in town since the apparition has cursed the street with its presence.

Elyria [OH] Republican 10 September 1908: p. 12 OHIO

NOTE: The cloak and the apparition's aerial abilities establish it firmly as a "Jack." You will also find the "gliding" characteristic in some of the following stories. I have found all but one of the persons mentioned in the article in census reports. Whether they were reliable witnesses or if they were witnesses to a hoax, it is impossible to say.

A similarly cloaked and bullet-proof creature appears in this story. The intruder is also unnaturally tall.

MAN IN BLACK
TWO SHOTS IN THE GHOST'S BREAST
Was it really a ghost?

Just ask Michael Colhane or Jack Murphy or Acting Police Sergeant Tom Walsh. If it was not a ghost this trio and two newspaper men who went hunting last night would like to know what it was.

Shortly after midnight a quintet of brave ones who didn't believe in ghosts resorted to the B.A. & P. railroad cut leading to the hill mines, just to show their contempt for the supernatural. By 1 o'clock the ghost hunters were returning down street with their ardor for displaying bravery considerably quelled and their opinions upon the existence of ghosts somewhat changed. They had seen something, but what, none of them can tell.

After spending some time prowling around in the darkness on the hills in Centerville the five ghost hunters determined to search the dark and uninviting railroad cut, crossing Main Street just on the border of the suburb. Under the bridge and up the track they went, joking at the expense of the ghastly apparition. The dark cut was thoroughly gone over and the hollow in which is located the deserted cabin supposed to be the abiding place of the ghostly one was examined, but nothing out of the natural was seen.

With their faith in ghosts badly shaken the searchers returned back down the railroad track east of Main Street and there awaited in what seemed to be the most likely playground for a ghost. But no ghost. Colhane must have had a hunch that something was doing under the Main Street Bridge, for he started back in that direction with Murphy at his heels, Walsh and the two other ghost-hunters bringing up the rear. The last three of the party took a side excursion around some freight cars in search of the satanic majesty and fell about 30 feet behind Colhane and Murphy. Just as these two passed under the foot bridge crossing Main Street moving westward, something happened. Colhane was still in the lead when a tall stately figure, garbed in a long dark robe or coat, came gliding down the steep embankment to the railroad track directly in front of the men. Now, Colhane is not a chump and up to that moment had no respect for the devil or his ilk. The specter appeared before him and Murphy, with a suddenness that sent a chill down their backs, but with good judgment they shouted: "Halt there! Hold!"

The strange figure slowly projected both hands upward and, with a noiseless movement, seemed fairly to glide over the rough ground in the direction of the hollow and the abandoned cabin.

Both men drew their guns and with the stranger being scarcely 10 feet in front of them blazed away directly at the breast of the tall figure. That both shots penetrated the form which has the semblance of humanity there can be no doubt in the world. The figure was not halted by the shots, but glided onward in the direction of the old cabin and again Murphy and Colhane shouted at the disappearing figure. When Walsh and the other two ghost hunters reached the spot there was no denying that Murphy and Colhane had undergone an experience out of the ordinary. Both were trembling and showed every evidence of being badly frightened.

They had a good look at the unearthly monster, whatever it might be, and declared that just as they fired a dull reddish light appeared about the breast, forming a splendid target for the shooters. The uplifted hands seemed to be transparent, the red blood being seen just as when one holds the hand before an electric light and the head of the creature was momentarily lighted with the same red dull glare that has been described by others who claim to have seen the strange apparition.

The ghost hunters are not even yet convinced that anything beyond the natural can exist on this earth, but they are certain that they saw something that was unnatural and that it acted like a visitor from another world. The strangest fact of all is that the two shots fired directly into the figure had no effect whatever in staying its flight. A few moments later the five men met two Finns coming down the railroad track who had also witnessed the strange apparition as it flitted across the hollow in the direction of the lonely cabin.

Is it a ghost?

Anaconda [MT] Standard 14 March 1901: p. 7 MONTANA

NOTE: This ghost was reported in multiple articles during March, 1901. In early April, an article told of a man claiming to be the apparition telling a bartender that he was done playing ghost since it was too dangerous. The bartender thought it was the liquor talking. Later that day a black robe was found hanging on a Main Street electric light pole. Stories of the ghost seemed to cease after this. [*Anaconda [MT] Standard* 7 April 1901: p. 18] This entity has a few features in common with what was called "The Van Meter Monster," which appeared in Van Meter, Kansas in 1903. It was said to look something like a bat, seemed impervious to bullets, appeared to generate light, and had a strange symbol upon its chest. It will be discussed in more detail in a forthcoming book. [Source: *Morning Olympian* (Olympia, WA) 21 October 1903: p. 4] You can also find the details in *The Van Meter Visitor: A True and Mysterious Encounter with the Unknown,* Chad Lewis, et al., On The Road Publications, 2013.

An Old-fashioned Ghost.

The Marysville (California) *Herald* says, "A merchant doing business at Industry Bar, relates that a figure having the similitude of a man, dressed in a cloak as an outside garment, has been seen in the vicinity of the Bar by a number of creditable witnesses. It has been questioned by many, and shot at by fifteen individuals at once, and still persists in its visits, saying nothing but 'Death to the murderer!' Great excitement prevails at the Bar concerning it, and some of our citizens propose going up to satisfy themselves in regard to the matter. One person saw it and discharged his pistol, confidently expecting to see it drop; but finding it produced no effect, he

became terrified, and fled, but the ghost kept beside him, seeming to glide rather than run."
Spiritual Telegraph, Vol. 3, 1854: p. 498 CALIFORNIA

BLACK FORM HAUNTS A VILLAGE
A Spook Terrorizes the Inhabitants of Downer's Grove, Ill.

Chicago, Aug. 14. A mysterious form in black has been haunting the streets of the village of Downer's Grove for the last six months, rattling doors and windows until the entire town is on the verge of hysterics.

Downer's Grove is a prohibition town and for that reason the inhabitants are all the more indignant at the ghost. There is not a saloon within two miles of the place where the ghost walks, and the people of the village say it is impossible for either a man or a ghost with a pull to get anything stronger to drink than ginger ale.

The ghost was first seen six months ago, and since that time it has been growing bolder. Its midnight peregrinations and perambulations have extended beyond the limits where it was first seen, the neighborhood of the village graveyard, to some of the main streets, and the townspeople are in terror over what it is going to do next.

Over a dozen people whose reputation for truth is above reproach have seen the ghost, and to none of them has it appeared the same.

To the men who have seen it the form generally appears as a woman. The young girls, on the other hand, generally see it as a man.

The principal "haunt" of the ghost is a cornfield north of the railway station, near the home of Dr. Gourley. It is here that the ghost appears to feel most at home, and to allow people to approach nearest.

Only one man has succeeded in getting near enough to the ghost to touch it. He is Dan Niley, and the experience he had with the uncanny prowler has nearly turned his hair white.

Niley was on his way home late at night when he saw what he took to be a negro hostler who works near the haunted field. He walked up to his supposed friend and accosted him, when to his horror he saw a shrunken form with a black cap drawn over its face.

Niley put out his hand to touch the apparition, but with a swish through the air that curdled Niley's blood the thing disappeared.

Night Policeman Karney has seen the ghost several times, but he has not tried to run it down. Several times the ghost has passed close to him in the form of a man in black.

Karney is a bit skeptical, but he says he is unable to account for the way it has of passing directly through houses and outbuildings. As long as it is thin enough to do that he considers it a waste of powder to shoot at it.

Another man who has seen the ghost close up is the night telegraph operator of the Chicago, Burlington & Quincy railroad. A few nights ago, while he was passing along the street north of the station, he heard the grass rustle beside him and the ghost went by like the wind.

The apparition was seen the last time on Sunday morning at 4 o'clock. It was broad daylight, and the man who saw it, Harry Courtright, was returning home. Courtright claims the ghost was only partly dressed, but the chilly air did not in the least interfere with its flight. It skimmed along over the tops of the grass like a hen hawk after field mice and with as little noise.

Harry Black also saw the ghost on the preceding night.

One family has been especially disturbed by the mysterious form. A Mrs. Millet, a widow, lives near the haunted field with her son and daughter.

The ghost seems to take special delight in rattling her doors and windows, and it was through the walls of her house that several persons have seen it pass, without taking the trouble to go around, as a well-bred ghost should.

The ghost is almost the sole topic of conversation at Downer's Grove just now. It has driven financial debates out of the corporation, and everybody is doing his best to solve the mystery without getting too near to it.

The part of the town where it has been most frequently seen has been almost deserted and children and grown people are beginning to give the place a wide berth.

In spite of the stories of its shrunken form and mysterious flying powers there were some people in Downer's Grove who think the ghost is identical with a negro hostler of the village, who has several times been met in the neighborhood of the ghost.

Others, however, say in refutation of this, that the negro has the rheumatism and can't run.

Plain Dealer [Cleveland, OH] 15 August 1896: p. 2 ILLINOIS

NOTE: A rarer motif found in stories of "Jacks" and giant ghosts is that of shape-shifting. Common forms are bulls, dragons, and dogs. In this story, the creature also appears in different shapes to attract the opposite sex. Dr. Gourley is found in the 1900 census, so at least one person in the story was real.

Like the lore of the banshee, European dwarf traditions were often left behind in the Old Country. There is a tendency in the rare miniature entity stories, to make the creature into more of a traditional ghost: a baby or a dwarf individual.

In *Haunted Ohio II: More Ghostly Tales from the Buckeye State,* I retold a story called "The Legend of the Dwarf," told by James Heinzman in *Haunting Tales from Fairfield County* (Lancaster, Ohio: Fairfield County District Library) 1981. The ghost was said to haunt a house in Perry County "on 37 between Junction City and the county line." The newly-weds who lived there saw a man "about 2 or 3 feet high with a long white beard who would run through the house." The dwarf crawled into bed with the couple: "he felt real cold." The husband shot at the creature on several occasions, but it didn't stop the visitations. When the couple decided to dig out the cellar, they found a "baby skeleton in the cellar wall." After that, the dwarf ceased to haunt them.

This next story also contains a menacing dwarf as well as an unusual poltpourri of elements: there are fearful noises, hurled crockery and other kitchen accoutrements, shrieks and hideous laughter. There is an invisible attacker and an apparition that tracks bloody footprints and hangs itself. Whatever it was, it does not fit neatly into either category of poltergeist or classic ghost.

DWARFISH SPECTER
Hanging in the Old Garret
The Ghost That Terrifies a Mississippi Family.
Many Bullets Have Been Fired Through the Suspended Corpse,
But Without Effect of Any Kind—Tragedy at the Bottom of the Mystery.

The old Bradfield place, as it is known to the people of the vicinity, stands on the outskirts of this place and has for years borne the reputation of being haunted, and been an object of awe to not only the ignorant of the community, but to the intelligent, who are supposed to be free from all supernatural terror. The phantom supposed to hold its nightly revels in the old house, which was erected some time in the fifties, is that of a dwarf, who trails about the place leaving tracks of blood on the porch and in the room. A poor family by the name of Claiborne, recently from Jackson, moved into the deserted house something less than a month ago, and for two or three weeks were not disturbed by the ghostly inmates, but a night or two ago they were awakened by a fearful din in the kitchen, which is connected with the main building by a slender passageway left open.

Thinking that burglars had made their way into the house, the father of the family, Alex. Claiborne, seized his pistol and went running into the kitchen, only to find the crockery and pans all flung to the floor and broken into fragments, but there was no one to be seen. Returning to bed, after a thorough search of the house, Claiborne was again aroused by a series of shrieks interspersed with bursts of hideous laughter, apparently issuing also from the kitchen, which caused him to once more search that part of the house, but likewise with no result.

The next day Miss Alice Claiborne was crossing the small passageway referred to before when she saw a small, dwarfish figure come out of the kitchen. It accosted her on the boarded way. She attempted to run past the specter, but it seized her by the hair and flung her off the passage on to the ground where she lost consciousness. On returning to consciousness, she related what had occurred to her father and mother, but they attributed the vision to the fright they had all received the night before, and reassured the terrified girl.

But late that afternoon, just before the lights were lighted, she ran screaming to her parents' room, declaring that the dwarf had accosted her in the hall, and again jerked her by her braided hair to the floor, and then vanished. Mr. Claiborne again soothed the girl with an expressed determination to catch the person who seemed bent on driving them from the house by instituting a reign of supernatural terror, though he was beginning to think that something out of the ordinary lay behind this matter, but being a complete skeptic in regard to the return of the dead, he was loath to attribute his daughter's visions to anything superhuman, so he resolved to keep watch himself in the kitchen, which seemed to be the haunted portion of the dwelling house.

Armed with a revolver, he seated himself in the kitchen and waited for some hours for the mysterious visitor, but it was not until after midnight that any manifestation took place. Then suddenly, and without warning whatever, he saw a bowed, humped figure moving along the wall about six feet from him. This he hailed, but it paid no attention to him, but continued to pass along the wall, as if groping its way and without once turning its head toward him. Finding that his calls to it won no attention from the phantom, Mr. Claiborne fired at it several times, but the bullets seemed to pass clear through it without any apparent effect, even to making the specter turn its head in his direction and at last summoning all his courage the man ran forward and attempted to clutch the mysterious figure, but found that his fingers only grasped the impalpable air, though the dwarfish figure remained in full view all the time.

It passed finally from the kitchen into the house, whence it proceeded up the stairs to the garret, where, to Mr. Claiborne's amazement and horror, he found it suspended to the rafters by a rope about the neck. He endeavored to reach the ghastly sight, but found himself held back by a hand that clutched his arm with so icy a grip as to detain him where he stood. He struggled with this invisible but powerful grasp for some minutes, but finding that it finally sought his throat he succumbed to its supernatural force and finally fell senseless.

The next day Mrs. Claiborne insisted on leaving the house, feeling convinced that the ghost who held sway there had determined on driving them forth, but her husband had resolved on solving the mystery of the phenomena they had witnessed there, and declared his intention of staying. Mrs. Claiborne, therefore, stayed with her husband, and was engaged the next morning in making up a batch of bread, when she saw enter the kitchen the dwarf before described and who proceeded to rummage the kitchen as if looking for something. The phantom overthrew in its search the flour-barrel, various jars and bags, leaving its track in the scattered flour, then, rushing on the woman, finally upset her in the midst of the confusion.

When the figure had disappeared Mrs. Claiborne sought her husband and declared her intention of quitting the place at once and accordingly moved out with her goods and children that afternoon. Mr. Claiborne decided on remaining one more night in the haunted house, and persuaded a couple of neighbors to stay with him on his vigil. The three waited in the kitchen several hours without seeing anything of the phantom, when they heard a voice faint and shrill, as if coming from a distance, calling to them by name to come upstairs, when, on proceeding to the garret, they found the dwarfish, humped figure hanging by the neck from one of the rafters. The two neighbors were so persuaded that it was a real body they beheld that they were for rushing forward and cutting it down, but Mr. Claiborne, who had had experience with it before, fired shot after shot into it with no other effect than to cause it to vanish as an image from a mirror, amid loud laughter from some invisible spirit.

The place is owned by a gentleman in Rochester, N.Y., who in 1881 took it for debt from a family named Bradfield, who in turn inherited from one Josiah Bradfield, who was a little man, hideously deformed by a hump on the breast and back. Josiah Bradfield was married to a girl of the neighborhood who was famous for her good looks and whose choice of the dwarf was a mystery to all who knew her. This girl was found one morning dead in her bed of an overdose of some drug, with a letter purporting to be written by her, saying she had resolved to take her life. Six months after her wretched husband was discovered hanging in the garret of the old house, having committed suicide, it is said, from remorse over the manner in which he had treated his young wife. That the phantom is that of Josiah Bradfield is beyond a doubt in the minds of the people. The Claiborne's have moved out of the house, and say that whoever doubts the truth of their story has only to pass a while in the old Bradfield place. *Cincinnati [OH] Enquirer* 5 October 1892: p. 12 MISSISSIPPI

NOTE: After this lengthy (and somewhat chronologically muddled) account of paranormal phenomena at the old Bradfield Place, in the end we are treated to a historical "explanation" that comes straight from a sensational Gothic novel serialized in the papers. I've encountered a number of historical poltergeist cases in which farfetched explanations are given. Is it because the phenomenon was so unbelievable, so traumatic, the witnesses would grasp at any straw to explain it? It could also have been a fiction-writing reporter's nod to a sensational genre.

AN ACCOMMODATING GHOST
A Massachusetts [sic] Dwarf Who Appears and Disappears in Night or Day
He is Cut in Two by a Workman's Spade.

Special Dispatch to the *Globe-Democrat*
New Haven, Conn., Jan. 11. In the town of North Haven there has been for the last thirty years rumors of strange and supernatural sights in the vicinity of Shear's brickyard. Many men and women who have been riding and walking along the highway after nightfall have seen the strange figure of a dwarf about three feet high. Sometimes he would be dressed in one color of clothing and then of another. When people told of what they had seen they were received with incredulity by some, and others would put faith in the stories. Night before last, Owen McNulty, an Irishman; Oscar Jansen, a Swede; Septi Maganzo, Pasco Servisco, and Lorenzo Partisco, Italians, five laborers employed in the brickyard, were going home about 7 o'clock in the evening. Suddenly there appeared in the road before them the figure of a man about three feet high, dressed in black velvet clothes of the fashion of 100 years ago. The coat was trimmed with fur, and on his head was a cocked hat. McNulty had a spade on his shoulder. He said: "Boys, I guess I'll stop the chap," and so saying he made a thrust at the figure with his spade, but it passed through and the dwarf vanished. The men were much frightened and crossing themselves, fled for home. They

went the next day to see if their senses had played them false, when the figure appeared again in the full light of day. McNulty again lunged at the object with his spade and cut it in two. It went up into the air about forty feet and the pieces reunited with lightning rapidity and then vanished into the air. They then went home and told the woman with whom they boarded. She said that it was not strange, and that many other people had seen the same thing. All five are industrious men, who positively assert that the story is true in every particular. The diminutive ghost carried a lantern when it was first seen at night; but the next day its hands were empty. There is a tradition that many years ago a sailor of dwarfish stature sailed up the Quinebec [Quinebaug] River, his boat was capsized and he drowned.

Kansas City [MO] Star 14 January 1886: p. 3 CONNECTICUT

NOTE: "Massachusetts" in the headline appears to be a misprint. Once again, we see the imposition of an improbable "tradition" (a sailor in a velvet suit and cocked hat?) on a story of a sighting. I found McNulty and Jansen in the census reports for 1880, but not the three Italians.

Few of the fairy traditions of the British Isles came to these shores. While immigrants managed to smuggle to the New World some Black Dogs, Kobolds, and the odd banshee or gnome, it seems as though the Brownie, the Leprechaun, and the fairies were left behind on the pier, waving a sad farewell to those bound for the Land of Opportunity. In his books on fairies, Sir Arthur Conan Doyle printed only a few letters about fairies sightings in the States including this explanation of a fairy photograph.

The following letter from a young lady in Canada, daughter of one of the leading citizens of Montreal, and personally known to me, is interesting on account of the enclosed photograph here reproduced. She says:

"The enclosed photograph was taken this summer at Waterville, New Hampshire with a 2A Brownie camera (portrait lens attached) by Alverda, eleven years old. The father is able, clear-headed, enthusiastic on golf and billiards; the mother on Japanese art; neither interested in psychic matters much. The child has been frail and imaginative, but sweet and incapable of deceit.

"The mother tells me she was with the child when the picture was taken. The mushrooms pleased the little girl, and she knelt down and photographed them. As an indication of their ordinary size, they are *Amanita muscaria*.

"There was no such figure to be seen as appears in the picture.

"There was no double exposure. The picture astonished them when developed. The parents guarantee its honesty, but are mystified.

"Do you think shadows, etc., can explain it? I think the line of the right shoulder and arm especially are too decisive to be thus brushed away." I rather agree with the writer, but it is a point which each reader can decide for himself upon examination of the photograph. It is certainly very vague after the Yorkshire examples. [The Cottingley Fairies.]

The Coming of the Fairies, Sir Arthur Conan Doyle, 1922, p. 160-1 NEW HAMPSHIRE

NOTE: You will find a copy of the photograph, with the complete book here: http://ebooks.adelaide.edu.au/d/doyle/arthur_conan/fairies/complete. html. It shows a tiny child's figure, rather like a doll in a floppy hat among the vegetation. It certainly is not as clear as the Yorkshire examples since those images were cut out of magazines and photographed by Elsie Wright and Frances Griffiths.

A Texan man wrote Conan Doyle with a more detailed and fantastical story:

...A gentleman named Matthews, writing on January 3, 1921, from San Antonio, Texas...declared that his three daughters, now married women, could all see fairies before the age of puberty, but never after it. The fairies said to them: "We are not of the human evolution. Very few humans have ever visited us. Only old souls well advanced in evolution or in a state of sex innocence can come to us."...

These children seem to have gone into a trance state before they found themselves in the country of the fairies—a country of intelligent beings, very small, 12 to 18 inches high. According to their accounts, they were invited to attend banquets or celebrations, excursions on beautiful lakes, etc. Each child was able to entrance instantly. This they always did when they visited Fairyland, but when the fairies came to them, which was generally in the twilight, they sat in chairs in normal state watching them dance.

The father adds: "My own children learned in this way to dance, so that at local entertainments audiences were delighted, though they never knew from what source they learned."

The Coming of the Fairies, Sir Arthur Conan Doyle, 1922, p. 152-55 TEXAS

Returning to the theme of black-clad entities, some do not wear the theatrical and concealing robe or cloak, but a proper Men-in-Black suit.

A Ghost Story

The era of ghosts and goblins it seems has not wholly passed away. The following account of the latest manifestation of this sort we find in the *Ballston Democrat*. Our readers are at liberty to believe just so much of it as they please:

"Something of the ghost order—vouched for, by the bye, by reliable individuals—occurred at the axe factory of Messrs. I. Blood & Co., a short time since that may be as well jotted down, even if it is not deemed credible. It has been necessary for some time back, for the proprietors of the axe factory to keep the grinding shop in operation for the most part of the night, in which some fifteen men were employed.

About twelve o'clock one night some time since, one of the men at work saw a man dressed in plain black, but whose countenance was pale and livid, enter by one door and pass through from one end of the shop to the other without the least apparent noise. On mentioning the fact to his comrades they had seen nothing of the kind, and the occurrence was considered as some optical illusion. It was but a few nights afterwards, however, and at the same hour, another workman saw the same apparition, and informed his shopmates of the fact, but, as before, no other person had witnessed it.

By this time some curiosity was excited to know who it was who thus noiselessly and without any invitation paid these midnight visits, and the door was afterwards carefully shut and barred. But doors and bars did not seem to exclude the white faced man dressed in black; and but a few nights afterwards as another person was at his work the same incorrigible individual entered the shop without being perceived, and took a stand by one of the workmen, who, on looking over his shoulder saw his white face and shining black clothes as he stood behind him to excellent advantage. In an instant the figure had vanished; but not so with the trepidation of the workman the apparition had created. He left his seat in quite a hurry, and did not stop his running until he had reached his residence in this village, a distance of more than a mile. Since then it has been impossible for Messrs. Blood & Co. to induce men to work in the grindshop after dark.
Daily Ohio Statesman [Columbus, OH] 9 July 1853: p. 3 NEW YORK

NOTE: The name seemed a little too good to be true, but I. Blood & Co. was an axe and scythe company taken over in 1837 from the founder, his father Sylvester, by Isaiah Blood in Ballston, New York.

Well before the UFO age, in the 19th century we find mysterious visitations from sinister men dressed in black. In the following case the entities are accompanied by the same bizarre, poltergeist-like events Keel and others experienced when the Men in Black came to call.

This account, from 1863, contains motifs found in later UFO cases (Hopkinsville, for example): shooting at intruders without effect, a frightened dog, doors mysteriously malfunctioning, and showers of missiles on the roof. The skeptical editor satirically suggests a political ("Union vs. Confederate") explanation.

Very Strange If True! Two Ghosts in
Wapello County!

We learn, by a gentleman of unquestionable veracity, that great consternation prevails in Adams Township, in this county, occasioned by the nightly visitations of two seeming men, at the residence of Mr. Wm. Spaulding, who lives five miles east of Blakesburg. These visitors, be they who they may, and whether in the flesh or spirits in human shape, make their appearance about seven o'clock in the evening, and remain until about five in the morning, their first appearance being on Friday night, a week ago. They seem medium sized, heavy set men, *dressed in black!* On their first appearance, on Friday night, the family and some of the neighbors, were boiling molasses about forty rods from the house, when about seven o'clock, suddenly, clubs, cobs, (they had been shelling corn during the day) and small sticks, began to fly in a shower, from a certain direction, occasionally hitting some one of the persons present, but generally falling in one small place. Once a candlestick, held by Mrs. Spaulding, was hit, nearly knocking it out of her hand. No person was then visible, but they heard something walking about with a heavy tread. About one o'clock, they quit boiling, and two of the men, Harmon Wellman and J.M. Spaulding, started out in the direction from whence the missiles seemed to come, armed with clubs and brickbats, to find and chastise these strange and curious intruders. No sooner had the men started than the missiles came, larger and thicker. The fire of missiles was returned by the men, but without evidence of their hitting anybody. The party about the kettles returned about this time (one o'clock) to the house. After their return, the missiles seemed to strike the fence and the house with great violence. Spaulding and one of the men went out to turn out the horses, taking their guns with them. No sooner were they out of the house, than a large club fell near them, seemingly coming from behind. One of the men wheeled, and saw a man standing near enough to be distinguished in a dark night, at whom he instantly shot. The man ran and disappeared. They turned out the horses and returned to the house. Nothing more was seen of the men that night, although they were heard walking near the house. The next night, and for the four succeeding nights, the same state of things existed, two being seen on Tuesday night. Missiles struck the fence and house, but left no dents and marks distinguishable by daylight. In the meantime, Mr. Spaulding and his neighbors became alarmed by such strange phenomenon, and from time to time, met at Spaulding's house to try and solve the mystery. On Monday night, J.W. Wellman, Wm. Hayne, Wm. Spaulding and his son, spent the night watching. Sometime in the night, one of the men looked out of the window and distinctly saw, by the light of a bright moon, a man standing before the door. After sitting awhile, they looked out again, and saw the man prostrate on a plank, lighting a dark lantern with a match. Getting their revolvers and guns ready, the party prepared to open the door, but strange to say, the four powerful men could not open it. They afterwards remained quietly in the house until 5 o'clock in the morning. One night, Mr. E.B. Day took his dog, a very sagacious animal, and tried to set her on, but she trembled, ran between her master's legs, and refused to make any demonstrations against the ghosts.

The above are the leading facts as related to us, of the most strange phenomenon. Mr. Spaulding at first attributed the persecution to political enmity, but certain evidence of the absence, in other places, of those he only could suspect, at times when the visitors were seen and engaged in their operations, satisfied him that he must look for some other solution of the mystery.

We give the facts precisely as they are related to us, merely expressing, by way of comment, our decided conviction that no Union men, in or out of the flesh, have resorted to that mode of converting Mr. Spaulding and his political friends from the error of their political ways. The story is a strange one, and we await, with considerable anxiety, further developments. In the meantime, an opportunity is afforded to the curious to speculate on the subject of ghosts! We don't believe in ghosts, and if we did, it is against all ghostly rules to visit in couples, and they have generally been clothed in white, invariably so as far as our recollection serves us. It is barely possible that some evil disposed persons have been playing rather a fatiguing and protracted trick upon Mr. Spaulding and his friends. Most of the

phenomena can be accounted for without resort to the supernatural. To persons laboring under apprehension of danger, everything, particularly in the night, seems unnatural and distorted. Ghosts can be manufactured with the greatest ease. It is also extremely difficult to aim accurately under such circumstances, and a person would stand many chances of escaping to one of being hit. And so we might speculate upon all these occurrences, supposing them to be real occurrences. As to that we repeat, we merely give what is related to us. *Ottumwa Courier.*
Burlington [IA] Hawk Eye October 31, 1863: p. 2 IOWA

NOTE: I found William Spaulding, E.B. Day, and several Hayneses and Wellmans in the 1870 census. Here we see the usual disclaimer: "We don't believe in ghosts," followed by a joke about white clothing and a rational explanation about the difficulty of aiming in the dark, which, to be fair, answers the question of why people would risk their lives to play pranks like this: statistically they did not believe they could be shot.

The showers of corn-cobs are echoed in this 1880 account from Belle Center, Ohio, which also tells of a mysterious gnome-like creature seen on the farm just before the cobs began falling.

BUGABOO BUSINESS
DOINGS OF SPOOKS IN LOGAN COUNTY
SHOWERS OF CORN-COBS, CLUBS, STONES AND OTHER MISSILES FLYING MYSTERIOUSLY THROUGH THE AIR

Belle Center, Ohio, July 23. About three miles north-west of town there is a farm known as the Zahller Place, one of the oldest in the State, and owned by the heirs, one of whom occupies it. On last Friday afternoon the folks went blackberrying and two of the children went to a picnic nearby. About five o'clock the children returned and they say as they came into the yard a man of small stature, bow-legged and very ragged, came out of the kitchen, walked past them, opened the garden gate and went in. He then jumped over the picket-fence into the barn-yard and disappeared in the barn. The children becoming frightened at his strange actions went to a neighbor's house about half a mile distant and returned home in the evening. When their parents returned, they related their story. Mr. Zahller tracked the man through the garden and barn-yard by noticing three large-headed nails in the impression of his boot-heel. At the barn all traces were lost.

Now comes the mystery: Mrs. Zahller went to the barn-yard to milk; corn-cobs commenced falling near like someone was throwing at her. Mr. Zahller was standing nearby but didn't notice them. She asked him if he saw that. He answered no. Just then a large one hit near him, but he could not see where it came from. During Saturday the children were hit with corn-cobs, pieces of bark and small stones every time they attempted to go into the barn yard. Two of the family—one a boy of seven, and the other a young lady of eighteen—seemed to attract the most. When they came near the missiles were sure to fly. The boy, especially, was hurt about the face with small stones.

One of the neighbors, coming to witness the shower, was hit in the back by a wooden pin that had been used to fasten a large gate. A trace-chain that had been plowed up and was hung on a corner of the corn-crib, near the barn, also went sailing in the air in search of something to light on. Hundreds of people have been to see this sight since Saturday and all came away satisfied that they saw chips, small stones, corn-cobs, &c., falling near them, but unable to explain where they came from. One man says he saw corn-cobs start from the ground and soar over his head and light on the ground without the least noise. Another one says he was standing near a chicken house, the door of which was open, when some half dozen cobs came flying out. The house was searched, but nothing found...Some say the flying pieces are not noticed until they either strike them or fall on the ground nearby. The strangest thing is that they light as easy as a feather, no matter how large the article is. One man brought home a piece of an old walnut rail about a foot long and two by four inches thick. That, he says, he tried to aggravate the spirits, and said in a loud voice, "Don't throw anymore corn-cobs; throw a club this time." Just then this piece lit on his shoulder as easy as a feather and rolled to the ground. The whole neighborhood is excited, and watch the barn from morning until night, trying not to believe it, but at the same time convinced that they saw something, they know not what.

Cincinnati [OH] Enquirer 24 July 1880: p. 7 OHIO

NOTE: This account, accompanied by a follow-up story, which includes a ghostly woman in white seen in the vicinity, is found in *The Face in the Window: Haunting Ohio Tales*, while this next story was published in *The Headless Horror: Strange and Ghostly Ohio Tales.*

The UFO-MIB connection is even more pronounced in this 1873 letter from Zanesville, Ohio to a New York newspaper.

VERY LIKE A WHALE

Zanesville, Ohio April 5, 1873

To the Editor of the *Herald*:

A most extraordinary phenomenon was observed near the village of Taylorsville, a few miles from this city, about a week ago. Mr. Thomas Inman, whom your reporter can vouch for as a respectable farmer of unquestionable truth and veracity, related the circumstances to the writer, and, with his son, who was also an eye witness, is willing to make oath to the truth of this statement.

One evening about two weeks ago, while Mr. Inman and his son, a young man, were returning to their home from Taylorsville, they saw a light, which they describe as looking like a "burning brush pile," near the zenith, descending rapidly towards the earth, with a loud, roaring noise. It struck the ground in the road a short distance from them. The blazing object flickered and flared for a few moments and then faded into darkness, as a man dressed in a complete suit of black and carrying a lantern emerged from it. The man walked a few paces and stepped into a buggy, which had not been observed before by either Mr. Inman or his son. There was no horse attached to this supernatural vehicle, but no sooner had the man taken his seat than it started to run, noiselessly, but with great velocity along the highway and this it continued to do until it reached a steep gully, into which it plunged, when buggy, man, and lantern suddenly disappeared as mysteriously as they came.

This phenomenon is certainly an extraordinary and unexplainable one, and sounds more like the vagary of a crazed brain than anything else. But both Mr. Inman and his son, who are sober men and not given to superstitious notions, agree precisely in their statements and maintain that they are strictly true. If it was an optical delusion, superinduced by a meteor or "Jack o' lantern," is it not strange that the same fancied appearances could be conjured up in the minds of two men at the same time? Here is a chance for scientists to explain the fantastical optical and other illusions and delusions which follow in the train of, and are suggested by, some strange and unexpected sight or occurrence.

W. A. Taylor.

New York Herald 8 April 1873: p. 7 OHIO

NOTE: The title is drawn from a dialog between Hamlet and Polonius in William Shakespeare's *Hamlet,* Act iii Sc. 2, where the two men are looking at clouds:

Ham. Do you see yonder cloud that's almost in the shape of a camel?
Pol. By the mass, and 't is like a camel, indeed.
Ham. Methinks it is like a weasel.
Pol. It is backed like a weasel.
Ham. Or like a whale?
Pol. Very like a whale.

The horseless buggy and the falling, blazing brush pile sound like something out of a novel by Jules Verne. Still, it is odd that the narrator specifies that the alien man appears dressed in black. This, in an era when many men wore black as a matter of course, seems a peculiar distinction to make, as if to point out the high strangeness of the man.

I will finish this chapter with an unclassifiable creature. Some might picture this as a walking shock of cornstalks; I see it as a spidery heap scuttling into the road.

A clerk of William Talbottom, of Macon, Ga., while returning from the residence of his sweetheart last Sunday night was attacked by a ghost. His horse suddenly became frightened and turned to one side of the road. Something like a pile of cornstalks, but with hideous face, was coming right toward him in the middle of the road. He could not discern any feet or legs, but he heard a thunderous tramp. He drew his revolver and fired five shots at the object, which neither spoke nor moved, but would not yield the road. So he gave it a wide passage, laying whip to the horse, and got into town so frightened that he has not slept or eaten since.
Juniata Sentinel and Republican [Mifflintown, PA] 20 March 1889: p. 2
GEORGIA

FURTHER READING: The definitive work on Spring-heeled Jack is 'Spring-heeled Jack,' Mike Dash, *Fortean Studies 3,* Steve Moore, ed., 1996: 7-125. The paper is online at http://www.mikedash.com/extras/forteana/shj-about.

6.

Killed by a Specter

Jacks and Giants

And now the mist seems taking shape,
Forming a dim, gigantic ghost,
Enormous thing!—There's no escape.

-Richard H. Dana-

America is a giant country and it has always been a country of giants: the ravening Native American Wendigo and the immense skeletons of the Mound Builders, so often mentioned in the papers as en route to the Smithsonian Institute, where they cryptically and invariably fail to arrive. Or the stone Cardiff Giant, a mammoth hoax that found a colossal audience for the original fake *and* P.T. Barnum's copy (guaranteed to be genuine.) Mr. Barnum's sideshow also brought America The Shields Brothers, known as The Texas Giants; Anna O'Brien, called "The Irish Giantess;" and the Nova Scotian giantess, Anna Swan and her colossus husband, Captain Bates. Americans look up to their titanic Tall Tale heroes, Paul Bunyan and his Blue Ox, Babe, and Pecos Bill, even if they are literary creations.

With the feverish 19th-century interest in giants, both stone and flesh-and-blood, came a wave of giant ghosts. Common sense would suggest that these are the result of misjudging the height of something moving in the dark, or perhaps deliberate hoaxes involving stilts. I would suggest further that these giant ghosts share some common traits with Spring-heeled Jack. He was clad in black, belched fire, had the ability to make impossible leaps or glide without touching the ground, and was sometimes described as a giant or increasing in size before the witnesses' horrified eyes. He was also bullet-proof. While not all of the ghosts in the following stories could be classified as "Jacks," many of them share similar characteristics.

There is a folklore motif found particularly in the British Isles, where supernatural animals, usually Black Dogs or spectral calves, grow in an instant from ordinary to mammoth size. Possibly this motif has influenced these stories. A surprising number of giant ghosts carry clubs—they are virtually the only ghosts who carry weapons—which would suggest that they are somehow related to the Fee-Fi-Fo-Fum Giants of European fairy tales. The giant ghosts are also particularly aggressive and violent apparitions, another trait they share with Spring-heeled Jack.

Let us begin with a long and dramatic story of a giant ghost who embodies many of the characteristics mentioned above.

A GRAVE YAWNS
And a Real Ghost Walks Abroad in Elkhart County, Ind.
The Weird Visitor is Eight Feet High and Wears White Robes
Shooting Parties Fill It With Buckshot With Harmless Results
Carries a Club and Haunts the Cemetery

Benton, Ind., July 26. Wearing a long white beard and robe, and carrying a huge club, a real ghost, eight feet high, is abroad in Benton Township, Elkhart County. Night after night it has been seen for the last week and night after night searching parties of farmers have fired at the fearful object with shotguns. But that it is a real ghost is proved by the fact the shot whistled harmlessly through the ghost and it disappeared only to reappear in a different place, waving its long white arms and shaking its club at pursuers.

It has been seen by hundreds, it has been fired at by terrified searching parties and it has each time vanished and then flashed its fearsome presence in another place.

Last Tuesday night it made its first appearance. On that evening John W. French and his good wife made a call at a neighbor's some miles away from their farm. The evening was spent in storytelling and jollity and it was well along toward midnight when Farmer French helped his wife into his big farm wagon and climbed up beside her to start home. A few miles along the lonely country road over which they had to travel is an old church, moss grown and weather beaten, and beside it is a graveyard well filled with the bones of those who once tilled the soil in this locality. Ten years ago an aged man who lived alone not far from the old church and visited the graveyard almost daily to pray over the resting place of some relative was foully murdered for the store of gold he was supposed to have hidden about his hermit abode. The robbers and murderers escaped justice and the luckless greybeard was buried in the graveyard where he spent so much time.

And just as the lumbering wagon of Farmer French drew within sight of the white headstones in the churchyard the horses reared back on their haunches and snorted in terror. French was alarmed, and suspecting highwaymen had been scented by the horses, he reached for a shotgun which lay in the bottom of the wagon for just such an emergency. But before his hand touched it he was startled by a scream from his wife.

Clutching his arm she pointed straight ahead and gasped: "Look, John, look!"

Far down the road, just beside the glimmering monuments of the old graveyard, he saw an apparition. It was that of a man with a long white beard sweeping over his breast. The figure appeared to be eight feet in height and in one hand it carried a club, such as the brains of the old man had been beaten out with ten years before. Slowly raising one arm the ghost with a majestic sweep beckoned French to come ahead. He was too startled to do anything except try to restrain the prancing horses, which were straining at the harness in attempts to break away and run. A cold sweat started out all over the body of the farmer as he realized that he was at least looking at a ghost, and then the sound of his wife's voice came to him begging him to return the way they had come and escape the doom which seemed impending. French was still too much scared and excited to control the horses, and as he gazed steadfastly at the fearful white object in the road it slowly began to move toward the wagon. The club was now raised to its shoulder, as a soldier carries a rifle, and it seemed to move forward without touching the ground, like a winged thing. Then the farmer recovered his faculties and, whirling his team around, he lashed the horses into a run and began the trip to the house of the friend he had just left. As he did so a great roaring noise as of thunder filled all the air and maddened the frightened horses, so that they ran over the road like wild creatures. The noise came from the ghost, which followed close behind the wagon. Though fainting with fear Mrs. French could not resist the temptation to look behind and see whether the spook was following. She saw it about ten feet behind the wagon and as she screamed it vanished. A few minutes later French drove into the barnyard of his friend and told his tale to the frightened people. No ghost could then be seen and some of those in the house were inclined to doubt the story and laid it to imagination. But Mrs. French could not be induced to pass the graveyard again that night, and the couple stayed for the night with their friends. The next day the story was repeated over the countryside and by night everyone from Millersburg to New Paris had heard of the Benton ghost. The old church and graveyard were visited during the daytime by hundreds, but no trace of the ghost could be found. Parties of boys and young men boldly ventured to stay in the graveyard all night and watch for the apparition, but as the shades of night drew on and the shadows of the headstones began to lengthen across the grass most of the watchers left the place under various excuses. A peculiar, creepy feeling, common to those who ever pass a cemetery at night took possession of those who remained and it soon amounted almost to a panic, so that every man in the crowd left for home and vowed the ghost could do as it pleased. Night came on with the great wall of blackness which shuts down over everything in the country at night. The moon at times struggled through the clouds which overspread the heavens and shed a faint radiance on the tombstones in the lonely graveyard and the long rank grass which flourishes in the city of the dead. Absolute silence reigned when Milton Moon, a farmer of Benton Township, strode sturdily along the highway which passes the graveyard and over which Farmer French's team went flying the night before. Moon had not heard of the ghost, or if he had, it did not scare him. He was perfectly familiar with the lonely road, for he had traveled it for years. He knew just where the old church was, for he had spent many hours in its shadow, and he felt no qualms about passing the deserted graveyard which he had so often passed after dark. Moon walked boldly ahead, his thoughts on a business venture which he contemplated, when suddenly he heard a wild roar and rumble like 10,000 bolts of thunder. Stopping in amazement he looked up and the sight which met his eyes turned him sick and giddy. All the blood in his body seemed turned to ice and his brain reeled.

Fifty feet before him he saw a ghost, a figure over eight feet tall, with flowing white robes and a patriarchal beard which reached its waist. As he gazed, stupefied and almost insane, Moon observed that the figure was transparent and through it he could still see the dim outline of the old church looming up in the darkness. In its right hand the awful apparition grabbed a club, murderous, fearful. And as it swept toward Moon, as though borne on the wings of the wind, and the thunderous roar continued, he sank to the earth and knew no more until he awoke in the farmer's house surrounded by his friends and with a doctor bending over him. In broken words Moon told the awful story of his fright and of the ghost which had almost bereft him of reason, and when the narrative was done he again swooned at the memory of the fearful object. Ever since he has been under the constant care of a physician and his condition is grave.

When this tale was spread broadcast throughout the neighborhood the countryside seemed to flame with a desire to trace the mystery to its source and discover the cause of the apparitions, which had so terrified French and Moon. Meetings were hurriedly held and posses organized to hunt down the spectral creature with the long white beard and menacing club. Many farmers and hired men positively refused to join the expedition when they had learned of the fate of Moon, but enough brave men were found to make a goodly showing and armed with shotguns and rifles they set out Friday night to hunt down the ghost. A leader was chosen and he divided the men into squads of three and four, posting them at various places along the road near the old churchyard. Each squad was ordered to challenge the ghost should it appear, and on its failure to halt to fire directly at it. With these instructions well understood the men separated and waited for developments, which they felt sure would come.

When the main party was thus divided some of the watchers were not so bold as they had been at the outset. The little groups kept close together and whiled away the anxious hours telling ghost stories and weird tales of apparitions of bygone years. The history of the luckless old man, whose ghost they thought they were awaiting, was recounted by those who had known him and the horrible story of his murder by robbers was retold. That he had come to haunt the neighborhood where once he toiled and suffered all were agreed and the fact that the tall ghost carried a club was taken to indicate that he was to be revenged upon the countryside for his sudden taking off. While these stories were causing shudders to chase up and down the spines of the more timorous in the party, John Martin, a farm hand, startled one of the groups with a cry, "There it is!" Less than twenty feet away stood the ghost, evidently looking directly at the watchers. Its long arms hung motionless and in one hand was grasped the club. It did not attempt to approach the group of men huddled there in the darkness with hands tightly clutching their shotguns and hearts beating so loudly they could almost be heard. Martin was the first to recover himself. Raising his shotgun to his shoulder he called in a loud voice: "Who stands there? Speak, or I fire." No answer came from the spectre, but instead one of the long arms slowly raised and the figure began an almost imperceptible advance. This was enough for Martin and his friends. Four shotguns rang out at once and four loads of buckshot passed through the white figure and rattled among the tree trunks behind it. In a flash the figure disappeared and darkness more intense than before, supervened.

The noise of the guns aroused the other watchers in distant spots and their lanterns could be seen flashing among the trees as they approached where the ghost had been seen. A meeting was held and Martin and his friends related their adventure. Extra caution was ordered and all through the long watches of the night the men lay around in the darkness near the deserted churchyard watching for the ghost, which did not come. The next night the party was again reorganized and under the same direction watched once more and once more the awful apparition was seen. It was further away than on the first night and as it approached the thunderous roar which Moon and French had described was plainly heard. A volley of shots was sent through the spectre when it came within firing distance, but they whistled through it as harmlessly as on the previous night and at the same instant the ghost disappeared.

The stories told by the members of the posse when they returned to their homes created intense excitement. Women refused to go out of doors at night and half the country people are sitting up all night to watch for the coming of the tall ghost with the big club. It appears in various places, but usually somewhere near the graveyard or the old church where the murdered man lies buried. Each night searching parties go out to run down the specter and each night they return with the same tale. The ghost of Benton is talked of at night in country homes and wayside villages and still it stalks abroad, spreading terror and dismay in its wake.

Plain Dealer [Cleveland, OH] 27 July 1896: p. 4 INDIANA

NOTE: This is good, strong, dramatic stuff. Unfortunately none of it is provable, although it was widely reported with varying degrees of detail. I can locate what seems like independent verification for only one of the cast of characters (Milton Moon's grave). But the story checks all the boxes in the giant ghost category: Robed, tall, carrying a club, elusive, and bullet-proof. These entities are also often found in connection with cemeteries. The thunderous sound, which, like the roar of a tiger, can paralyze a witness, is another intriguing feature.

We find another ghost that roared in this story of a "black ghost" unmasked.

THE BLACK GHOST A DISAPPOINTMENT
A Boy on Stilts, with a Sheet, Was Impersonating the Powers of Darkness

The mysterious figure known as the black ghost, which has for several weeks frightened the residents of Upper New Rochelle by appearing on the highway in the vicinity of the Thomas Paine monument, has at last been identified. The figure has turned out to be a clever impersonation arranged by some of the mischievous boys of the neighborhood. The apparition appeared in the highway for nearly every night for a period of two weeks and caused excitement in the neighborhood. Some persons who met the figure declared that it was eight feet tall, wore a white shroud, and, when approached, belched forth fire and roared like a lion.

A few nights ago the ghost sprang from behind a tree and stopped Mrs. Paulson, who was driving home alone from New Rochelle, and frightened her nearly into hysterics. Mrs. Paulson has since been suffering from an attack of nervous prostration. Several persons from Manhattan who have country homes in that vicinity saw the figure while driving, and their horses shied and nearly ran away.

The end of the mystery came on Saturday night, when a farmer while on his way home encountered the figure, which sprang from behind a stone wall. The farmer, instead of running away, struck the object a sharp blow with his whip, which felled it to the roadside. As the figure fell it gave a yell of pain, and then scampered away. The ghost proved to be a boy who lives in the neighborhood. He left his spectral paraphernalia behind, consisting of stilts five feet high, a sheet, and a black mask.
New York Tribune 17 November 1902: p. 4 NEW YORK

Three years later, a leaping apparition armed with a club was reported to be terrorizing western Indiana.

HEADLESS GHOST
An Apparition That Wields a Big Club in Indiana

Near Hillsboro, in western Indiana, there is a strip of wild, hilly country known as Red Hills, which for several years, according to the stories of reputable and reliable people, has been haunted by a headless ghost. Quite recently two farmers, driving through the hills after nightfall, were attacked by the ghost, which jumped into their wagon. Both deserted their team and fled in wild dismay. More recently a gang of coon hunters were stampeded, and none of them can be again persuaded to venture in that locality after night. Other people profess to have seen the same apparition, which came bounding toward them, frequently leaping 10 and 15 feet into the air, but disappearing when close at hand.

Recently, says the *Cincinnati Enquirer,* William Pithoud, a farmer, makes declaration that as he was driving homeward the ghost appeared armed with a huge club, and began belaboring his horses. Pithoud jumped out and fled in terror, never stopping until he reached the home of Harry Barton, who armed himself with a rifle and furnished Pithoud with a weapon. Together they returned to the scene of action, and they found the horses lying in a ditch, quivering with terror and showing every indication of having had a rough time.
Akron [OH] Daily Democrat 13 December 1899: p. 6 INDIANA

As I have previously remarked, killer ghosts are very rare. Yet if a ghost were to be violent, we would expect it to be a giant ghost.

KILLED BY SPECTER
Weird Legend of Wisconsin Mining Days
Haunting the Old Military Road at Ridgeway, Wis.,
an Uncanny Spirit Has Caused the Violent Deaths
of Three Persons.

In the little town of Ridgeway, lying about twenty miles from Madison, Wis., excitement during the past several weeks has been at high pitch. The cause of this agitation is the reappearance of an individual known as the Ridgeway ghost. For many years the ghost at different times has caused a reign of terror throughout that section of the country. That this apparition has given tangible evidence of its existence is shown by the fact of its having been the cause of three deaths, one of the victims being John Lewis, father of Evan Lewis, one-time champion wrestler of the world. It is a strange, weird tale, bearing all the earmarks of a ghost story. Nevertheless, in many incidents, facts bear out the reports in the case. One mile east of Ridgeway, on the old military road, there stood an old deserted farmhouse. For years a mere shell of boards, so shrunken and hardened by the summer suns that decay and worms never affected it, the house stood until some men at noonday, when the ghost could not walk, tore it down. This was the one-time home of an old miser of the lead mining days, named Holbein, who mysteriously disappeared one day, leaving no clew to his fate. Ghostly manifestations were at intervals reported as having taken place at the old house, but the lead miners were a hard-headed lot, afraid of neither man nor devil, and the stories of lights in the house and moanings at the roadside made little impression. It was not until the mining days were long over that the startling, unexplainable, terrible manifestations of the ghost were made. One night, as Dr. Cutler, a Dodgeville physician, was returning from a visit beyond Ridgeway, which is six miles from Dodgeville, he was suddenly affrighted to see a dark figure sitting on the buggy tongue between his horses. The reins slipped from his nerveless grasp, and the horses dashed away at full speed, the specter riding the pole nothing discommoded by the shaking he was getting. Down a hill, up another, dashed the frantic horses, and lo, the spectre vanished.

The doctor's story of the occurrence met with little credence. He was known to be one who loved the flowing bowl. He had taken a drop too many, said his scoffing friends. It was a dream, a spectre of *delirium tremens*, of mania, *a potu.* [Insanity arising from the use of spirituous liquors] But the doctor declared that he was sober. He recalled the fact that a year previous, when he really was a little full, while passing the self-same haunted spot, he had become aware of a dark and silent stranger sitting beside him in his carriage. For a mile the stranger rode, saying never a word, and all at once he was gone. All the time, the doctor had asked no questions of his drunken wits and had considered this nothing more than a strange experience. He was now convinced that the man beside him on the seat and the thing on the pole were not of this world. Whereat the people laughed—in the daytime. But not long afterward the reputation of the doctor received a sudden and terrible vindication, as he was himself to later vindicate it, almost as terribly. John Lewis, father of Evan Lewis, champion wrestler of the United States, known in the world of sports everywhere, was a prosperous and respected farmer living in the vicinity of Ridgeway, a man of sober life, of undaunted courage, and blessed with the tremendous physical strength his son has inherited. Sixteen years ago last fall he was returning home after nightfall, having spent the day assisting a friend in butchering. The night was not dark and when he drew near the haunted spot he determined to cut across lots to reach his home. He was approaching the stone wall at the roadside to climb it, when his attention was arrested by the sight of a figure that seemed to have gathered itself together out of the just now tenantless air, and stood confronting him in a menacing attitude. He knew of no enemy, and highwaymen were unknown in that retired quarter of the state. He decided that it must be someone trying to frighten him. So he hailed the figure, and no response being made he advanced upon it. The figure did not budge, but stood a towering shape of blackness, a gigantic and grisly thing.

Some unaccountable awe and the uncanny hugeness of the thing made Lewis decide to avoid a conflict, and drawing his butcher knife from his pocket, he started to pass by, when the figure, raising an arm with a forbidding gesture, stepped athwart his path. Obeying a hasty impulse that was more of a ghastly and soul-chilling terror than it was anger, Lewis let drive his keen knife, only to find himself piercing the empty air. In the morning a neighbor found Lewis lying inside the stone wall in a semi-conscious condition. Of what happened after he had struck with the knife, he had but vague impressions. He said he had been hurled in the air as if in the vortex of a cyclone, pounded, beaten, crushed into insensibility. Beyond the awful pain and the awful fear, he remembered nothing with distinctness. He died a few hours after he had been carried home, his neighbors having it that his heart had been literally torn to pieces with the shock. Whether it was the shock of fright, whether it was his physical injuries that killed him, none is ready to say with certainty. As he lay dying,

he asserted his belief that his death was occasioned by a supernatural being. Thus did the death of John Lewis make the first vindication of the reputation of Dr. Cutler, of Dodgeville, and the scoffing ceased. But a second time and a third was the doctor to be vindicated. Returning home one night, a dressmaker encountered the ghost and being pursued by it, soon after died of the shock occasioned by the intense fright. At last Dr. Cutler himself, finally and triumphantly vindicated his word, though at the cost of his own life, for dying as a result of fright, he became the third of the victims of the implacable spectre of the old military road. And now the mysterious apparition has again made its appearance and the good people of Ridgeway await with much anxiety the result.
Belleville [KS] Telescope 20 April 1900: p. 6 WISCONSIN

NOTE: This is perhaps the best-known ghost in Wisconsin. Dennis Boyer, author of *Restless Spirits*, Prairie Oak Press, 1997, has looked at the stories and says that they run in 40-year cycles starting in the 1850s. The specter was still being reported in the 1970s. The scene where the doctor suddenly becomes aware of the ghost sitting beside him in his carriage is a rare and early example of a phantom hitchhiker tale. Evan Lewis was the first American Heavyweight Champion in catch-as-catch-can wrestling. He was known as "the Strangler," for his perfecting of the "stranglehold" move.

Just as female ghosts may materialize as Women in Black or Women in White, giant ghosts are similarly monochromatic. White or black robes, cloaks or shrouds are their usual garb. Is this a peep into the closets of the Afterlife or was it a convenient and intimidating method of concealment for hoaxers?

SAW A TALL GHOST.
Apparition That Is Troubling a County Orphan's Home.

Wabash, Ind., Jan. 2. The Cass County orphans' home has gained the reputation of being haunted and the inmates are in a state of panic. Mrs. Carney, the matron, is skeptical and wants ocular demonstration of the ghost's existence. The servant girl who says she saw the apparition last Thursday night in the rear of the home describes it as that of a man 7 feet tall, clad in pure white.

When it came to the clothesline, she says, it had to stoop. The screams of the children who were with her aroused her and all fled precipitately. The home is just across the road from a cemetery and the servant girl

insists that a buried enemy has returned to plague her.
Dubuque [IA] Daily Telegraph 2 January 1901: p. 1 INDIANA

NOTE: A buried enemy who needs to stoop for a clothesline seems suspiciously corporeal.

An Apparition
The Strange Creature Creating an Excitement Near Mexico, Mo.

The neighborhood of Hopewell Church, near Mexico, Mo., is much excited over the appearance in the locality of a strange creature, which is thought by the credulous to be a ghost, and which is a puzzle at least to the most skeptical. The apparition is simply that of a lean monster man, between eight and ten feet in height wearing a long cloak, and going about with his head bowed in an abstracted way, but occasionally glaring at those it meets with small, glittering eyes, said to resemble those of a cat or some wild beast. The negroes believe the apparition to be a ghost; the white people do not know what to say. There appears little doubt, whatever the creature may be, that it has actually been seen a number of times. The school at Hopewell Church is about abandoned because of fear of the monster and even sturdy farmers go about armed in apprehension of it. John Creary, a well-known old resident, declares that the other afternoon as he was returning from Mexico to his home he had a good view of the queer being, who was about fifty yards ahead of him, walking in a leisurely way along the middle of a big road, in mud almost knee deep, his head still lowered and his long black cloak flowing in the breeze. All at once, and in the twinkling of an eye, he disappeared in the thick woods as mysteriously as he came upon the scene. Mr. Creary says for the first time in his life, although a soldier under Gen. Grant, he was really frightened, and it was all he could do to control the horse he was riding, so great seemed its fear of the object. Mr. Cyrus Hagger and wife, who were returning home from church Thanksgiving eve, were surprised by the monster's peering with its cat-like eyes into their buggy and leaning against it, almost crushing the vehicle. The lady has not yet, it is said, recovered from the shock. Mr. and Mrs. H. both claim on this occasion a white cloak was worn. A large number of others have seen the strange creature, and a large party is scouring the neighborhood of Hopewell Church, hoping to capture it. The creature is thought to be located in the rear of Philip Brown's residence.

Jackson [MI] Citizen Patriot 17 December 1883: p. 2 MISSOURI

NOTE: *The Daily Los Angeles [CA] Herald* adds the following information:

[Dispatch to *St. Louis Globe-Democrat*] The newspapers of the city are represented in the searching party, which includes one or two St. Louisans, and a report from the expedition is awaited with much interest. The creature is thought to be located in the hills in the rear of one Philip Brown's residence. The Mexican party is under the leadership of Bob White and Merkel. No services will be held in the Hopewell Church tomorrow. *Daily Los Angeles* [CA] Herald 27 December 1883: p. 1 MISSOURI

NOTE: The "lean monster man" irresistibly suggests the creature from "Canon Alberic's Scrapbook" by M.R. James: "a body of fearful thinness, almost a skeleton, but with the muscles standing out like wires."

Regrettably, I have not found any trace of the people named except Robert Mitchell (or Morgan) White, owner of the *Missouri/Mexico Ledger* newspaper and a mention of a Philip Brown in a Kansas City, MO paper of 1898. It is too common a name to give any certainty and the specific reference suggests a local insider joke.

This next lurid apparition appeared only a few years after the beginning of the natural gas boom in Indiana. At the time, the Trenton Gas Field of Indiana and western Ohio was the largest in the world.

GHOST IS GENUINE.
Gruesome Specter at an Abandoned Gas Well.
Fearsome Sight Seen by Umstott
A Man Ten Feet High Holding In His Arms a Beautiful Woman With Her Throat Cut

Elwood, March 20. A few miles west of this city is an abandoned gas well, the abiding place of a genuine ghost. Many adventures have taken place there lately. The well was one of the first drilled and before it was completed an accident occurred by which one man lost his life and the well was never finished. A year passed after the death of this man and then someone started the report that strange things were happening at the old well. Finally a choice assortment of ghost stories were floating around the neighborhood. Recently Jabez Umstott saw a headless man one night while passing the place after nightfall, and he found plenty who would testify that he was telling the truth.

"Spectral Form of Giant Size."

Last week while returning home he was horrified to see standing in the road by the well a spectral form of giant size. The form was that of a man fully ten feet high, and in his massive arms he held a beautiful woman. Across her white throat there was a cruel cut, from which the life blood was flowing fast. The awful apparition held a large knife in its long hands, which bore the red stain of murderous guilt. The poor man was unable to move hand or foot and stood there spellbound until the forms slowly disappeared. He was dumbfounded and could scarcely believe his senses, but after telling his adventure he found several who had seen the same thing. The inhabitants of the vicinity do not go near after nightfall alone, and the road leading to the well is deserted after night.

Logansport [IN] Pharos 20 March 1894: p. 1 INDIANA

NOTE: "Jabez Umstott" might sound like a joke name to modern ears, but the surname was quite common in Ohio, Missouri, and Kansas. While I haven't studied the question extensively, I have noticed that areas in Ohio during the gas boom produced larger-than-average numbers of apparition and monster stories. Something for future research, perhaps.

A HUGE GHOST.
The Terrible Apparition Which Persecutes the Citizens of Elizabeth, N.J.

[Boston Herald.]

A ghost twelve feet in height, with fiery eyes and horns, has been disturbing the peaceful citizens of Elizabeth, N.J., with the most unseemly pranks. The apparition has been repeatedly seen of late, and a vigilance committee, armed to the teeth, scours the streets nightly, hoping to lay the specter with cold lead. Unfortunately, this ghost is extremely difficult to catch. Its agility is something amazing. Fences fifteen feet high afford no obstacle to the gigantic bounds by which it is accustomed to travel. One day last week it was actually cornered by the vigilance committee, but it made its escape by climbing a lightning rod to the roof of a church and leaping to the street on the other side. People have suggested that it must have a spring in it somewhere. It is rumored that several young women have been kissed by the naughty ghost, and the girls are afraid to venture out of doors after dark. There is something anthropomorphous about the spook after all.

Xenia [OH] Daily Gazette 30 January 1886: p. 4 NEW JERSEY

NOTE: This ghost is one of the most "Jack"-like in our collection, with his agile leaps, his amorous ways, and his fiery eyes.

TOWN TERRORIZED BY BLACK DEVIL
Mysterious Giant Figure Keeps Georgetown, Del. Guessing—
Frightens Women and Children.

Georgetown, Del., May 18. More than seven feet in height and swathed in a long black cloak, closely wrapped around its face, a mystery has been exciting some parts of Georgetown where it has followed women and young girls and jumped out from behind trees at them.

The "Devil in Black," as it is called, first appeared several nights ago, when a dozen or so persons saw it during the course of the evening. From behind a tree it jumped at Mrs. William Curdy and sent her screaming with fright into a neighbor's house, while a daughter of Joseph Carnel also was chased by the mysterious stranger until she fell almost unconscious into Fred Rust's grocery store.

The men of the neighborhood, informed of the affair, led by William Curdy, ran across fields, jumped fences and through backyards with the "Devil" but a few yards ahead of them, but, while crossing the big ditch known as the Savannah, the figure completely disappeared, and despite search, could not be found.

Again it was seen by several young girls and last night it made its appearance and was seen closely by Mrs. Carl Josephs, who heard a noise as she passed her woodshed. She turned to look and distinctly saw the "Devil" walk out of the shed and after her.

Almost fainting with fear she ran screaming into the house while her husband ran into the yard with his gun and fired at the tall figure, which was plainly distinguished at the woodshed. In a second it was gone with no trace of injury from the gun. Many superstitious declare that bullets cannot hit it, but some of the more determined men declare it is the work of a practical joker and expect to put a load of shot into it at their first opportunity.

Fort Worth [TX] Star-Telegram 9 May 1909: p. 5 DELAWARE

In some cases there might have been a grim natural explanation for what appeared to be a giant ghost. This man, tarred, feathered, and fleeing for his life, was mistaken for a phantom.

APPARITION
Travelers Thought a Man Coated With Tar and Feathers—Caused an Accident.

Lawrenceburg, Ind. March 19. Lee Kennedy, the negro who was tarred and feathered Thursday night for an attempted assault on a white girl, came near causing a fatal accident during his wild flight from his tormentors.

Coat after coat of the sticky mixture had been applied to the person of the culprit until his dimensions were enormous and as he shambled rather than ran away on account of his cumbersome covering he resembled a giant bear in his waddling motions.

While running along the pike nearly a mile beyond the place where he had received his punishment he met Joseph Topher, Edward Christy and Mr. Bennett driving homeward in a wagon drawn by a team of horses. The animals became frightened, jumped and threw the occupants of the vehicle out, injuring all three of the men, but Mr. Bennett more seriously than his companions. Mr. Christy, who held the reins, succeeded in stopping the terrified horses and prevented the injuries becoming probably fatal.

While all three of the men distinctly saw the singular looking object that dashed past them not one could divine what it was. Mr. Topher said it looked more like an ostrich with wings extended.

All day yesterday several parties searched for the disgraced darky, but the only trace discovered was a large pile of feathers and a quantity of tar on the roadside six miles distant from the scene of the punishment, where the poor fellow had evidently rested for the first time in his terrified flight and had plucked the clinging mixture from his denuded form.
Cincinnati [OH] Enquirer 20 Mar 1897: p. 4 INDIANA

We will finish this chapter with a strange story of a giant, flaming ghost—a bridge to the following chapter on fiery phantom devils.

Iowa's Remarkable Ghost Story.

Davenport, Iowa, July 22. A ghost story of an unusual style comes from a Swedish settlement on the Rock Island Road, northwest of this city. There are any number of people willing to vouch for the truth of the story, and it is certain that part of it is true beyond all question. A man named Richardson lived on a small farm near the village of Tiskavilla [Tuskawilla] in a humble but contented way. He was industrious and well-liked by his neighbors. On Wednesday of last week his youngest child, a daughter, ran screaming to a neighbor's before daylight, saying that a huge man, all covered with fire, had come into the house and carried off all but herself. It was supposed the house was on fire, and aid was quickly afforded, but the house was found to be all right. Nothing at all was disturbed, but no one was about. The horse and buggy remained in the stable. The clothing left off by members of the family on going to bed was found where it had been left. The vicinity was thoroughly searched, but without avail. No train had stopped, and no water was near. It seemed as if the ground had opened and swallowed the family up. A neighbor's family moved into the house to take care of the things and the child and were nearly scared to death the first night. They assert that suddenly the house was filled with a strange white light and the voice of Richardson was heard calling his daughter. She responded and instantly the light disappeared and a great shower of small stones fell upon the roof. The same scene has been enacted nightly since and the whole community is aroused. The child does not appear to be in the least alarmed at the voices.

The New York Times 23 July 1885 IOWA

NOTE: Of course the disembodied voice of the missing man harkens back to the fictional tale of the disappearances of Oliver Lerch/Larch and David Lang. See "The Difficulty of Crossing a Field," by Ambrose Bierce. The light might be interpreted as a spook light or a UFO, while the abrupt shower of stones is a poltergeist prank common to the point of tedium. An early eye-witness account of a stone-throwing poltergeist in New Hampshire can be found in *Lithobolia: Or the Stone-Throwing Devil*, online at http://w3.salemstate.edu/~ebaker/chadweb/lithoweb.htm.

7.

The Devil Went Down to Kentucky

Fiery Phantom Devils

From his brimstone bed, at break of day,
A-walking the Devil is gone,
To look at his little snug farm of the World,
And see how his stock went on.

-Robert Southey, *"The Devil's Walk."*-

The Devil has long walked this land. Some say he was found here in the guise of shaggy Native American wood-demons. The earliest Puritans brought with them their rough-legged Robin Goodfellows and woodwoses as well as the notion that the Devil aped the clergy in a sober suit of gentlemanly black, claiming souls with the stroke of a pen. Some say the Devil died at Salem, but in the 19th century, he reappeared, reverting to his bestial nature in a cloud of sulphurous smoke.

In February of 1866, something extraordinary was reported from a small Kentucky county, seemingly his Satanic Majesty in all his devilish glory.

The Old Fashioned Satan, with Horns and Tail, Broke Loose in Bracken County, Kentucky.

A correspondent of the Mt. Sterling *Sentinel* gives the following account of a fiery fiend visible in Bracken County. Is it a Freedmen's Bureau incarnate?

BRACKEN CO., KY., Feb. 17, 1866.

Mr. Editor: The people of this neighborhood are in the greatest state of excitement in consequence of a remarkable visitation, or apparition, of some demoniacal personage in our midst. I am not a believer in the doctrine that disembodied spirits can "revisit the glimpses of the moon," nor do I believe that epoch designated in prophecy, when the chains of Satan are to be unloosed, has arrived. But the things whereof I now write are of such strange import, so inexplicable, that I have determined to put you in possession of a full and explicit narrative of them, merely premising that every word is true, and the facts sworn to, as witness the accompanying affidavit. What it is, I am unable to say. I merely give the facts, such as I am personally cognizant of, and leave it to wiser heads than my own to unravel the mystery.

On Monday night last, after myself and family had retired to rest, we were suddenly aroused by a great outcry from the negro quarters—which are immediately to the rear of the house—in which prayers vied for supremacy with blasphemies; men, women and children screaming "fire!" and "murder!" at the top of their voices, all conspiring to create a scene worthy of a pandemonium. Terribly startled, my wife and I sprang from our bed. The room was illuminated as brightly as by a flood of sunlight, though the light was of a bluish cast. Our first and most reasonable conclusion was that the negro cabins were being consumed by fire. We rushed to the windows and beheld a sight that fairly curdled the blood in our veins with horror, and filled our hearts with the utmost terror. My daughters, shrieking loudly came flying into my room, hysterical with fear. This is what we beheld:

Standing to the right of the upper cabin near the fence that separates the negroes' garden from the house-yard; was a creature of gigantic stature, and the most horrifying appearance. It was nearly as high as the comb of the house, and had a monstrous head not dissimilar in shape to that of an ape; two short very white horns appeared above each eye, its arms were long, covered with shaggy hair of an ashen hue, and terminated with huge paws not unlike those of a cat, armed with long and hooked claws. Its breast was as broad as that of a large sized ox. Its legs resembled the front legs of a horse, only the hoofs were cloven. It had a long tail, armed with a dart-shaped horn, which it was continually switching about. Its eyes glowed like two living coals of fire, while from its nostrils and mouth were emitted sheets of bluish colored flame, with a hissing sound like the hissing of a serpent, only a thousand fold louder. Its general cover, save its arms, was a dull, dingy brown. The air was powerfully impregnated with a smell of burning sulphur. The poor negroes were evidently laboring under the extremest terror, and two of them, and old woman and a lad, were actually driven to insanity by their fears, and have not recovered their reason up to this writing. I do not know how long this monster, demon or devil, was visible after we reached the windows—possibly some three seconds. When it vanished it was enveloped in a spiral column of flame that reached nearly to the top of the locust trees adjacent, and which hid its horrid form completely from view. The extinction of the flame was instantaneous, and with its disappearance we were relieved of the presence of this remarkable visitor.

It would be impossible for me to attempt to describe the effect of this visitation upon the members of my family. Suffice it to say, that my wife and two daughters are firmly persuaded that it was the veritable Satan. For myself, I would willingly believe that we all, by some curious coincidence, had been the victim of a horrid nightmare, did I not know that we were fully awake, and actually witnessed that which is above recorded. Again, if ours had been the only family visited by this unearthly creature, I should have kept silent, and, perhaps tutored my mind into the belief that it was a hallucination.

But precisely the same apparition made its appearance at my neighbor's, Mrs. Wm. Dole, appearing there in precisely the same shape in which it presented itself to us, save the head, which appeared to those who witnessed it at Mrs. D. 's to resemble that of a horse. At Mr. Adam Fuqua's another neighbor, its head was that of a vulture. On Tuesday night it appeared at Mr. Jesse Bond's, there wearing the head of an elephant. At all these places, it made the same appearance as at my house—excepting only the change of the head—and disappeared in the same manner. These parties are all reliable ladies and gentlemen, and at my request have made oath to what they witnessed.

What it is, what its object, what its mission, is something that passes my poor comprehension. What I have above written is simple, unadorned truth. You are at liberty to use this in any manner you may esteem proper.
Respectfully your friend, NATHANIEL G. SQUIRES.
State of Kentucky, Bracken County— *Sct* :
This day personally appeared before the undersigned, John G. Finley, Justice of the Peace, within and for the county and State aforesaid, Nathaniel G. Squires, Minerva Squires, Sarah D. Squires, Lucy Squires. Martha W. Dole, Adam Fuqua and Jesse Bond, who, being duly sworn according to law, declare that the statements in the foregoing letter are true as far as it refers to each of them. And I certify that the affiants are credible and reliable persons, and their statements entitled to full faith and credit.
John G. Finley, J. P. B. C.
Weekly Vincennes [IN] Gazette 17 March 1866 KENTUCKY

NOTE: The Freedmen's Bureau was an organization set up by the Federal Government to help former slaves adapt to freedom. It offered practical aid like food and clothing, as well as education and help in finding work. The Bureau quickly found itself overwhelmed by the immensity of need and by 1866, its scope and funding were reduced. There were many bitter complaints in the southern press about the Bureau overstepping its bounds, including a vitriolic attack in the *Louisville Daily Democrat* published the same day as the date this letter. I suspect that the reference in the article is comparing the Bureau to an out-of-control beast, the terror of the status quo. To speculate about the descriptions: African Americans were sometimes described by the prejudiced as "apes." "Vultures," in the form of carpetbaggers were traveling South to pick over the carcass. And horses and elephants could be wild creatures, running away and trampling on the rights of ordinary citizens.

The imagery in this piece is quite astonishing, but it is consistent with omnibus monster reports or stories of strange wild animals composed of bits of multiple species, so often found in the period papers.

Less than a month later, an arrest was made and it seemed as though the horrifying mystery was solved.

The Devil Caught and Caged

The Nashville *Banner* says:

The Kentucky "old-fashioned Satan with horns and tail," is no longer at large. The Giascutus has been taken in out of the wet. The "Squier's family" and Mrs. Dole, and the rest of the Bracken County people, who were scared out of their wits and their movable effects by this monstrous visitor, may rest in peace. The luminous eyes, the gnashing teeth, the scaly hide, the cloven feet, the horrid horns, the terrific tail, will trouble them no more forever. Satan is bound, and his name is Oden.

A man bearing the name of Oden, a resident of Carlisle, Nicholas County, Kentucky, procured a horse-hide, with which he clothed himself, and having furnished himself with a phosphorous substance, to imitate the devil's eyes of fire, started forth to alarm the timid. He would approach a dwelling, making a strange noise, causing the inmates to leave hurriedly. He would then enter the house and appropriate what valuables he could find. He was shot at repeatedly, but being protected by a coat of mail the shots failed to take effect. Finally a number of persons surrounded and succeeded in lassoing him and he is now confined to the narrow walls of Carlisle Jail, to answer to numerous charges for theft, which will be arrayed against him.

Macon [GA] Weekly Telegraph 9 April 1866: p. 2 KENTUCKY

NOTE: The Giascutus is a joke monster. It lives on hillsides and has one set of legs longer than the other. A James H. Oden, age 29, is found in the Nicholas County 1860 census, as well as a William C. Oden, age 49. Both are listed as farmers living in Carlisle; James has 4 children under the age of 7, including an infant and an estate valued at $200—making him desperate enough to steal? William C. has 6 children aged from 4 to 18; he owns over 1,000 acres and his estate is worth $6,600. W.M. Oden, age 27, is a laborer and has a 1 year old son. His estate is worth $500. Oden is a neat explanation for the February 1866 story. However Carlisle is about 40 miles from Brooksville, the seat of Bracken County, rather a long way to go for a robbery. I also find it curious that a sneak thief would go to so much trouble to scare people away. A black mask and a pair of gum shoes would have been less conspicuous. And how did he work the rest of the effects: the paws and cloven hooves; the height as tall as a house; (The comb of the house is the roof ridge.) the very theatrical spiral column of flame to the treetop? How did he avoid suffocating in the fumes from the bucket of sulphur used to create the blue flames?

I owe a tip of the horns to that extraordinary Fortean researcher Theo Paijmans for discovering these fiery devils. I was very excited to run across the first Bracken County story only to find Paijmans's masterful article from *Fortean Times* when I went online to look for more details. He comments on the Oden story:

> "Imaginative as Oden's ruse was, he certainly was not the first to hatch such an elaborate scheme. Mike Dash has noted in his study of Spring-heeled Jack that in the 1840s a Georgia man had disguised himself as the Devil in order to rob a wealthy woman, but paid for it with his life, and I have found several other cases. There was the 'demon' captured in Moscow [Russia] in the 1800s who wore "horns, tail, fiery eyes and all" but turned out to be a rather creative thief. There was the similarly dressed burglar in Maple Grove, Wisconsin, who was fatally shot in 1877 by the boy in the house he intended to rob. And there was the thief dressed as the Devil who was again fatally shot by two boys in Huntsburg, Germany, in 1897." [You'll find the Paijmans's full story with his citations at http://www.forteantimes.com/features/articles/5581/blasts_from_the_past_the_news_that_time_forgot.html]

Despite my skepticism about the efficiency of this disguise, as Paijmans points out, there are other reports of similar thieves.

> One night last week a man was aroused by an unusual noise in his yard, and went out and found that someone had broken open his meat house and was making off with his meat. He hailed the supposed thief, but found to his astonishment that he had waked up the most unearthly looking four-legged customer he ever beheld. At first he was tempted to leave the field to the intruder; but not liking to loose [sic] his meat, he conclud-

ed to make at him. He was met by a most ferocious growl. He at once ran to the house, got his gun and blazed away at the monster. The shot had about the same impression on it as would be produced by shooting green peas against a brick wall. The devil uttered an infernal growl, shook his chains, spit sparks of fire from his mouth, and filled the air with the smell of brimstone. The unearthly manifestations of [the] demon made the hair stand on the man's head; but he could not bear to lose his bacon. He then, nothing daunted, determined to have another fire at the devil, and took the precaution to put a Minnie ball in his gun. The shot took effect directly in the eye of the monster, and he rolled upon the ground a lifeless corpse. Upon examination, it was found to be a negro man, wrapped in a mule-skin, which he had padded and fixed up, to render it impervious to shot, and the fire and brimstone was but an artifice intended to frighten away intruders, while he committed the robbery.

Flake's Bulletin [Galveston, TX] 22 March 1866: p. 1 TEXAS?

Note the date. The next story is a decade later:

The town of Maple Grove, Wis., is excited over a recent Sunday occurrence there. The people were mostly at church, and in one house a twelve-year old boy was the only occupant. During the absence of the family a man came to the house completely enveloped in a beef hide, with horns, tail, and all complete, and so fitted that nothing else could be seen. It was known in the neighborhood that the occupants of this house had money, and there was there at the time about $200. The object disguised in the hide told the boy that he was the devil, and that he had come after his money and he must give it to him. The boy answered that he could not have the money. The devil then told the boy that he would have him and kill him if he did not bring out the money. The boy then stepped into the house as if he was about to comply, but instead of bringing the money he brought a gun and shot the man dead in his tracks. The boy then ran to the nearest neighbor, and, finding only a woman there, told her he had shot the devil at his house. The woman went with the boy, and found that the devil whom the boy had shot was her husband.

Galveston [TX] Weekly News 11 June 1877: p. 3 WISCONSIN

NOTE: Both of these stories have parallels in folklore and the lack of specific individual names suggests that these should go into either into the fictional tale box or the folklore category of ostension, where a fictional event actually occurs.

With the arrest of Oden, the Devil-Impersonator, peace should have come to Bracken County. But in 1868 there was another visitation.

The Devil in Bracken County, Ky.

Brooksville, Ky., October 19, 1869 [sic]
To the Editors of the *Enquirer.*

A wonderful phenomenon has recently made its appearance on Willow Creek, in Bracken County, about two miles from Brooksville, and has been seen by quite a number of the worthy citizens of our county. Our people have been in a constant state of excitement since it first made its appearance.

On the 10th inst., as one of our citizens, a prominent tobacco merchant residing in Brooksville, was returning home from the southern portion of the county, where he had been buying some crops of tobacco, and, being belated, was riding along the road, when suddenly he beheld a frightful object in the middle of the road immediately in front of him. I will give you the description of it as I heard it from his lips.

"The object was about six feet in height, and walked upright. The face was at times that of a man, very pale, with curls of flame falling over his shoulders; eyes of sulphurous blue, changing constantly in size, one moment large as a tin-cup, and then gradually decreasing in size until it was almost invisible. Its arms were those of a man, and hands deadly pale. In one hand it held a torch, and in the other a sword that seemed to be about four feet in length. Its lower extremity was that of a horse, with legs well proportioned, and hoofs as those of a horse. Its tail, which was about three feet in length, was of flame. Its breath was a solid sheet of fire, which vibrated with the heavings of its breast, like the pendulum of a clock. It was certainly the most frightful object I ever beheld. It walked off to the side of the road, and then vanished. When it disappeared I immediately put spurs to my horse and galloped by the spot where I had seen it. When I arrived at the summit of the hill, about two hundred yards off, I looked back and saw the object in the spot where I first beheld it. I stopped my horse and watched it for a moment; it walked over to the left side of the road, and, mounting a rail fence that stood there, commenced running toward me. I did not stay to see the remainder of the drama."

He immediately rode to town, and having told the adventure to some of the citizens they immediately formed a party and started out to see the strange visitant. Lawyers, doctors, preachers and tradesmen, armed with guns and pistols, made their way *en masse* to the scene of this strange adventure. When they arrived at the spot, some of them beheld the specter and others could not see it. It was, when they saw it, on the fence, and running rapidly along up and down it past the crowd, for the distance of a quarter of a mile. As it passed the crowd, several fired at it, but with no effect.

About eleven o'clock it vanished, and was seen no more that night. Since then it has been seen every night at the same place. Hundreds of visitors have been on hand every night, and the excitement is at a very high state now, and is increasing. The cause of this is beyond human conjecture. It has been only about a year ago since it was seen in this county before. The county is astir, and the people are eager to get rid of their unwelcome visitant. This is the whole narrative.

Will not some philosopher explain the cause of this wonder?

Yours truly,

JOSEPH PEYTON [Another virtually identical version of this article spells the name Payton.]

State of Kentucky, Bracken County, S.S.

We, the undersigned, make oath and say that the above statement is substantially correct, and has been examined by us.

Lucius Langdon

Jonathan C. Soule

James S. Wolfe. X His Mark

Sworn to before me this the sixteenth day of October, 1868. John P. Jones, J.P.

Cincinnati [OH] Enquirer 22 October 1868: p. 2 KENTUCKY

About two months later, the Devil went down to Virginia.

A Ghost—or Something—in Prince William County, Va.

[Correspondence of the Alexandria *Gazette*.]

Prince William County, Va., Dec. 12. It becomes my duty to chronicle a most singular and extraordinary series of nocturnal visitations on the part of some ghostly apparition, to the farm of one whom I shall call Silas Brown, Esq., a peaceable and intelligent citizen of this county. Mr. Brown lives in what is known as the forest of Prince William, near the village of Independent Hill, and his residence is completely surrounded with the growth indigenous to that section of the county.

For the past few weeks visions of an alarming character have been seen in the neighboring forest, but more particularly in the copse adjacent to Mr. Brown's barn and stable. At numbers of times has an immense figure been seen passing to and fro near the barn, with large horns and terrible claws, which it contracts to a sort of hoof, and has assaulted Mr. Brown, when he attempted after dark to feed his horses and stock, in such a manner and with such violence that he has been compelled to flee to his house for safety. The figure, to the best of Mr. Brown's recollection, seemed about three times as large as a man in its front, and having a back converging from its neck and shoulders horizontally to the distance of some six or eight feet and supplied on each side with huge and tremendous arms. It is of a pale blueish color when first seen, but upon being irritated by the near approach of any person becomes a deadly white, and issues from its surface a small volume of smoke, accompanied with a sickening smell. This ghoul or unnatural and horrible animal or demon, has been seen as often as four times near Mr. Brown's stable; and when seen, it has lingered till its deadly effluvia has completely impregnated the surrounding atmosphere. One evening Mr. Brown, desiring to have another beside himself see this terrible visitant, induced a courageous gentleman whom I shall call Siger, who happened with his wife to spend the evening at Mr. Brown's, to go to the stable to feed his horses. Mr. Siger, not believing the story, went without hesitation, when, upon entering the stable, he was alarmed by the fall at or near his feet, with a deep rumbling sound, of a tremendous stone. Mr. Siger, without looking to see whence the rock came, picked the stone up, and it was so hot that he was compelled to drop it. Upon looking up he beheld the unearthly monster not over fifty yards from him, and the air became quickly filled and inoculated with brimstone (!) Not wishing to be thought a coward, he did not mention anything of this at the house, but upon walking home with his wife the same night he told her of what happened at the stable, and instantly she became alarmed, and was carried home in a state of apparent insensibility.

The neighborhood is in a terrible state of excitement, and steps have been taken to investigate this frightening matter.

By your next issue it may be possible that some clue can be gained to the identity and character of this hideous monster. K.

The Alexandria [VA] Gazette 15 December 1868: p. 2 VIRGINIA

NOTE: Ripping as this yarn is, I have my suspicions that it is a teaser article meant to stimulate sales of the "next issue," as I have seen in articles referring to a "rat baby" or "devil kid," whose "full particulars will appear in Saturday's edition." Only they never do.... This original article was published in the *Petersburg [VA] Index* 18 December 1868, p. 4 and the *Burlington [IA] Daily Hawk Eye* 5 January 1869: p. 2, but I have not found a follow-up. And the author does not give any real names. Note the inclusion of a hot lithobolia rock. A stone-throwing devil, indeed! [See *Lithobolia: Or the Stone-Throwing Devil*, online at http://w3.salemstate.edu/~ebaker/chadweb/lithoweb.htm.]

Like the second Bracken County devil sighting, this "hobgoblin" in Alabama carried a sword and had eyeballs of fire.

Gazed on a Huge Hobgoblin

[Birmingham (Ala.) Cor. *Globe-Democrat*]

A dozen colored men and women were badly frightened in Central Park early yesterday morning by a ghost. They were going home from a church festival about 1 o'clock and passed through the park near the old Exposition building [the state fairgrounds.] As they were passing near the building they saw a ghost of a giant stature, with eyeballs of fire and carrying a flaming sword, emerge from the back door. The horrible-looking monster stood on the steps for a moment, then walked slowly around the building to the main entrance in front. There it disappeared inside the building and was seen no more.

The colored people who saw the gigantic phantom say it was completely enveloped in a sheet of blue flame, and that its eyes were like two great balls of fire. The party stood helpless and speechless with terror until the ghost disappeared, and they ran home as fast as they could go.

The mysterious monster has been the one subject of conversation among the colored people of the city to-day, and it will be a long time, it is said, before a colored man can be induced to go near the old building after nightfall.

Cincinnati [OH] Enquirer 27 July 1890: p. 16 ALABAMA

NOTE: If it weren't for the date, I would think that these witnesses had seen a Ray Harryhausen-ized version of the immense statue of Vulcan, the fiery god of the forge, holding a spear that stood at the Alabama State Fairgrounds. The statue, commissioned by the Commercial Club of Birmingham, was the Birmingham contribution to the St. Louis World's Fair of 1904. But it wasn't even a gleam in the eye of sculptor Giuseppe Moretti, who began designing it in 1903. Meant to symbolize the Birmingham iron and steel industry, it was cast entirely of locally produced iron and displayed at the St. Louis Exposition "Palace of Mines and Metallurgy." It is very curious that these witnesses saw a figure that corresponded in so many ways to the idea of the God Vulcan.

I have found several other similar fiery devil stories, most notably from New York, Chicago, and Missouri, but what are we to make of these terrifying creatures from Kentucky? Could there be any literal truth to these flaming emissaries of Hell? The capture of the thief, Oden, from Carlisle seems to offer a neat and rational explanation; a counterbalance to the fantastical nature of the other stories. But we need to take a closer look.

Initially I thought perhaps the Kentucky and Virginia monsters were designed to scare slaves so that they would not run away. There were several Underground Railroad sites near Augusta, Kentucky where escaping slaves could cross the Ohio River to Ripley, Ohio where the Reverend John Rankin had a safe house. But the dates of the devils' appearances are too late; slavery had already been abolished. There was, however, bitter resentment in the county over some high-handed behavior by the Freedmen's Bureau. Could the devils have terrorized the populace in retaliation for the Bureau's activities?

Further, perhaps my newspaper sources are defective, but I cannot find the Bracken County stories in a single Kentucky newspaper. One would think that the advent of his Satanic Majesty would have been the top local news, particularly in Kentucky, a state noted for its fire-and-brimstone preachers.

But what of the witnesses? Shockingly, they do not exist. I have looked at a number of different types of records for Bracken County: the census, cemetery logs, business directories, Masonic lodge lists, Civil War muster rolls. *None* of the names in those official-looking affidavits can be found in any of these sources. We might expect some people to slip through the cracks of history and disappear, but over a dozen? And all of them witnesses to a satanic visitation? With our narrators disappearing in a puff of sulphurous smoke, it seems reasonable to conclude that these devil sightings are a species of very tall tale.

This then begs the question, if the first Bracken County devil was a hoax story; what of Oden, the thief-in-a-skin? Was this again, ostension in action; a hoaxer copying a hoax?

The impetus for the Bracken County stories is unclear unless they were a purely literary exercise, a kind of proto-science-fiction. They could also have been created to mock religion or, conversely, superstition. Possibly they were an insider joke we cannot grasp. Or were they simply a diabolical yarn, the brainchild of an ingenious editor?

If a 19th-century editor were casting about for a tale of a startling monster that would sell papers, where would he have found inspiration? I suggest that the author went to a book that everyone in the community knew practically by heart; a book nearly as familiar to 19th-century Americans as The Bible: *Pilgrim's Progress* by John Bunyan, first published in 1678. With the exception of the Bible it has been translated into more languages than any other book in the world. It was wildly popular in the Victorian era; you would expect to find a gilt-stamped copy in most parlors in the United States. Generations of Sunday School children knew the stories and, what is more important for our purposes, had seen illustrations of them, in particular that of Christian's combat with the fiend Apollyon. Like the Bracken County devils, Apollyon is a smoking hybrid, made of different animals representing the elements water, air, fire, and earth.

> He espied a foul Fiend coming over the field to meet him; his name is Apollyon...Now the Monster was hideous to behold; he was cloathed with scales like a Fish (and they are his pride); he had wings like a Dragon, feet like a Bear, and out of his belly came Fire and Smoke; and his mouth was as the mouth of a Lion....Then Apollyon straddled quite over the whole breadth of the way and said, I am void of fear in this matter, prepare thyself to die; for I swear by my infernal Den, that thou shalt go no further; here will I spill thy soul.
> And with that he threw a flaming Dart at his breast...
> *Pilgrim's Progress*, John Bunyan, Chapter IX.

The analogy is not perfect; the Bracken County devils do not have wings. But some of the most vivid illustrations of this scene do not show wings or minimize them, like "Christian cast down by Apollyon," a wood engraving by Frederick Shields found in the 1864 edition. [See a copy here: http://www. victorianweb.org/art/illustration/shields/3.jpg.]

Another possible source for images of giant flaming fiends were the magic lantern shows and moving panoramas of *Pilgrim's Progress*. The glass slides of the lantern shows, a popular Sunday School entertainment, were thrown onto a screen or wall, while the moving panorama consisted of many paintings on an immense roll of cloth, each scene slowly cranked before the audience, accompanied by narration and music. Seen by flickering lamp or gaslight, the pictures must have seemed alive.

Panoramas toured from about 1850 through the 1890s; they visited Mobile, Alabama and various cities in Ohio in 1860. I have not found an advertisement for a panorama in Kentucky, but Bracken County lies on the Ohio River and would have been an easy stop. A *Pilgrim's Progress* panorama visited Portsmouth, Ohio, about 70 miles upriver, in the 1870s.

Another possible source of inspiration lay 40 miles down the Ohio River, at Dorfeuille's Western Museum in Cincinnati, where, from about 1827 to 1867, those wishing to go to Hell could see an animated, clockwork version of the Inferno modeled in wax by sculptor Hiram Powers, complete with a jolly, long-horned King of Terrors who assured visitors that he was very glad to see them all in such a hot place. There was smoke and fire and there were hissing snakes and howling-demon effects: advertisements speak of "unearthly sounds, horrid groans, and terrible shrieks." The diabolically clever Powers also installed an electrified rail to give unwitting visitors a shock.

Mrs. Trollope, who came to Cincinnati in 1827, wrote about "Dorfeuille's Hell:"

> He has constructed a pandemonium in an upper story of his museum, in which he has congregated all the images of horror that his fertile fancy could devise: dwarfs that by machinery grow into giants before the eyes of the spectator; imps of ebony with eyes of flame; monstrous reptiles devouring youth and beauty; lakes of fire and mountains of ice; in short, wax, paint, and springs have done wonders. *Domestic Manners of the Americans,* Mrs. Trollope, 1832, p. 69. It is said that Mrs. Frances Trollope, an English author, suggested to Hiram Powers the idea of an exhibit blending Dante's *Inferno* with Milton's *Paradise Lost.*

While it is stretching credulity to think that a giant clockwork devil was striding around Bracken County, I think that we can argue that the devilish imagery found in magic-lantern entertainments, book illustrations, wax-works, and panoramas was pervasive enough to have inspired a written fantasy. Possibly the statements: "a scene worthy of a pandemonium" and "a hissing sound like the hissing of a serpent" offer a clue as to this story's origins.

Given the date of the spectacular devil tales of Bracken County, it is curious to find a modern urban legend, also originating in Kentucky, about a strikingly similar entity. Sometime in the late 1940s or early 1950s, a legend grew up around the Pope Lick Railroad Trestle, east of Louisville—about 120 miles from Bracken County. The Trestle is a railroad bridge about 80 feet high and over 700 feet long. Inevitably it has become a teen hangout and a place for adolescent dares. There have been a number of deaths, either by train or by falls, but I have not been able to establish an exact count. Deaths, fences, and police warnings do not seem to stop the dare-devils.

And there may be a devil to dare. The sinister creature of the Pope Lick Trestle is described as large and hairy, with the body of a man and the horned head of a goat. It is said to wail like a train whistle and some Boy Scout campers said that it screamed and threw stones at them. Farmers used to find their sheep torn to shreds. Is it, as some folklorists have suggested, a Bigfoot, or is the legend a memory of one of the fiery devils of Bracken County?

For more on the Goat-man legend, see http://beforeitsnews.com/beyond-

science/2012/11/goat-man-sightings-in-kentucky-texas-maryland-2440036.
html?currentSplittedPage =1. For a modern case of a "Minotaur" sighting in
Ohio, see http://camp firetell.blogspot.com/2012/10/the-ufo-and-minotaur.
html.

The Devil did not die at Salem; he merely decided to move west. With good
whiskey and first-rate bloodstock and devilish fine fiddling to recommend it,
Kentucky looked like paradise to his Satanic Majesty. Scholars of panics might
suggest that the devils were a projection of the stresses of Reconstruction, the
usual "mass hallucination" trigged by a few malefactors in disguise. Yet the
fact remains that the alleged witnesses, those "credible and reliable persons" of
Bracken County, did not exist.

For the sake of wonder-lovers everywhere, I would have liked for the
Bracken County devils to have had some sort of objective reality: a thief in
the ultimate super-villain costume with a pot of smoldering sulphur, or a mad
inventor tinkering with a steam-powered robot in his secret lair. If, as I suspect, they were the fantasy of an unknown Bracken County editor, they were a
marvelously nightmarish creation—you could practically smell the brimstone.
Perhaps someday we will discover their origin, but for now, at least, I fear that
the chill hand of historical fact has quenched those fiery devils of Bracken
County.

FURTHER READING: Miraculously, one of the best-known *Pilgrim's
Progress* panoramas survives today. In these pictures Apollyon's wings are not
always visible and he looks very much like the descriptions of the Bracken
County devils. See http://www.tfaoi.com/newsm1/n1m487.htm and http://
www.sacomuseum.org/panorama/

Here are some examples of glass magic lantern slides depicting *Pilgrim's
Progress*. http://www.cinematheque.fr/uk/museum-and-collections/actualite-
collections/dons-acquisitions/pilgrim-progress.html.

For an overview of the influence of *Pilgrim's Progress*, see http://www.christian
itytoday.com/ch/1986/issue11/1124.html.

8.

A Face Blue and Terrible
Ghostly Window Peepers

Sometimes she would glance nervously at one of those seven long
windows, half fearing to see a strange face looking in at her—
a face not of this earth.

-*Taken at the Flood: A Novel*, Mary Elizabeth Braddon-

It is the stuff of nightmares: the shock of seeing a disembodied face peering
in at the window or pulling aside a curtain to find a ghastly visage pressed
against the glass.

The face in the window was a common motif in 19th-century fiction,
from sentimental newspaper stories usually involving husbands or wives
thought long-dead (cue the gasp and the hand to the throat), to the sinister,
scowling face in Conan Doyle's "The Sign of the Four" and "the white face
of damnation" in Henry James's *The Turn of the Screw*. The chaos of various
wars brought genuine stories of lost soldiers peeping in the windows of their
remarried wives. And ladies alone at night were often startled into hysterics by
strange faces staring in at them.

It was a similarly prevalent—and ambiguous—image in ghost lore. Do these
phantoms gaze hungrily at the feast of family life within? Or do they watch
with more malign intent? None of the ghosts in this chapter were a welcome
sight.

SINGULAR GHOST STORY
Mother and Son Driven Crazy By a Supposed Visit From the Grave

Philadelphia, June 19. A special dispatch to the *Times,* from Snydertown,
Penn., says: "Last night Mrs. Moore, a widow, who lives with her young
son at Brush Valley, near here, was startled by hearing a shriek, followed
by agonizing yells, in the room next to her own, which was occupied by
her son, a youth about 16 years old. In a fright she ran into the room and
found the boy almost dead with fear and trembling in every limb. She qui-
eted his fears and questioned him, and, after considerable delay, he told
her that at about midnight, while listening to the furiously raging storm,
he was startled by seeing through the dim light of a lamp which burned
in the room a man raising the window. Almost paralyzed with fear, he sat
up in bed, unable to move until by the aid of a vivid flash of lightning he

perceived the features of the man to be similar to those of his father, who was killed in the mines five years ago. With the shriek that had so startled his mother, he sank on the bed and the intruder fled hastily. When the mother had heard his story she turned her gaze toward the window and beheld the identical face pressed against the pane. With a loud yell she sprang to the window, and raising the sash, jumped through and striking the ground 25 feet below with terrible force, injuring herself fatally. The shrieks and moans of the young Moore brought a few neighbors to the spot and they carried the limp body of the woman into the house and after a few hours' labor succeeded in bringing her to sensibility. As soon as she fixed her eyes on her son she burst into a violent fit of laughter in which the son joined, and which lasted until both fell to the floor exhausted. On the part of young Moore the fit of laughing was then followed by violent spasmodic attacks. He foamed at the mouth, barked like a dog, and made vicious snaps at those who attempted to quiet him.

A young farmer named Herrick went up to him, and while attempting to quiet him caught hold of his hand. No sooner had he done so than he too was seized with fearful spasms, and writhed on the floor in intense agony, exhibiting the peculiar symptoms manifested by the others. The few other neighbors who had come to the scene were so badly frightened as to be of little assistance and they fled precipitately, leaving the three maniacs alone in the room. Mrs. Moore was stark raving mad, and soon the two young men were busy at work demolishing the furniture and striking one another. One of the women who had at first rushed to the house ran home and returned with her father, an old Army Sergeant named Billheimer, who ran into the room, and grasping Herrick, threw him to the floor, and, putting his foot upon his breast, bound him with the bed ropes. He then secured young Moore in a like manner. Mrs. Moore was bleeding from the wounds received from falling out of the window and lay on the floor insensible. Lifting her in his arms, Billheimer carried the woman to the open air, the storm having ceased. One of the neighbors had mounted a horse about one hour before and ridden at full speed across the rough country roads in search of a doctor. After a long search he found one and brought him to the stricken family. The young man Herrick was taken home by his father in the morning, and another physician attended him. No hope is entertained of Mrs. Moore's recovery. Her son was unusually violent this morning and could scarcely be held by four men. The case has occasioned much excitement among the farmers and throughout the neighborhood. Mrs. Moore and her son are practical, steady people. Young Herrick is not so violent, but arrangements are being made for his removal to an asylum. Mrs. Moore was in a sinking condition this evening, and she will hardly live until morning. *New York Times* 20 June 1883.

Daily Illinois State Register [Springfield, IL] 21 June 1883: p. 1

PENNSYLVANIA

NOTE: Due to the lack of first names and relatively common surnames, I have not been able to find any more about the participants in this sensational story. I located several Billheimers from Pennsylvania in Civil War databases, but it is impossible to tell which one this intrepid man might have been. The "contagious" madness is a minor, but noticeable theme in the 19th-century press. So is the mad-dog-like behavior of the maniacs.

'BLUE MAN' IS LIVELY GHOST
Strange Story Told of Mysterious Creature That Bullets Do Not Hurt.

Louisville, Ky., Feb. 26. The bullet proof "blue man" or the mystery of South Eighth Street. That might be the title of a strange story told guardedly in the downtown section, says the *Courier-Journal*. There is a sick man in the house on South Eighth Street, the account ran. Every night recently a face, blue and terrible, has been pressed against the pane of the sickroom window. Always it has come between the hours between 7 and 9 o'clock.

It has been shot at and the bullets struck thin air. When the image appears members of the family run to the outside, but never have seen anything more than darkness.

A fortune teller has been consulted. She declared that when the "thing" got what it wanted it would disappear.

What does it want?

A woman leaning on her front gate talking to her neighbors had heard of the "thing."

"It's been seen almost every night looking in Mrs. Fogel's window," she said. "It's a terrible thing to behold and the inside of its mouth is all blue."

Two young men, Reese Carrell and a companion, were talking in their front yard. Mr. Carrell was called inside.

"Have you heard about the 'blue man,' the ghost that looks into Mrs. Fogel's window?" he was asked.

"Ghost!" he exclaimed. "I'll say it's the ghost. I've only been knocked down once in my life and it did it."

Mr. Carrell's companion was Clarence Fogel, son of the house where the "Blue man" visits.

A HUSKY "GHOST"

"It's been around here every night for the last two weeks," young Carrell explained. "One night, when I came home at about 11 o'clock I saw somebody standing on our front step. I thought it was my father and I walked right into him.

"'Looking for the "blue man," Pop?' I asked, and just then it hit me in the chest. I was knocked against the fence and when I got up it was gone."

The next night "It" stole the elder Carrell's trousers from his bedroom. It had opened the shutters, put a washboard under the window and crawled in. The following night the Carrells laid in ambush.

Young Carrell heard a noise in the yard. He ran out with his shotgun and caught the intruder in his neighbor's back yard.

"I wasn't more than twenty-five feet away from it and I fired directly at it. No effect whatever. He jumped over the fence."

That was the first time. Later, he shot at "It" again without avail. Doubting his son's aim, the elder Carrell shot at the stranger on his next appearance.

"I never missed a rabbit or a bird in my life," the father declared, "but the shots went right through him."

"Do you think it a ghost?" the father was asked.

"Ghost? What would a ghost want with my pants? Here's my idea about spirits. If a man dies and goes to heaven, he doesn't want to come back. If he goes to hell he can't!"

Mr. Fogel is the sick man of the story. He formed an ideal background for the tale of the uncanny blue face, his countenance emaciated from his illness and his dark, intense eyes staring from hollow depths.

The First Visit.

"I knew the first time he came," Mr. Fogel reported. "It was some time between midnight and daybreak. I was lying awake. All at once three shafts of light came through the shutters. They were the color of the flame you see in the stove there. They stayed several minutes and then disappeared."

The lights were followed by rattlings of the shutters a few nights later. Mr. Fogel has heard the mystery walking around his house on several occasions since. He has tried several windows, but thus far has not been able to get in.

On one of the "blue man's" first visits he was seen by a little child of the Fogel family. She saw the form in the yard and, thinking it was her father, ran to it. The form disappeared into the darkness.

On another visit, a dog in the Fogel back yard challenged passage over the coal shed.

"If it's a ghost, it's a strong one, for it kicked the little dog up against our house so hard that it almost came through," Mr. Fogel declared.

Clarence Fogel, the son, said he surprised the "thing" just outside the house. It was about 4:30 o'clock.

"I ran in the house, got my revolver and ran out again. It was still there. I wasn't twenty feet away when I fired directly at its body. It ran through the back yard and disappeared."

Police of the sixth district have been called. One patrolman, it was said, fired seven shots at close range and the "blue man" never budged. But the Fogels and their neighbors keep their weapons ready and loaded from 7 o'clock at night, the time of the earliest visit, until dawn. They agreed that they would solve the mystery and turn "It" over to either an undertaker or the guardian of the spirit realm whence the mystery came.

Miami [FL] Herald 27 February 1921: p. 7 KENTUCKY

NOTE: Despite the chilling image of the blue face at the window (was it done with phosphorescent paint?) the creature is unusually corporeal for a ghost. Yet, once again we find an apparition that is seemingly bullet-proof. There were so many stories like this that it raises three questions: 1) Were the people giving chase just not very good shots? 2) What kind of bullet-proof armor would have been available for fake ghosts? and 3) Why would you dress up to play ghost when there was a real chance of being shot?

The Ghost at the Window

[Galena (Ill.) Spe. Corresp. *Globe-Democrat*]

Mrs. Charles Rindesbacker, of Stockton, this county, has just returned here from Mankato, Minn., where she was visiting relatives, having been summoned home by reason of the sudden death of her sister, a young lady who had long been in poor health, resulting from an injury received in childhood. A remarkable incident occurred, singularly, as it was afterwards learned, at the precise time of her sister's death, at the house where she was sojourning in Mankato, the particulars of which Mrs. Rindesbacker related to the *Globe-Democrat* correspondent, as follows: "On the evening of my sister's sudden demise, which occurred a week ago to-day, I was sitting, in company with the lady relative at whose house I was sojourning, in Mankato, near a window, in the family reception room. It was a clear night outside, and lamps had not been lighted. We were both engaged in conversation concerning a contemplated drive next day, when suddenly, as I sat gazing at the dim objects outside, I was startled on observing the face of my lately deceased sister peering into the room through the window from the outside. I could see nothing but her head and two hands, which were held open at the side of her face, as though to shade the moonlight and enable her better to see into the room. I was speechless for the instant, but finally uttered the word 'sister,' at the same time directing the attention of my cousin toward the window. The latter saw and recognized the well-known features, and, overcome with fright, made a sudden outcry, when the face gradually receded from view, and before we could gain our senses had entirely disappeared. It was no hallucination, you may be assured," continued Mrs. Rindesbacker, with emphasis. "The face was that of my sister, plain and distinct. It was white, and had a death-like expression, and the features and everything connected with them were as clearly seen and recognized by my cousin, as well as myself. We are neither of us superstitious, nor are we at all inclined that way, yet I am as certain that the countenance we saw was that of my sister, and that it was of supernatural origin as I am as sure that I live this morning. I had the curiosity to look at my watch, and found that the time was 8 o'clock, and calculated that the apparition must have appeared five minutes earlier. On the following morning I received a telegram which read: "'your sister Jennie died last night at 7:55. Come home at once.'"

It may be added that Mrs. Rindesbacker is an intelligent, respectable, and thoroughly trustworthy lady, and that her story is fully believed by all except the most incredulous and is the all-engrossing topic of conversation at her home in Stockton.

Cincinnati [OH] Enquirer 8 September 1889: p. 15 ILLINOIS and MINNESOTA

Although the witnesses seemed frightened by the spirit, I find this story of an elderly farmer's ghost staring in the windows at his young family to be oddly touching.

LAVERTY'S GHOST
A Weird Apparition Frequently Seen in Parke County.

It will be remembered that a few weeks ago Aquilla Laverty, the wealthiest farmer in Parke County and one of the heaviest land owners in the state, fell from the third story of his granary and sustained injuries from which he died, says a dispatch from Clinton, Ind. Though nearly 90 years old, the land prince had a girl wife and was the father of a babe less than a year old. He was very eccentric, and notwithstanding his vast wealth, was a hard worker. He could bind more wheat, "shuck" more corn or plow more land than any of the hundred or more men in his employ. He was unfriendly with his several children by his first wife, and a few months prior to his death he had been defendant in a law suit brought by them. [The four surviving adult children's complaint was that Laverty had not turned over a bequest of $5,000 from their mother's estate. Laverty settled out of court for a hefty sum.] After the suit the old man would have nothing to do with the children by his first wife.

But no sooner was he laid in his grave than the discarded children began to set about to get a share of the vast estate. Their father had made a will bequeathing $50 to each of them and the remainder of his fortune to his girl wife and the babe. The elder heirs at once employed attorneys and began an effort to break the will. The probable litigation has been the subject for much newspaper discussion throughout the state.

Now it is said the ghost of the venerable old farmer comes back each dark night, and can be seen stalking about his old haunts on the farm. The litigants are alarmed, while many residents in the locality and tenants on the farm are looking for other locations.

Those who do not believe in ghosts hoot at the various startling stories relative to the venerable farmer's early outings from the spirit land, but this does not disabuse the minds of the superstitious, who with mouths standing ajar, like graveyard gates, insist that their eyes cannot deceive them, and that they actually saw the ghost of Aquilla Laverty, in robes of snowy white, flitting from house to barn, to field, and along all the familiar paths he used to tread before he made a will and was called from labor to rest.

Gossip goes that when Mr. Lavery was in this vale of tears and taxes "he had a will of his own," which could not be broken, and now that he has been transferred to the land of immortality, comes back occasionally to resist any attempt which may be made to break the will he left. Some of the residents are frightened at the hair-raising recitals of those who claim to have seen the ghost, and, owing to this fact, there is an encouraging epidemic of remaining indoors of nights throughout what is known as the "Laverty settlement."

As the story goes, the celestial visitor first makes his appearance in the third story of the elevator, at the spot where a few weeks ago Mr. Laverty had his fatal fall. There, with lantern in hand, the phantom will waltz about a few moments and then glide away to another part of the premises. Often peculiar tramping is heard in the stables, followed by the low, ecstatic neighing of the horses, in a manner indicative of equine delight. The superstitious residents, who are so much concerned about the mysterious visitor, who only floats down when the nights are darkest and the hours are stillest, insist that the faithful old work horses recognize their late master and, with instinct superior to human intelligence, neigh their friendly greeting to his spirit as it floats into the barn. From here the weird spook goes from one part of the farm to another, apparently on a tour of inspection.

The unwelcome spook prefers to operate in the blackest darkness, and each night when he makes his appearance down on the farm, begins his work by snuffing out all the lamps and candles burning on the estate. The lamps are no sooner relighted than they go out again, and no matter how often the frightened natives apply the match to them, they refuse to burn and shed light while the silent, unwelcome visitor roams the premises. If Mrs. Laverty gets up to give the crying little heir a dose of soothing syrup she is forced to grope through the darkness while the ghost of his ancient papa peeps through the window and dances about in apparent glee.

The affair has created a reign of terror in the vicinity, and is the main topic of conversation. The men seek refuge indoors as soon as darkness falls and whole families sleep with their heads covered up, while the watch dogs deposit their caudal appendages between their rear pedals and seek safety under the houses.

Logansport [IN] Journal 27 January 1897: p. INDIANA

There was a complicated back-story about the Laverty children and the widow.

"The discarded children were at the funeral, but the father was scarcely cold in his grave when they began a contest to break the will. The best legal talent to be found in Parke and Vigo Counties was retained. A complaint alleging insanity, duress, and kindred claims, was filed, and all was ready for the struggle when it became apparent, that another heir was to be born. Investigation disclosed the fact that no provision had been made for the heir unborn. According to the Hoosier statutes, this fact alone would invalidate the will, and the litigation was brought to a sudden stop. The announcement of the facts excited great interest, and the arrival of the peace-making heir was waited with considerable anxiety by the other heirs, their friends, and, in fact, all who were familiar with the case. March 4th, the last, an infant heir was ushered into the world to play its role in the domestic drama. The birth of the child, of course, invalidated the will, and then it was decided that after the statutory allowance had been sent off to the girl widow all the heirs would share alike. The young widow was chosen administrator, and the work of dividing the big estate was practically completed, only awaiting the approval of the court.

An Heir was Born But Died.

The infant heir, which had been named Cecil Frederick Laverty, was apparently a healthy child, with merry, dancing eyes, strong lungs and a good appetite. All the other heirs loved it, because its advent into the world averted what would have been a long, bitter and costly family quarrel. The little one seemed likely to live to the age when it would come into actual possession of its share of the vast estate. But a mysterious providence sent it into the world on a mission of peace, and when his mission was performed called its spirit back. The child sickened and, notwithstanding the best physicians were called, death resulted in two days. The death of the infant heir gave rise to a new complication in the settlement of the estate, and its share will have to be divided among the other heirs.

Syracuse [NY] Herald 12 September 1897: p. 17

NOTE: Aquilla/Aquila Laverty, born in 1822, was one of those energetic, self-educated land barons one finds in such abundance in 19th-century county histories. He was one of the richest men in Indiana. Although Laverty's father lost the family property before his death and his son got only a limited education from the local log cabin school, Laverty swore to recover the family fortunes. He seemed to have a golden touch. All of his enterprises—prospecting for lead, building flatboats, and farming—prospered. His first wife, Elizabeth died in 1890. Four of his seven children lived to adulthood: George, Irene, Erminnie, and Kit Carson. He took his time about remarrying, wedding Lillian Mann [1872-1950], a former servant in the Laverty home, on 30 January 1895. Their son Aquila Jr. was born 25 March 1896. Cecil was the posthumous "heir." By all accounts the second Mrs. Laverty was devoted to her elderly husband, and there was no hint that she was a gold-digger. Her appointment as executrix of the contested estate shows the respect the Laverty children had for her. She never remarried and managed the Laverty holdings with great acumen. [Source: *Portrait and biographical record of Montgomery, Parke and Fountain counties, Indiana: containing biographical sketches of prominent and representative citizens: together with biographies and portraits of all the presidents of the United States*, (Chicago: Chapman Brothers) 1893.

The next story begins with a ghost with an unusual request.

DECLARES GHOST OF MURDERED MAN APPEARS ON WESTSIDE AND WANTS TO START DICE GAME
Strange Apparition Startles H. Reichardt From Slumber

The Westside in the vicinity of the Market Street Bridge is agog over various hair-raising stories which are being told in barber shops, saloons and at the engine house and which have the effect of sending those who hear them home with frequent backward glances. Almost everyone in that vicinity whistles loudly when walking home after night and each day there is some one with a newer and more harrowing tale of something that has occurred in the place where the ghost is supposed to walk.

It is said that in the rooms above the saloon where Frank Potmeyer was killed years ago is a stamping ground for ghostly wraiths who hold night revelry there, opening and closing bolted doors, wakening occupants of the rooms by passing hands over their faces and frightening passers-by by showing white, ghostly faces at the window.

One of the many harrowing tales told is that of Herman Reichardt, proprietor of the Bismark Café who occupied the building. It seems that Reichardt went home late one evening and going to bed fell into a deep slumber from which he was awakened by a hand passing over his face. As he opened his eyes something shook him by the shoulder and said, "Here, come on and I'll shake the box with you." Reichardt rose, but not to shake the box with the spectre sport; instead he hurried into his clothes and departed and the next day moved leaving the ghost in full possession.

Considering the time when it happened the experience of Reed Schuman is still more weird and unexplainable. Schuman says he is willing to make affidavit that he saw the profile of a man's face pressed against the window as he passed opposite the place a week ago last Sunday. Shuman says it was broad daylight and that he could scarce believe his eyes, but there was the apparition plain and distinct.

He narrated the incident in the Carter Barber Shop on the following day when his story was greeted with derisive laughter. Later in the week a colored barber was telling Shuman's ghost story to a customer he was shaving.

"An' he saw a man's face in the window right up there and I—" At this juncture the colored barber looked up at the window and as he did so his razor fell to the floor with a clang and with a wild yell he bolted from the shop and dashed across the bridge. Towards evening he returned to the shop and there told of how when he looked up at the window as he was shaving a customer, he saw, plain as day, a man's face pressed against the

window. The face was wan, emaciated and a look of blood curdling horror was written on it and the barber said as he looked two lank, bony hands were raised and one stroked a long, straggly beard on the face while the other beckoned to the barber. As the tales are told in the shop customers gather closer to the fire, voices are lowered and it is told that two timid men stayed in the shop all night rather than venture out and cross the bridge after listening to the ghost stories. The affair is taken seriously by some while others declare it is the work of some imaginative yarn spinner.
Logansport [IN] Journal 10 March 1906: p. 1 INDIANA

NOTE: Here is a squib on Frank Pottmeyer's murder:

The jury trying John McIntosh for murdering Saloon Keeper Frank Pottmeyer last October, when Pottmeyer's brother and a sister were also shot down by McIntosh, brought in a verdict to-day, sending the murderer to prison for life. The jury was out twelve hours.
Indiana State Journal [Indianapolis, IN] 26 January 1898: p. 1

I found a short notice from the Chicago *Daily Inter Ocean* 11 October 1892: p. 4 about Herman Reichardt, a local saloon keeper, who shot a man's legs out from under him when the man struck him, but there is no proof it is the same man.

It is rare to find a newspaper story giving an explanation for a ghostly face in the window. This article lacks concrete details, but a "moving picture enthusiast" is a novel explanation.

LOCATING A "SPECTER"
"Ghost" That Frightened Neighbors Routed by House Owner

From the *Chicago News*
There is that face in the window again, declared a frightened woman as she pointed out a ghastly looking figure in the window of the house across the street in a congested district of Chicago. A little group of women and children had gathered on the corner to discuss the mystery of the neighborhood. For the last two weeks everyone in the block had been terrorized by the appearance of a face in the window on the second floor of an old tumble down house long vacated on account of a story current in the neighborhood declaring it to be haunted. No one could be paid to go inside the place and children hated to pass it even in the daytime.

But now since this new development the fear of the excitable populace was at its zenith. All felt sure that the ghost of a man said to have been murdered there had come back to haunt his old home. When the news of the ghost came to the owner he decided to investigate and learn the real trouble. He boldly entered the old place despite the repeated and urgent pleadings of the women who declared that he would never be seen again if the ghost got him.

In he went and mounted the creaky stairs to the second floor expecting every moment to encounter the spectre. He entered the front room where the spook had been seen and after about two minutes came out smiling serenely. Reaching the street he went at once to the house directly across the way and called on the people in the second flat. Then he came out and explained to the frightened neighbors.

His investigation of the house had disclosed no ghost at all but merely a ray of light seeming to come from a building across the street. At that place he found nothing more ghastly than a moving picture enthusiast who had been amusing himself night after night by casting on the curtains of the haunted house a pale yellow reflection resembling the figure of a man. He knew the excitable nature of his neighbors, was familiar with the story of the haunted house and decided to have a little fun out of it.

The next night the "ghost" did not appear. That week the owner sold the place and it is now undergoing repairs to make it habitable for the new owner.

Washington [DC] Post October 3, 1909: p. 12 ILLINOIS

In *The Face in the Window: Haunting Ohio Tales*, I devoted a chapter to the faces and images which appeared on glass window panes in the United States beginning about 1871. These were literally faces *in* the window glass, rather than a ghostly face seen outside, although the effect was equally startling. The images usually appeared very quickly, appeared to be embedded in the glass and typically could not be seen from the inside. Often they appeared in the wake of bereavement or, it was claimed, they were "lightning daguerreotypes," images etched by a lightning strike. The phenomenon was a recurring theme in the newspapers through the 1910s, although there are a few reports from the early 1920s. We sometimes hear reports of it today, like the Virgin Mary image on the glass windows of a health center in Clearwater, Florida in 1996. How much of this is self-deception, how much simple human brain pattern matching, I am not qualified to say. At this historical remove, I doubt that anyone could sort out the riddle of these images.

I will say that, in many cases, the images of faces in glass appear to have some element of psychokinesis or PK: a severe stress—a death, a murder, a shock—somehow creates an image of a known person, recognized instantly by the immediate family and sometimes, without prompting, by others. This particular story also contains an "omen of death" element. One oddity is that this image is described (somewhat ambiguously) as visible from inside the room. Every other example of this sort of image I've discovered can only be seen from the outside. Another enigma....

LEFT A PICTURE ON THE PANE
A Strange Memento of the Death of Husband and Children

Pittsburg, Pa., August 16, 1890. A mystery surrounds the home of the late James Dougherty, at Swissvale. Within four weeks the father and three children have died. The mother refuses to remain any longer in the little home.

Midway between Swissvale and Hawkins stations on the line of the Pennsylvania Railroad, and on a street which leads toward the railroad tracks back of the public school building, stands a little one story frame house. Surrounding this little home is a garden of probably half an acre.

This, until a few days ago, had been the home of the Doughertys—the father, mother, and three children. It was always the father's delight returning from a hard day's labor at the Carrie Furnace, where he was employed, to meet his little ones down near the river bank. Taking the short cut through the fields and over hills he would take the children one at a time, place them on his back and carry them to his little cottage.

He had always been a most devoted husband and kind father.

July 5, the second child was taken ill with a fever. It lingered for a few days then died. In just one week from the death of the first child another one, a little boy, was stricken down with the same malady and died within a few days. Hardly a week had passed after the death of the second child when the last and youngest child and the father's favorite, was stricken with pneumonia and in a few days passed away.

THE FATHER GOES TOO

The death of the three children occurring in as many weeks was a severe blow to the parents.

Last Monday morning the husband departed for his work at the Carrie furnace early in the morning. As he left his wife he bade her the usual goodbye. With the parting salute, "Bear up, dear," he vanished over the hills on his way to work. This was the last seen of him alive by his wife. That afternoon while engaged at work on a high trestle in one of the departments at the furnace he missed his footing and fell backward to a pile of iron below. He was killed instantly.

Just before the sad news was brought to the unfortunate woman she happened to be near the window in the front of the house.

She was horrified to see imprinted on an ordinary pane of glass in the window before her a picture of her husband as lifelike as if he stood before her himself. On his back was the favorite little girl and in his hand his dinner pail, just as had been his custom in days when all was bright.

The woman was frightened by the sight, and was in the act of notifying her neighbors when a messenger stopped her on the threshold and announced to her the death of her husband.

AFRAID TO STAY IN THE HOUSE.

The news completely prostrated her. The husband was buried yesterday, and Mrs. Dougherty left the house before night, saying she was afraid to remain there. She is now with friends.

Crowds of people have visited the house. The crape still flutters from the door, and one spectator after another files up to the window to see the sight. Every one expressed himself to the effect that it is a wonderful likeness of Dougherty and his favorite child. The picture has the appearance of being ground in the glass. It is near the centre of the pane. It is in such a position that it would really be seen by a woman sitting inside the room and watching the path over which her husband would return home.

New York Herald 17 August 1890: p. 11 PENNSYLVANIA

9.

The Spook on a Bicycle
Spirits of Road and Trail

The way to dusty death

-*Macbeth*, William Shakespeare-

A s we have seen in many of the stories of Men in Black and giant ghosts, supernatural visitations often take place out of doors. There is also a long tradition of ghosts appearing to travelers. Outside of large cities, traveling in the country meant a lonely, dark, and perhaps dangerous journey. While we hear very little in the newspapers of the traditional "phantom hitchhiker" so beloved of 20th-century folklorists, a traveler by foot, horseback, bicycle, wagon, or carriage never knew exactly who that dim figure might be, glimpsed just ahead in the dusk. The road ghost in this first story belongs to a familiar type of British phantoms of the highway.

A GHASTLY SPECTER
Terrible Experience of a Mississippi Man

Jackson (Miss.) Special.

Our town is much excited just now by a bona fide ghost, which is to be seen nightly on what is known as the old North Road. This road is little traveled now, as a better one has been made of late years nearly parallel to it, though some hundred yards apart. However, owing to the fall of an immense oak across the new road during the recent storm, travel has temporarily been resumed over the old one.

Jim D., a milkman, driving his wagon to town early one morning, was the first to see the ghost. On being interviewed, this man stated to your correspondent: "It was just a little after daybreak, and there was a very heavy fog, which prevented my seeing very far ahead, so I was not able to see where she came from, but I suddenly saw, almost under my horse's nose, a little woman in a checked sunbonnet, hobbling along the road. The horse seemed to see her about the same time that I did, for he sprang back with an awful snort, or rather screech. He's the steadiest animal that ever wore harness, but he began to rear up then, and take on so I could hardly hold him, and the sweat just rolled off him until he was as wet as if he'd been through the river. I was too busy quieting the horse to look after the woman, but when I got him started again, there she was still pegging along just in front of us. The bonnet flapped about her face so I could not see it, but from her walk and humped figure I could tell she was an old woman. She was holding her hand up to her head as if it hurt her, and I could hear her moaning to herself in a piteous sort of way that made my flesh feel mightily creepy. I called out to her to know what was the matter, and if she didn't want to ride, but she didn't seem to hear, and just kept straight on till I got mad. 'Hello, there,' I said, 'would you mind getting out of the way? I'm in a hurry, and I'd like to pass you.'

"As she still didn't seem to hear or notice, I turned out and tried to drive round, but though I got faster and faster, the old woman kept ahead, until we reached that old clearing where a house used to stand on the side of the road when she turned around and gave me one look. And, I tell you, sir, I'll never forget that sight as long as I live. That old woman's face had the awful greenish, corrupted look of a person that's been dead a long time, and right across her long, skinny throat there was a dreadful cut, from which, as I am a living man, the blood was still oozing in big black drops. I was sitting there in the wagon staring at her, all the blood in my body freezing, and my hair standing up like a brush heap, when she vanished right before my eyes as completely as if the earth had opened and swallowed her up."

Several have watched the road since then and seen the little old woman suddenly appear, always just as day is breaking in a certain part of the road, and after going a few hundred feet, vanish near the old clearing. She responds to no greeting, and seems unconscious that anyone is near, until just before disappearing, when she glances round, revealing her unearthly dead countenance with the bleeding gash across her throat.

A certain gentleman of this place made the boast that he would fathom the mystery surrounding her, and had the courage to accost her, even endeavoring to lay hold of her garments; but, in his own words, his hand and arm felt as if they had encountered an electric fluid that fairly paralyzed them, and he fell back fainting, and half dead from the shock, while the specter calmly pursued its way. The gentleman still keeps his bed, and is suffering from the nervous attack brought on by his encounter with the ghost. As there seems to be some connection between the phantom and the cleared space spoken of, and on which a house evidently once stood, conjecture has been rife concerning this house and its history. But the oldest inhabitants have no recollection of any building ever having been there within their memory and say that the place has always presented the same

bare and desolate appearance as now, no grass, no verdure of any sort ever having been known to spring up within its circuit.
St. Paul [MN] Daily Globe 6 April 1890: p. 19 MISSISSIPPI

NOTE: Here we have the typical road ghost: an old woman, a figure that cannot be overtaken, no matter how fast the pursuit, an entity that does not answer when spoken to, and whose face is concealed—at least until the last, horrifying moment. This is reminiscent of the folktale retold as "May I Carry Your Basket?" in *Scary Stories to Tell in the Dark* by Alvin Schwartz and of a class of Welsh spirits found on mountain roads called the "*Gwyllion.*" They take the shape of old women and are described as "female fairies of frightful characteristics, who haunted lonely roads in the Welsh mountains and lead night-wanderers astray. They partake somewhat of the aspect of the Hecate of Greek mythology, who rode on the storm, and was a hag of horrid guise." *British Goblins*, Wirt Sikes, (Boston: James R. Osgood and Company) 1881.

This next road ghost, too, has a phantom wagon-driver who hides her face.

A SPECTRAL VISITOR.
An Apparition That is Greatly Exciting the People of Richmond, Texas
An Emigrant Wagon Which Nightly Passes Through the Streets of the City.
The Citizens and Officers are Unable to Unravel the Mysterious Affair.

The entire city is agog over an apparition which is said to visit Main Street every night about 12 o'clock, and which takes the form of a large old-fashioned wagon of the sort known as emigrant's or "prairie schooner," and drawn by two oxen, says a Richmond, Texas, special to the *St. Louis Republic*. The phantom, as it is believed to be, is a common-place spectacle enough and would attract little notice were it not for the hour of its visit, and the extraordinary phenomena attending its appearance. About two weeks ago the people residing on Main Street were awakened at the hour mentioned by the creaking of a wagon as it went along, but thought nothing of the occurrence until the thing was repeated the next night and the night after, when their curiosity concerning its errand began to be aroused. Several prominent citizens waited on the fourth night, and when the wagon approached hailed the driver, who could be somewhat indistinctly seen sitting rather back in the vehicle. No response was given to their hail, which was repeated several times, and at last with some peremptoriness, determined to solve the question for themselves, the men ran forward and attempted to lay hold of the oxen's heads, when, to their utter amazement, nothing was to be found on the spot where the moment before the huge team was to be seen. It was gone as completely as a shadow before the sun, but twenty or thirty feet further on was presently seen wagon and oxen jolting on as composedly as ever.

Dumbstruck at the occurrence, the men resolved to thoroughly investigate the matter before speaking of the puzzling thing they had just witnessed, as they feared the story would meet with only incredulity and ridicule. They ran after the wagon, but failed to overtake it before it was swallowed up in the night, and were unable to find it again. The next night all were at their posts a full hour before the apparition made its appearance, and the watchers of the night before, joined by others whose slumbers had also been disturbed by its passage, waited, guns and revolvers in hand for the coming of the mysterious vehicle. It was seen coming promptly at the usual hour, appearing all at once just beyond the first house on the street, and moving along at a leisurely pace.

The oxen appeared to be very weary and dispirited, and every now and then the sound of a whip snapped in the air could be heard, but no other sign of life could be heard or seen about the wagon itself. A dark figure sat on the seat, which was pushed back under the canvas, but whether the driver was a man or woman could not be decided. Several of the keenest-sighted declared it to be a man with his hat drawn down far over the face, concealing the features, while as many others were quite as positive that the figure was that of a woman wearing a dark sunbonnet.

But whatever the sex of the driver, the shadowy figure paid not the slightest attention to the crowd collected and standing on both sides of the street, but pursued its way without so much as a turn of the head in answer to the questions plied to it. The oxen plodded on without a sign that they heard the shouts, and did not pause even for a moment. Twenty men sprang into the streets as the wagon neared; twenty pairs of hands were put out to grasp its side, the harness of the team, the team itself, but only empty air did they grasp. There was not even a trace of the phantom to be seen at that spot, though it could be distinctly perceived disappearing in the distance. In the meantime that portion of the crowd that had remained on the sidewalk continued to call out to those who had essayed to stop the wagon, and, seeing the mysterious vehicle as plainly as ever, could not but wonder at the discomfiture displayed by the others.

These spectators declare that the wagon moved placidly through the midst of the eager hands that grasped at it, and to them no reason was visible why they could not have stayed it.

Excitement now became almost uncontrollable, and it was impossible to keep the matter quiet, so that on the following night the street was lined from end to end with a crowd determined to solve the mystery or know the reason why. Each man carried a weapon, and across the street was stretched ropes, and even a roll of barbed wire attached to stout posts, not to be uprooted by any gentle means. Punctual to its tacit engagement the strange team made its appearance, and as the night was brilliantly lighted by the full moon, the white canvas with the dark body below was more clearly outlined than ever. As it approached them, Officers Gray and Connelly stepped out into the street and directly in front of the oxen and called upon the phantom driver to halt. The next moment the men were seen to stagger back and stretch their length upon the ground while the wagon seemed to pass directly over their bodies. So sure was the crowd that this had happened that a volley of shots from half a hundred guns were poured into the vehicle. But without even a momentary check the team pursued its way through ropes and wires as if they had been but shadows of the things they were. The crowd ran after the wagon until it disappeared, close to the river as mysteriously as it had come.

In the meanwhile the officers had been taken up unconscious, but unhurt in any way. It was hours before they could be restored to their senses. Both were genuinely frightened out of their wits. Mr. Gray says:

"Those that like may continue to investigate the wagon, or ghost of one, and what it carries, but they may count me out. I have nothing more to do with it, for while I'm not afraid of anything I can hold onto, I'll admit I'm a very poor hand at tackling the unreal. No, I won't describe what I saw, for I can't, and besides I don't want my mind to dwell on it; but I'll tell you how I felt, and that was as if I'd stumbled on an iceberg in the dark only the air about that ghost's team was colder than any ice I ever saw."

Connelly confirms this statement about the inexpressible chill that came sweeping from the apparition, but says that as he fell back, overpowered by it, he caught a glimpse of a number of dead faces in the wagon, and that the driver is a skeleton with burning eyes.

The ropes and wired fencing, which had so little effect on the passage of the phantom, were found to be unbroken and in their original position. Nonplussed anew, and thoroughly alarmed, the citizens resolved to watch whence the apparition came, and stationed some twenty men the following night just beyond the spot near which the team had been first observed on each occasion, but failure again resulted. The strictest watch was kept for the coming of the phantom, but though all could swear it had not passed them, it was presently seen traveling slowly down the street just beyond their post. Where the wagon goes is likewise a mystery as yet unsolved. It simply disappears before the eyes of the watchers as if it had never been. The excitement produced grows hourly, and the majority of the people, even the educated intelligent class, is very nearly convinced that the occurrence can have but one origin, and that a supernatural one, though what the object or meaning of the apparition is all are equally at a loss to conjecture.

The negroes are even more wrought up, and meditate an early exodus, as they believe that the destruction of the town is thus foreshadowed. To avert this or to prepare for it this portion of the populace spends the night and the greater part of the day in carrying on religious services, weeping and shouting for mercy, and likening the place to Sodom and Gomorrah. They are completely demoralized and cannot be induced to go to work.

There are a few skeptical spirits in the community who persist in expressing their belief that the people are being very cleverly hoaxed by someone, who by means of refraction and ingeniously disposed mirrors causes the reflection of such a team to pass down the street every night. In proof of this they point out the fact that the phantom is not visible under the electric light that has been placed on the street, though on the other side of it the apparition is distinctly seen. But the theory is too far-fetched to gain credence with the masses who are beginning to feel rather proud of the sensation created by it, and which brings in hosts of visitors from all over the country to see the thing for themselves. Richmond is one of the oldest towns in the state and was connected with many of the thrilling events of Texas' early history.

Col. Dan Thurber, one of the first settlers in the county, speaking of the mysterious travelers, says that in 1847 a similar excitement prevailed over a phantom wagon that traversed the village for seven days and heralded an outbreak of yellow fever that depopulated the country. He says that at that time it was believed that the wagon carried a family of pioneers, or their ghosts, to speak accurately, that had been taken with the fever while coming from Louisiana, and smitten and dying had passed through the village, but were not allowed to stop even to bury their dead or procure medicine for the sick, but were forced to drive on out into the country. The oxen came back in a couple of weeks, still hauling their load, but the wagon was filled only with the dead and decaying bodies.

As to the truth of this dreadful story Col. Thurber could not be

positive, but knows such it was at the time spoke of. Other old settlers admit that they have heard this story, and with that of the ghost wagon they are well acquainted, one or two even remembering having seen it in 1847. These are confident that the appearance presages evil to the community. It is now nearly a week since the phantom began its slow journeying, and according to tradition has but one more trip to make.
Algona Upper [Des Moines IA] 2 March 1892: p. 2 TEXAS

The northern wilderness scarcely seems like a natural place for a haunting, yet the indigenous peoples abandoned fertile hunting grounds because of a suicide's ghost.

ALASKA INDIANS WON'T HUNT IN GHOST LAND

Seward, Alaska, Aug. 1. An immense section of country drained by the Wood River, in the proximity of the Nenana, has been for years practically a game sanctuary.

Twenty years ago or such a matter a white settler committed suicide in the region, and the Indians say his ghost wanders over the country constantly uttering deep wailing sighs that bring bad luck to anyone unfortunate enough to hear it.

Naturally, no inducement would lead Indians to hunt or trap there, and only very urgent necessity ever takes one near the district.

As the country is rather difficult of access and no white man lives nearer than 100 miles, the game has been long unmolested by human foes and seems indifferent to the presence of the ghostly denizen. The region is a natural feeding ground for game and as a net result of these conditions it has become much overstocked.

A forest ranger who chanced to pace through the district recently counted 60 bears in one day and great numbers of foxes, lynx, wolverine, mink and small fur-bearers, besides a pack of black wolves.
Sun [Baltimore, MD] 2 August 1919: p. 5 ALASKA

From New Mexico comes a story of what may be either the "spirit of the canyons" or a treasure guardian. He seems to be dressed like a Spanish friar.

STRANGE STORY OF MYSTERIOUS MAN OR SPIRIT
Albuquerque Citizen Sure He Has Seen in Tijeras Canyon
Ancient Guardian of Sandias.

A prominent Albuquerque citizen, one who does not wish to have his name mentioned in this connection but one in whose word the utmost confidence can be placed, yesterday returned from an auto trip in the Tijeras Canyon with a strange tale to tell of an aged patriarch who evidently makes his home in some cave in the Sandias a few miles from the entrance to the canyon and lives the life of a recluse and a hermit, keeping himself from the eyes of man. The automobile party in question was returning to the city at dusk last evening and had reached a point on the return trip about four miles from the mouth of the canyon when a strange sight was encountered. An old man with flowing whiskers reaching to his waist, wearing a strange flowing garb and depending upon a staff for support was seen to emerge from behind a large rock, closely followed by a burro. Evidently he was not aware that anyone was near and at first sight of the strangers he seemed inclined to flight, but on second thought he stopped and regarded them gravely for a time and then made some strange signs with his hands which were not understood. A moment later he moved a few steps to his right and then apparently disappeared through solid rock.

While the members of the auto party felt somewhat "creepy" at seeing the apparition, it was decided to investigate. A careful search failed to reveal any opening or cave into which the man could have disappeared, and it seemed that the earth had literally swallowed him up. The searchers would have been inclined to doubt their senses had not the burro been there as evidence that at least a part of the apparition had been real.

From the old man's appearance it was judged that he must be of a very great age. Some inquiry was made at two houses in the canyon but no satisfactory information was obtained. At one house there were mysterious shakings of the head and intimations that the rocks were inhabited by the spirit of an old man who at one time was protector of the mountains and all they overlook. The tale was told that either he or his spirit had been seen once many years ago and that during the Spanish occupation he used to come out of his hiding to visit the Spanish padres in the valley.

Whatever the story, the members of the auto party are sure that they saw a venerable old man of strange appearance and that he disappeared before their very eyes into rocks where there was apparently no place to hide.
Albuquerque [NM] Journal 9 May 1916: p. 8 NEW MEXICO

NOTE: Given the complexity of the canyons and rock formations, it might have been easy for a hermit or wild man to disappear. However, the legend seems to have been current for years before this story, as seen below.

IMPERSONATOR OR WIZARD APPEARS AGAIN
IN MEXICO

Albuquerque, N.M., Sept. 23. An interesting story has been unearthed to confirm the legend of the old man of Tijeras Canyon, the story no doubt being the foundation for the impersonation which someone is apparently attempting....At least this is the assumption of those who during the past week, have seen the man in his strange garb in the canyon.

One of the oldest Indians at San Domingo traveled all the way to Albuquerque recently to explain the story after having heard that after many generations the protector of the Rio Grande Valley had again been seen. It was impossible to convince the Pueblo that the old man is not what he seems to be.

He held stoutly to the opinion that there has again appeared the wizard who hundreds of years ago first took up his abode in the mountains east of the valley, and thereafter for many decades occasionally appeared to right the wrongs of the Indians, settle differences and in other ways act as the protector of the tribes living in the Rio Grande.

According to the Indian's story, the legend has been handed down for at least 300 years, the first appearance of the wizard dating before the Spanish occupation. He was called the Wizard of Sa-Id-Nas and was reverenced by all the tribes in the Rio Grande.... The old man was regarded as a spirit, as no one knew how he existed. The story is that he was always old, but that he apparently grew no older.

The San Domingo Indian asserts that even in the lifetime of his father, the old wizard was seen in the northern end of the valley, although long before that he had ceased to offer his services because, as the story runs, the Indians had at one time spurned his advice at the bidding of a young and hot-headed chief, who a short time later mysteriously disappeared.

If someone is attempting to impersonate the Wizard of Sa-Id-Nas at the present time, the impersonator has certainly secured from the Indians the story for...the San Domingo Indian's story of the wizard's appearance as handed down in the tribe and the description given by those who have recently seen the apparition agree perfectly.

Columbus [GA] Daily Enquirer 24 July 1916: p. 1 NEW MEXICO

NOTE: The Tijeras Canyon area is believed to be the location of an immense treasure of gold and silver—the so-called Gran Quivira hoard.

Modern forms of transportation quickly became the haunts of the up-to-date ghost.

THE MYSTERIOUS LADY
A Veritable Ghost
An Impalpable Presence Boards a Street Car Nightly.

The Detroit *Free Press* says: The conductors on the First Street route have a nice little sensation all to themselves. About ten nights ago the conductor of the last car down, having no passengers beyond Twentieth Street, was standing in the front door talking to the driver, when he heard a rustle of silk, and looked about to see a woman seated in the car. He wondered to himself at her agility in boarding the car while the horses were on a trot, and after the car had passed along several blocks he started forward to collect her fare, and to ask her where she desired to stop off. She had her face turned away from him, and as he put out his hand to touch her shoulder the lady vanished. The conductor's hair stood up, and the driver felt cold chills run up his back. Every night since then, as half a dozen conductors allege, the ghostly passenger boards the last car, providing there are no other passengers, and after riding a few blocks she suddenly vanishes. Some of the drivers have remained on the rear platform to see where she got on, but the first thing they know she is in the car. They described her as being richly attired in winter clothing, having a shawl, hood and muff, and so closely veiled that a glimpse of her features is impossible. Whatever the general public may think of the affair, it is certain to the minds of ten or fifteen conductors and drivers that they have a real ghost on their hands.

Indianapolis [IN] Sentinel 23 August 1873: p. 7 MICHIGAN

NOTE: Once again, even in a street car, the female road ghost remains faceless.

The development of the safety bicycle and pneumatic bicycle tires brought the bicycling craze of the 1880s and '90s to enthusiastic wheelmen and women. In a surprisingly short time, stories of ghosts on bicycles began to circulate, almost supplanting stories of phantom horseback riders. Here is an unusual story of a wheelman's wraith.

A GHOSTLY BICYCLIST
A Wheelman's Story of an Effort to Overtake a Phantom Who Rode an Old-Fashioned Wheel

"I used to ride in races and only last year I spun around the track at my home in the east, but I was cured of the sport in a rather remarkable manner," said a visiting bicyclist at the races of the Garden City Cyclers to a *San Jose News* reporter.

"The story is a strange one," he continued, "and I have never told it to any one yet that I think really believed it, but so firmly am I convinced of the reality of an incident that was frightful in some of its details, that for fear of a repetition I have not had the courage to ride in a race since. "The races were run on a half-mile horse racing track that had been rolled and otherwise partially prepared for the purpose. I had never been especially fast, but just before the event I had bought a new pneumatic tire racer, one of the first seen in that part of the country. The machine was a beauty, full nickeled and with the object of making a display more than anything else, I entered for the five-mile race with a fifteen-minute limit, the conditions being the same as those of the last race in San Jose yesterday that Wilbur Edwards won.

"There were seven starters in the race and we had ten laps to make. I thought we were making rather slow time, and from some remarks that I overheard from the judges' stand when we passed on completing the eighth lap I was certain that it would be no race, as the winner would not make the distance within the time required. By this time I was well winded and was sure that I would not come out first, but I did not feel in the least disappointed, as I had not expected to win the race when I started.

"In the beginning of the ninth lap, however, as I was tolerably well in the lead, I thought I would spurt a little, so I forged ahead and was allowed to make the pace for a while, each of the riders having done this in turn before me. I had been in the lead seemingly only a second when to my surprise I saw just ahead of me a strong-looking rider on an old-style solid-tire wheel. I had not seen him pass and did not know that any such man had entered the race in the first place.

"The stranger was well in the lead and I felt so much ashamed of myself to think that I was plodding behind on a new style racing pneumatic while he was making the pace at a swinging gait on a solid tire that I just dug my toe nails into the track, so to speak, and did my utmost in an attempt to pass him. It did no good, however. I could not decrease the distance, although spurred on as I was, my speed, as I afterwards learned, became something terrific.

"When I passed the grand and judges' stands at the end of the ninth lap for the finish there was tremendous cheering. I could not understand what it was all about as I did not consider that my efforts on a pneumatic flyer to catch a man on a solid tire with a spring frame were worthy of much applause. I did not have time to look around and see what the rest of the riders were doing.

"On I flew like the wind, every muscle strained to the utmost in my endeavors to catch the stranger, who kept swinging along about ten feet in the lead. I felt that he must tire out at last, so I did not relax, but rather increased the immense strain to which I was putting every fibre of my being. When we neared the grand stand I could hear thunders of applause rolling up to greet us, and when I was within fifty yards of the scratch I made a last desperate effort to pass the stranger.

"In the strain that was upon me I shut my eyes and paddled like lightning. When I was certain that I had crossed the tape I looked up just in time to see a terrible spectacle. The wheel of the rider ahead struck something. He was thrown forward and struck on his head. I was sure his neck was broken and blood gushed forth from his nose, mouth and ears. The sight was horrible and in my exhausted state I could stand the strain no longer. I fainted and fell from my wheel.

"The next thing I knew I was stretched out on a blanket in the rubbing-down room with a crowd around me. As soon as the boys saw that I had recovered consciousness all of them began to talk to me at once. They congratulated me on my wonderful victory, all declaring they had never seen anything like it before. They all wished to know, however, why I had exerted myself so much when I was so far in the lead. I had left all the rest of the riders far behind, and yet I swept forward and saved that race, coming in just inside of the fifteen-minute limit.

"When I spoke of a rider that I was trying to catch all were dumb with amazement. They had seen no such wheelman and the judges had given me the race. When I described the man I saw and his wheel he was recognized as being identical in appearance with a man who was killed under similar circumstances several years before in a five-mile race on the same track. It is scarcely necessary to state that I almost fainted again when I learned that I had been urged forward by a spook. I have never had the courage to get in a race again for fear that there would be a repetition of my former terrible experience. I had before heard of ghostly riders on horseback, but it was my first and I hope it will be my last experience with a spook on a bicycle."

Plain Dealer [Cleveland, OH] 24 October 1892: p.6 CALIFORNIA

NOTE: Wilber Edwards [1872-1951] was a record-setting speed-demon from San Jose, California who set the "paced" world speed record for one mile on a bicycle: 1:34 minutes, on 9 February, 1895.

10.

A Vat of Acid
Homicidal Hauntings

Let them appear in sickly fires, to mope
About in mists and exhalations foul,
Like the unquiet ghosts of murder'd men
Through clammy vaults and churchyards.

-W. Martin-

If we judge by the newspapers, the 19th century was one long orgy of slaughter. Headlines shrieked of Awful Murder, Horrid Murder, Appalling Murder, Murder of the Century! There was, of course, no *CSI: 19th Century*, no DNA evidence, and barely any fingerprinting. Criminals might be identified by Bertillonage, a collection of detailed body measurements, invented by a French criminologist in 1879 or the notion of criminality being visible in the face, as popularized by Cesare Lombroso. Arsenic could be detected by the Marsh test, first used in court in the 1830s, but poisons' ready accessibility made the 19th century a poisoner's paradise.

With so little forensic science, the public fell back on rotting corpses, dreams and ghosts to solve murders. It was popular to surprise the accused with some part of his victim (preferably the head in a vile state of decomposition) to shock him into a confession. Scott Jackson and Alonzo Walling, who decapitated Pearl Bryan, were confronted with Pearl's headless corpse so the police could see their reactions. (See *The Headless Horror* for the outcome.)

Another crime-solving method, which, to judge by the papers, was widely credited, was the "evidence dream." Someone would dream of a murder victim who described the death and perhaps the murderer, as we will see in the story about the notorious Parkman-Webster murder in this chapter. Sometimes the ghost in the dream would tell where their body was hidden or helpfully describe incriminating evidence, such as stolen property. Séances were also held to try to entice the deceased to assist the police. It was axiomatic that the ghost of a murder victim would haunt her murderer until he confessed or went mad. And it was common knowledge that some atrocious crimes never died, but were replayed in a ghastly Grand Guignol fashion beyond the grave.

A HAUNTED HOUSE.
GHOSTS SAID TO BE STROLLING AROUND THE
DRUSE HOMESTEAD.
THE MURDER OF THE LITTLE LAKES RECALLED
AN APPARITION WHICH WALKS IN THE SWAMP.

On a rise of ground sloping toward a swamp fringing the more northern of two bodies of water known as the Little Lakes, in the town of Warren, stands a dilapidated frame structure, whose story of blood some half dozen years ago appalled the civilized world. Here it was that Roxalana Druse, assisted by a daughter of 17 and abetted by two shiftless nephews, butchered, hacked and chopped her husband, William Druse, and then, with true hell-born instincts, boiled, roasted and burned the remains and scattered the ashes in the swamp adjoining the premises. The story is a familiar one. [!!]

The miserable little frame farm house wherein this tragedy was enacted has literally been carried away piecemeal by morbid-minded relic-seekers. The wall-paper with which Mrs. Druse covered the blood-bespattered walls has been torn off and carried away; the floor, which she daubed with liberal coats of paint to hide the crimson stains, has been hacked, sawed and appropriated by the army of clinker-brained individuals who have visited the place. Just what pleasure these people derive from these so-called relics it is difficult to determine. The snake-fence which once surrounded the buildings has also been carried off, but whether as relics or for fuel by some poor but dishonest neighbor is not known.

And now it is said that the old house is haunted. It would be difficult to imagine a more favorable place for spooks, even were there no horrible tale connected with it. Situated in the rear of a great barren field with a swamp at the back and the highway seldom traveled, however—some 500 yards distant, with toppling chimneys, flapping clapboards, creaking doors and great rents in the sides—the building presents a truly uncanny aspect. But when are added the details of a crime, the awfulness of which six years of retelling has not served to augment, a grewsomeness surrounds the premises which the stoutest-hearted yokel does not care to investigate.

It is said that upon storm-swept nights the place is visited by the wraiths of the murdered Druse and his demon wife. There are sounds of pistol-shots and groans, of wild yells and curses. There is the noise of a falling body, pleas for mercy, followed by the dull thuds of an ax chop, chop, chopping off hands, arms, legs. The whole horrid tragedy is again enacted. A brief silence ensues, and then issues forth from the house a ghostly apparition, which glides around to the rear of the building, follows a path swampward and disappears. It has been noted that the spook appears to be that of a woman, and it carries concealed a large package of some character. This is supposed to be the ghost of the murderess, and that the package she carries contains the head and cremated remains of the murdered husband.

Of those still living who were connected with the tragedy, the daughter, Mary, is slowly dying in prison of consumption; the little boy, Georgie, is still living with the kind-hearted farmer who adopted him; Frank Gates is living somewhere in the South and, Chester [also called Charles] Gates, the younger of the two nephews is making a good living from the sales of a liniment made from a favorite formula concocted by the old man Druse.

Idaho Falls [ID] Times 5 May 1892: p. 7 NEW YORK

NOTE: As may be seen from this story, murderabilia collectors are nothing new. While most news articles were as negative about the murderess as this one, the question of motive remains as Mrs. Druse never publically confessed. (One newspaper claimed that she admitted shooting her husband at the urging of Frank Gates, who then denied any knowledge of her actions.) There are stories that Mrs. Druse and her daughter Mary entertained men in the Druse home, which was not at all agreeable to Mr. Druse. It was reported that Mrs. Druse ruled the roost and that she boasted that she would get rid of her husband one day. Frank Gates testified that Mrs. Druse offered him a lot of money to shoot William Druse. There are also stories that Mrs. Druse and her children led a hellish life of abuse with a man described as both shiftless and psychotically violent. The daughter's description of her father's last morning tells of him threatening her mother, first with an axe and then saying he would cut her throat with his jack-knife. Mrs. Druse, who was described in the papers as looking as though she would not hurt a dove, shot him several times, then cut his head off, apparently while he was still alive. Mrs. Druse, after fighting "like a tiger," was hung at Herkimer, New York, 28 February 1887. The weights were improperly adjusted and she strangled to death, a spectacle so painful that it was the last judicial hanging in New York State. Thereafter, the condemned went to the electric chair.

As was common in these cases, Mrs. Druse did not rest in peace:

A Herkimer correspondent claims that the ghost of Mrs. Druse now haunts the cell in the Herkimer jail in which she was last confined, and

tells of moans and murmurs and cries of "Oh! Oh!" such as Mrs. Druse uttered when the black cap was drawn over her head.
Olean [NY] Democrat June 30, 1887 p. 1 NEW YORK

The Parkman-Webster murder, with its wealthy victim, gruesome dismemberment, and novel forensic evidence, was the crime sensation of 1850. This anonymous lady claimed to have witnessed the aftermath of the murder.

A recent writer narrates the following significant dream, relative to the Dr. Parkman murder, and which, in all its unpleasant details, was dreamed twice over: Dr. Webster, Professor of Chemistry in Harvard College, was convicted of the murder of his acquaintance—we can hardly say his friend— Dr. Parkman. A lady, well known in the literary world, and then residing in London, had, some years previously, paid a long visit to the United States, during which she became intimately acquainted with Dr. Webster and his family, who showed her much kindness and attention. After her return to England, she continued to correspond with the family; and one day, in the early autumn of 1848, a gentleman related to Dr. Parkman called upon her with an introduction from Professor Webster. On that night she went to bed at her usual hour, but soon experienced a horrible dream. She fancied that she was being urged by Dr. Webster to assist him in concealing a set of human bones in a wooden box; and she distinctly recollected that there was a thigh-bone which, after failing to break it in pieces, they vainly attempted to insert, but it was too long. While they were trying to hide the box—as she fancied, under her bed— she woke in a state of terror and cold perspiration. She instantly struck a light, and tried to dispel the recollection of her horrible vision by reading. After a lapse of two hours, during which she had determinedly fixed her attention on the book, she put out the light, and soon fell asleep. The same dream again occurred; after which she did not dare—although a woman of singular moral and physical courage — to attempt to sleep any more that night. Early on the following morning she called upon the writer, and told him of her fearful experiences of the past night. Nothing more at the time was thought of these dreams; but shortly afterwards the news reached England that Dr. Parkman was missing; that the last time he was seen alive he was entering the college gates; and that the janitor was suspected of having murdered him.

On the writer mentioning this to the lady, she at once exclaimed, "Oh, my dreams! Dr. Webster must be the murderer!" The next mail but one brought the news that the true murderer had been detected; and that, at the very time when the lady's dreams occurred, Dr. Webster must have been actually struggling to get the bones—the flesh having been previously burned—into a wooden box such as she had seen; and that, after attempting in vain to break the thigh-bones, he had hidden them elsewhere. *Cincinnati [OH] Enquirer* 22 February 1875: p. 2 MASSACHUSETTS

NOTE: Dr. John White Webster was a lecturer in the Medical College of Harvard University. He got into debt and borrowed money several times from Dr. George Parkman, a lunacy specialist and one of the richest men in Boston. When Dr. Parkman demanded repayment, Webster asked him to come to the Medical College on the afternoon of 23 November 1849. There, as he wrote in his confession, Dr. Parkman became enraged about the money Webster owed him. Webster claimed that he picked up a piece of wood in self-defense and bashed Dr. Parkman over the head, killing him. He then dismembered and tried to burn the body. Parts of it he threw into a privy. The janitor of the Medical School, Ephraim Littlefield, became suspicious of Dr. Webster's actions, watched him closely, and discovered the remains in the privy, leading to Dr. Webster's arrest. Webster was convicted and hung, although there are those who say that the hanging was faked and he was smuggled out of the country. The writer claims that he/she was told this story on the day after the dreams, but perhaps we should be skeptical of a dream related 25 years after the fact.

Stories of unnatural parents who slaughtered their children were a perennially sensational item in the press. In these next three articles, we can observe the progression of history into legend. First there is the bare-bones recounting of the ghastly facts. Then the addition of folk elements such as the barren graves and the black velvet band. And finally a madwoman overlooking the children's graves—and a ghost. In the ballad tradition, one would expect the blood-stained children to return to haunt their murderous mother, but strangely, the murderess is the only ghost.

NEW LONDON Oct. 20
The following tragical affair happened at the north parish in Killingworth on Wednesday last, viz. the wife of Mr. ___Higgins of that parish, being disordered in her reason, and being left in the house with three of her children, she called her son of seven years old to her, telling him she wanted to pin his collar, and immediately cut his throat, she then cut the throats of her daughter of five years old, and her infant which lay on the bed: Mr. Higgins soon after coming into the house, found her on her knees,

cutting her own throat with a dull knife, which with some difficulty he wrested from her; but she had wounded herself to that degree she died soon after.

Connecticut Gazette [New London, CT] 20 October 1779: p. 2
CONNECTICUT

THE MURDERED CHILDREN

About a mile and a half north of the Congregational Church, in Killingworth, on the old road which runs parallel with the main street, is a group of dilapidated houses. In one of these ancient dwellings there formerly lived a Mrs. Higgins, who was possessed of a most violent temper. October 14th 1779, after having quarreled with her husband, she grasped a common case-knife and cut the throats of her three children. The victims of this bloody tragedy were buried in the old cemetery, in the Union District. There was at that time a belief almost universally indulged in that grass would not grow over the grave of a murdered person; and it is said that for a long time the lot where they laid these children was barren as a desert. The natural sterility of the soil, however, is a sufficient explanation of the phenomenon. Mrs. Higgins subsequently resided in the Pine Orchard District, near the Union Church. On that edifice there was a clock dial with stationary hands, and she was heard to say: When those pointers come together and stand at twelve, my sins will be pardoned." She also cherished the strange hope that her husband, who was separated from her would return, and that she would again be the mother of three children in place of her dead offspring. She is reported to have made an attempt on her own life at the time of killing her children, but was prevented by her husband, and in after years always wore a black ribbon about her neck to cover the ugly trace of her savage rage. The story of her terrible deed was versified by a local poet, and within the memory of the living the aged women have been heard to sing in a mournful minor the sad song of this unfortunate woman. She was doubtless buried in the old cemetery in Pine Orchard district, but her grave, like that of her children, is still unlettered, and the historian looks in vain for the last resting place of her whom in charity he fain would call a maniac, not a murderer.

The History of Middlesex County 1635-1885, Hon. William H. Buell
(New York: J. H. Beers & Co, 1884) CONNECTICUT

NOTE: I have not yet located the poem or what sounds like a local murder ballad about the tragedy.

Over one hundred years later, the murders have not been forgotten and a ghost has arisen. We also see the distortions of history preserved in the newspaper.

A GHOST-HAUNTED COMMUNITY
The Scene of a Triple Tragedy Said to be the Home of Perturbed Spirits.

New Haven, Ct., Feb. 25. The residents of Killingworth, a quiet little town on the sound, are much exercised over a haunted house. On a lonely road near the center of the town stands an old house of peculiar construction. It was in this mansion that a decade [century] ago Mrs. Horace [Samuel was the correct name] Higgins cut the throats of her three children while they were asleep. They were buried in the village churchyard and, although the other graves there are covered in summer with an abundant growth of grass, not a blade ever grows on the graves of the children.

Their mother was adjudged insane and confined in a room overlooking the graves, and every night until she died she would stand at the window gazing on the clock in the church tower nearby, moaning and craving pardon for her crimes.

For many years the house had the reputation of being haunted, and it almost continuously remained tenantless until last summer, when the Ray family of Boston took it as a summer residence. The first night they slept there the two tenants were nearly scared to death by the apparition of a Woman in White standing at their bedroom window. Loud and unearthly noises echoed through the house. The next night Mr. and Mrs. Ray say they saw the apparition and they promptly gave up the house. Recently only these facts were learned by the villagers and since then several weird sights have, it is said, been seen in the old mansion.
Plain Dealer [Cleveland, OH] 26 February 1886: p. 3 CONNECTICUT

NOTE: I am deeply indebted to Paul Slade of planetslade.com for providing the following background and genealogical information for this case. The murdered children were William, aged 6; Sarah, aged 4; and Jane, aged 9 weeks. All three children are buried at Emmanuel Church Cemetery at Killingworth, Connecticut. Mrs. Higgins's name was Sarah and she was married to Samuel in 1769. Two other children, Ichabod and Martha, were not in the house at the time of the murders. Sarah did not die just after the murders, but is said to have died in or around 1810; she is buried in Union Cemetery in Killingworth. If her death date of 1810 is correct, Samuel, a farmer, who died in 1811, must have divorced her. He married Temperance, fourteen years his junior, in 1781. The couple moved to Vermont and had at least seven children.

One wonders how accurate the second of the articles was in preserving local traditions such as Sarah was bad-tempered and she had quarreled with her husband or if those were merely part of the stock child-murderess profile.

This next story purports to be from an oral family tradition. It is a touch theatrical, but gruesomely effective.

A True Story
No. 30 in a series of ghost stories sent to the *Dayton [OH] Daily News* ghost story contest in 1914.

The following story was related to me during the early days of my life so often, by my grandfather (now deceased) that I literally know it by heart.

"When I came to this country in 1872 from Warwick, England, I moved to southern Pennsylvania, and wishing to settle down for the remainder of my life, bought the old Turks Head Tavern in a little town of one thousand inhabitants. The hostelry was old even then and so I had the entire place gone over and all of the furnishings put in repair. I aided in this work myself and in cleaning out an old bureau drawer found a torn, yellow, old letter. For no particularly reason whatever, I put it in my pocket and forgot about it until one evening when after the place was in smooth running order, it again came to my notice.

"I read it over. It was the confession of what I thought must have been an insane woman. Either that, or some traveler with a peculiar idea of humor had written it to throw a scare into the proprietor, but somehow or other it had got pushed back in a corner of a drawer and was undiscovered until by me. I am not, or rather was not at that time, a bit superstitious and furthermore had no faith in the truth of the words, but nevertheless, my mind kept going back to it for several weeks until the thing got such a grip on my mind that I could think of but little else.

"One night, a month later, during the severest electrical and rain storm I have ever witnessed, I was sitting alone in the parlor on the first floor. The shutters banged, the house creaked, the lamp sputtered fitfully, and the wind blowing through the old eaves, made a mournful, haunting sound that was anything but pleasant.

"My mind reverted again to the letter and reaching up I took it from behind the clock on the mantelpiece, where I had secreted it. As I have said, I was not superstitious and I prided myself on my steady nerves, but I confess, as I took down that old yellow letter, my hand trembled. For the dozenth time I read:

"'Either I must kill the baby or I shall go mad. I loathe the sight of its pinched-up squalling face, its distorted limbs: I did not ask it to come into the world and its wicked father is not my lawful husband.'

"At this point in the letter I stopped for I thought that I heard a succession of sounds, like a baby squalling somewhere upstairs. Putting away the ridiculous idea, however, for I knew there was not a soul in the house under twenty years of age, I went on:

"'Listen to the little brat now. Here! I have it, this little penknife is just the thing; it will slip in without a sound and those contemptible little squeals will be silenced forever—.'

"When I had finished that sentence my breath nearly left me and the sweat stood out on my face, for at that moment the squalls came to an abrupt end, in an awful and piteous sigh, as though someone had just expired in terrible agony. I leaped from my chair and listened, but heard naught save the fury of the storm and the creaking of the timbers throughout the house. I sat down and resumed the ghastly letter:

"'Then when the little pig is dead I will wrap it in a sheet and when all is silent in the house I can steal down softly into the cellar—.'

"I leaped up from my chair again, trembling, and my heart seemed to jump from my breast, so violently did it beat. Yes, I was certain of it this time I could hear a door being opened stealthily, even above the fury of the storm someone was stepping softly along my hall upstairs. Now they were creeping down the stairs and I could distinctly hear every step creak under the weight. The letter dropped from my hand and I shivered from head to foot. I knew the words by heart and my trembling lips murmured the last sentence:

"'—and I will bury the brat in the cellar.'

"The footsteps sounded along the first-floor hall, down the cellar steps: and my heart stopped beating: and now, though the storm was at its mightiest, I could hear perfectly the grate of steel on gravel: then a brief silence and the footsteps were coming back. I could bear the horror of it no longer and reaching up to pull the bell-rope that signaled the servants I fell to the floor in a faint.

"When I recovered, my wife and a servant were chaffing my hands and sprinkling water upon my face. Then it all came back again suddenly and I nearly fainted again, but summoning my courage I jumped up, picked up the lantern and grabbing my man by the arm, rushed down into the cellar. He thought I was mad, but I made no explanation then. I quickly found a shovel, and something, I know not what, attracted me to a corner where a stack of cord-wood lay. I gave an order and in a few minutes the wood was cleared away. I dug into the soft gravel; I struck something that glistened in the yellow lantern light: and with cold sweat streaming from my forehead and before the horrified gaze of my servant, uncovered the skeleton of an infant child."

Dayton [OH] Daily News 20 January 1914 PENNSYLVANIA

NOTE: West Chester, the county seat of Chester County, Pennsylvania was known as "Turks Head" after the Turks Head Tavern, founded in 1762. (The name was changed to West Chester in 1784 when the town was formally laid out.) West Chester was the site of the notorious 1805 trial of Hannah Miller, known as "Black Hannah," for the murder of her infant child. She was hung at "Gallows Hill," the execution watched by over 2,000 spectators. Her ghost was said to haunt the site. One wonders if she inspired this story.

There is a sub-genre of ghost stories about dead husbands and wives haunting their living spouses, like the woman in the first story in this book who brought her husband a message from beyond the grave. This wronged wife had more reason than most to return.

Extraordinary Story.

We know the parties referred to, and know some of the facts to be true. Before the war there lived in this city a man and his family, consisting of a wife and son, the man was well known here in business circles and highly respected.

He was a man of wealth, but his home was for him the most miserable place on earth. His wife, who had once been handsome, sensible, industrious and cheerful, lost her health and temper and made all who associated with her unhappy. For a long time her husband did everything in his power to make her happy, but in vain.

His efforts seemed to increase his discomfort and misery. At last he became indifferent to her complaints and deaf to her scolding. This drove her mad; but still she lived with him. In time paralysis was added to her numerous infirmities of body, and she became almost as helpless as a child. The family removed to the country, and while the husband, his afflicted wife, and a waiting girl were sitting by the fire one evening, his wife rose from her seat and made an effort to cross the room, just in front of the fire, but her paralyzed limbs refused to serve her, and she fell so near the fire as to be in imminent danger of being seriously burnt. The girl sprang forward to rescue the prostrate and afflicted woman, but the husband forbade it and declared she should either get up herself or be burnt. She lay before the fire until the pain induced by the burning of her diseased flesh restored her senses. In her agony she turned her head, her eyes fell upon her husband, and, with the eloquence of one suffering excruciating pain, implored him to take her from the fire. With inhuman coldness he bade her get up herself. She made an effort to rise, but failed. Her husband then picked her up, to find her neck and shoulders burnt to a crisp. The woman died. In less than a year from her death her husband married again.

His second wife was handsome, sensible, and less than eighteen years of age. The happy couple took the usual bridal tour, and returned to the home of the bridegroom. One evening soon after their return, the bride sat in the very room which had been the chamber of the husband's first wife—she was gazing into the fire, which was smoldering on the hearth, when suddenly there rose before her the form of a woman, clothed in the habiliments of the grave, with the scar upon its neck and shoulder—the ghost, the spirit, or whatever it was, spoke not a word, but with its fleshless hand pointed first to the scar upon its neck and shoulder, and then to the smoldering fire upon the hearth of the young bride's chamber. She was so overcome that she could neither cry for help, nor flee. While she sat in this hopeless condition the object vanished. Soon she was fully recovered from her fright, and she left the room, to return again with her husband. She told him of the strange and frightful object which had appeared to her, but he laughed, and pronounced it a delusion. Together they took their seats by the fire—the wife insisted that she was not mistaken, but the husband still laughed and doubted; not long, however, for the form again appeared, painfully distinct in form and feature. The husband doubted no more; fear froze his blood; he was motionless, speechless, helpless, unconscious, until his bride seized his arm and screamed, "Who is it?" All the time the form stood before them, pointing, first to the scar upon her neck and shoulder, and then to the fire—then it vanished; and as it vanished the miserable man exclaimed, as if in answer to his wife's question, "My God, it is Mary's ghost!" (Mary was the name of his first wife.) His new wife began to inquire how his first wife had been treated, and soon learned the story. She wrote to her father, who lives near the city, all the facts, and asked his advice.

He told her to come back home, and it is thought she will do so, although efforts are being made to fix the matter up. In the meantime the husband is very anxious to sell his "haunted house." *New Albany Ledger.* *Crisis* [Columbus, OH] 19 August 1868: p. 238 INDIANA

It is one of the myths of the past that people married very young. As we have seen, Mrs. Boyle, who was haunted by her husband's dead wife, was described at age 17 as "very young for a wife." The marriage of a 13-year-old girl would have been unthinkable, especially at this late date. Yet one rich old man did think of it. He had the wedding license in his pocket when he was struck down.

SEE SLAIN SUITOR'S GHOST
Farmer Williams' Intended Bride and Her Father Have Visions.

Dover, Del. Although the Maryland authorities have decided to forget the murder of aged Farmer Williams, new life has been given to this mystery of two states by the claim that the dead man's ghost is walking.

This newest phase to the crime is supplied by the 13-year-old girl, Elizabeth Walls, whom Williams meant to marry, for which he had procured the marriage license which was in his pocket when he was found hanging on the tree near Barclay, several years [months] ago. The child said she had seen the ghost of the old man several times since his burial.

Samuel Walls, the father, tells the same story of having seen the spirit of the dead man about the farm. These visitations of Williams, according to the Walls family, have occurred in the night time, and have so thoroughly aroused them that they declare a continuance of Williams' promenades will compel them to abandon the farm.

So impressed has the community become by the stories of the ghost's nocturnal visits that the Williams family has been advised to consult a medium as a means of solving the mystery of their father's death.

Hobart [OK] Daily Republican 6 October 1908: p. 6 DELAWARE and MARYLAND

NOTE: William Williams, a well-to-do aged farmer, seems to have been a nasty piece of work. Samuel Walls was a tenant on Williams's farm and was opposed to the match of the elderly man with his young daughter. Williams came to the Walls's home, secretly kissed and caressed the young girl and urged her to elope with him. She told him she didn't want to marry, but he bought a dress and told her it would be her wedding gown. He also stole her clothing from the family home and obtained a wedding license on June 20th. On the afternoon of July 15, 1908, he was found hanging from a tree near Barclay, eleven miles from where he was last seen—at the home of a son-in-law who did not want him to marry the girl for fear he would cut his children out of his will. Williams had left his buggy at this home and his daughter speculated that he had set off on foot for the Walls's home to get the girl away from her parents without them noticing. Williams was bruised and cut about the head and the coroner said the head wound had caused his death. Various suspects were suggested, but no firm evidence was ever found and the inquiry was dropped, perhaps out of distaste for the victim. [Source: *Philadelphia [PA] Inquirer* 17 July 1908: p. 1, 2]

On 1 May, 1897 Louisa, the wife of Adolph Luetgert, dubbed the "sausage king of Chicago," disappeared. Luetgert told their children that she was visiting her sister, but after Louisa's brother reported her missing, Luetgert claimed that she had run off with another man. The police investigation found that the couple had frequently quarreled, that Luetgert was in serious financial trouble, and that he had been courting a rich widow. The day following Louisa's disappearance, Luetgert's business failed and the sheriff confiscated the sausage factory. This was Luetgert's undoing, for the fact emerged that Louisa was seen entering the factory late the night she disappeared and Luetgert had not had time to clean up after that fatal visit. The building was searched and two of Louisa's rings, some bone fragments, and corset steels, were found at the factory. Luetgert was accused of murdering his wife and dissolving her body in a sausage vat full of acid. (Other rumors said he made her into sausages, which he then sold, but this, we hope, was not true.) The gruesome details captured the public imagination and the murder was labeled the "Crime of a Century." The jury could not come to a verdict at Luetgert's trial. There had been reported sightings of Louisa from around the country, leading to reasonable doubt as to whether she was really dead and if the bones were really hers. But Luetgert was found guilty at his second trial and he died in prison in 1899 after confessing to a lawyer that he killed his wife because he was "possessed by the devil," and in love with another woman. Louisa's ghost was said to haunt the factory where she had died.

MRS LUETGERT'S GHOST
Seen Stalking About the Once Famed Sausage Factory

Chicago Times Herald: Nearly four years have passed since the murder of Mrs. Louisa Luetgert by her husband, and just now her ghost is appearing in the factory building on Diversey Avenue, where she was slain. Several persons who live across the street from the structure are willing to testify to this fact. John Seifert, the watchman at the factory, August Beck, a saloon-keeper directly across the street from the building, and Gusted Haas, who lives in the house formerly occupied by Adolph Luetgert, are three of the many persons who have seen the apparition, and no one can convince them that there is no such thing as a ghost. Beck was the first to see it. He called the attention of Seifert to it and the two men watched the form from the window of the saloon.

VISION OF THE SPECTER

The locked door was thrown open, according to the story of the two men, and the shade of the woman entered the factory. Seifert declares that he immediately went into the building, and tried the door, but it was locked. He became frightened and hastened back to the saloon to tell Beck. Scarcely had the two men begun discussing the matter when Haas appeared and said that his children had been frightened by a woman who was in the rear of the factory.

Seifert is only a boy, and he feared to go into the place. He watched with the other men, and lights flashed before the windows. One moment a light would appear on the ground floor and the next it would be in the cupola, where Luetgert once had a bedroom. Seifert reported the occurrence to the police on Wednesday, the ghost having appeared for the first time on Tuesday night. Wednesday night Capt. Schuettler of the Sheffield Avenue station sent Detectives Quinn and Blaul to the factory. A light soon appeared at one of the factory windows, and the officers decided on an investigation. With their revolvers drawn and each with a lantern they entered the factory with Seifert.

SPECTRAL LIGHT SEEN

Immediately a light darted before them, as if it were a streak of lightning. It seemed to pass from the first floor down the stairway into the basement. The officers followed, and when they got to the basement they saw the light again. It was in the very place where stood the famous middle vat in which the body of Mrs. Luetgert is thought to have been disintegrated. Quinn rushed for it, but it vanished, and in less time than could be realized was in a corner fifty feet away. The officer again approached it and this time was able to get within a few feet of the apparition, which all the while was distinctly that of a woman, and the officer sprang for it. His arms were thrown about a small keg and his head went through a window pane. The light disappeared, but a crowd of men and women who were outside the building watching said they had no sooner heard the crashing of the glass than they saw the light appear in the top of the factory. The officers went back to the station, firm believers in ghosts ....

Agatha Tosh, whose notoriety in the trial of Adolph Luetgert is well remembered [She was a friend of Mrs. Luetgert and believed Adolph guilty from the start], has not seen the spirit. She conducts a saloon a block east of the factory, and declares that Beck has started the story in order to draw a crowd about the building with the idea of helping his business. The latter scamps this as a falsehood and makes his word stronger by declaring that he will move away if the apparition continues to appear. *Illinois State Register* [Springfield, IL] 26 March 1901: p. 8 ILLINOIS

In addition to haunting the site of her earthly dissolution, Mrs. Luetgert haunted her old house, which had been moved and divided into apartments.

One of the ghosts is described as a tall, corpulent man with black mustache, clad in a black suit with white linen shirt and collar, a black tie and a black derby hat. The other is said to be a woman in a gown of white lace with long, dark hair flowing loosely down her back. These descriptions fit Leutgert and his wife. Mrs. Leutgert was buried in just such a gown... [This is inaccurate, as Mrs. Leutgert was completely fragmented and, in any case, the bones disappeared from evidence after the first trial.]

Myra Berger is a pretty girl 18 years old employed as a switchboard operator in one of the Chicago Telephone Company's downtown exchanges....

"I have seen both ghosts many times," said the young woman as she sat in the parlor of her home. "One of my most harrowing experiences occurred only a week ago.

"I had come home from work a little late and was eating my lunch in the dining room. A light in an electric globe was burning over the table. The parlor was dark except for the light from the dining room. It was close to midnight when I heard a noise in the parlor, and I had a sudden startling sensation of not being alone.

"I glanced into the dim parlor and saw the figure of a man, tall, powerfully built, standing in a corner near the front window. While I looked, too frightened to scream, the figure came toward me. It paused directly under the arch between the parlor and the dining room and placed one hand on one of the pillars of the arch and stood staring at me out of wide open glassy, expressionless dead man's eyes. I could see it plainly. Its face was of a deathly pallor. It made no motion, uttered no sound—just stood and stared blankly at me.

"While it stood leaning against the pillar our little dachshund that had been lying on the floor near me saw it too, and jumped up growling savagely and started to circle about the thing, sniffing at it. All this had taken place in a moment. Then I screamed and ran into my bedroom, just off the dining room.

"My scream awoke my sister Hattie, who is my bedfellow, and my mother, who sleeps in a rear room. Both came running into the dining room, but the figure of the man had vanished into thin air."

＊ ⋯ ▬ ⋯ ＊

"I was convinced that the house was haunted the second night after I had taken possession of my flat," said [another tenant] Mrs. Harpling. "I had turned out the light in my room and had gone to bed. I was lying wide awake when suddenly a woman in white appeared at my bedside.

"Her gown was of lacy material and suggested a shroud, and her long, dark hair hung loosely down her back. I thought at first that I was dreaming and pinched myself to see that I was awake. I turned over in bed and tried to force myself to go to sleep, but it was impossible. I was convinced by this time that my visitant was a ghost. I turned again in bed and faced it.

"'What do you want?' I finally managed to say.

"I had heard that a ghost can speak only when spoken to. But the phantom made no reply. At the sound of my voice it glided slowly away and seemed to fade out into the moonlight through the closed window....

"One night with Mrs. Laden, who lives in the flat below me, I was standing at the head of the back stairs, which lead down to the laundry. The stairway was dark. Suddenly a little way down the steps a light appeared. It seemed to come from a lamp, the outline of which we thought we could see dimly. But to our horror the lamp seemed to float along in space with no visible hand to hold it. We heard footsteps descending the stairs, but saw no one...[They saw the light go into the laundry room and heard the tubs rattling, but, rushing downstairs, found no sign anyone had been there.]

＊ ⋯ ▬ ⋯ ＊

"My most terrifying experience," said Anna Berger, 16 years old, "was with the woman in white. One evening about 9 o'clock I saw the figure of the woman in her white gown and with her hair down her back standing near the fireplace in the parlor. I screamed at the top of my voice. The woman did not vanish, but seemed to drift like a white mist to the front of the room."

On the advice of her priest, one tenant sprinkled holy water to keep away the ghosts, but it wore off and "lately they have seemed to defy the holy water."

The Sun [New York, NY] 31 August 1913: p. 14 ILLINOIS

NOTE: For extensive detail about the murder from Robert Loerzel, author of *Alchemy of Bones: Chicago's Leutgert Murder Case of 1897,* see http://www. alchemyofbones.com/.

THE GHOST OF PEG ALLEY'S POINT

Peg Alley's Point is a long and narrow strip of wooded land, situated between the main stream of Miles River and one of the navigable creeks which flow into it. This little peninsula is about two miles long, from fifty to three hundred yards in width and is bounded by deep water and is overgrown with pine and thick underbrush. There is extant a tradition to the effect that many years ago a party of Baltimore oystermen encamped on the point, among whom was a man named Alley, who had abandoned his wife. The deserted woman followed up her husband, and found him at the camp. After some conversation had passed between them, the man induced her, upon some unknown pretext, to accompany him into a thicket. The poor wife never came out alive. Her husband cruelly murdered her with a club. The point of land has ever since been known by Peg Alley's name, and her perturbed spirit has been supposed to haunt the scene of her untimely taking off. About twelve years ago a gang of rail-splitters were at work on the point, and one day the foreman flatly refused to go back, declaring that queer things happened down there, and that he had seen a ghost. Mr. Kennedy, his employer, laughed at him and dismissed the matter from his mind. Sometime after this Mr. Kennedy had occasion to ride through the woods to look after some sheep, there being but one road and the water on either side. As he approached the point his horse started violently and refused to go on, regardless of whip or spur. Glancing about for the cause of this unnatural fright, he saw a woman rise up from a log, a few yards in advance, and stand by the roadside, looking at him. She was very poorly clad in a faded calico dress, and wore a limp sun-bonnet, from beneath which her thin, jet-black hair straggled down on her shoulders; her face was thin and sallow and her eyes black and piercing. Knowing that she had no business there, and occupied in controlling his horse, he called to her somewhat angrily to get out of the way, as his animal was afraid of her. Slowly she turned and walked into the thicket, uttering not a syllable and looking reproachfully at him as she went. With much difficulty he forced his horse to the spot, hoping to find out who the strange intruder might be, but the most careful search failed to reveal the trace of anyone, although there was no place of concealment and no possible way of escape, for which, indeed, there was not sufficient time.

Cincinnati [OH] Enquirer 6 November 1886: p. 11 MARYLAND

Mrs. W. Fred Pettit was murdered in 1889 by her minister husband, who administered strychnine, not once, but several times, possibly at the urging of his mistress, Mrs. Whitehead. The victim is said to still haunt her husband's former church. Shockingly, one of the first witnesses to the ghost of Mrs. Pettit, was the father of Mrs. Whitehead, who had swiftly disowned his daughter over the affair.

AN INDIANA SPECTER
Mrs. Pettit's Ghost Said to Haunt the Vicinity of Shawnee Mound.

The beautiful country neighborhood of Shawnee Mound, in Tippecanoe County, is much exercised over the weird ghost stories which are afloat in regard to the Shawnee Methodist Church, which is said to be haunted, says a telegram to the Chicago *News* from Crawfordsville. The people of Shawnee Mound compose the wealthiest and most enlightened class of country folk in this section of the State, and it is from some of the most reputable of the citizens that the stories come. The Rev. J.E. Clark is pastor of the haunted church, his predecessor being W. Fred Pettit, now serving a life sentence in the Northern Penitentiary for the murder of his wife by strychnine poison. It is the ghost of this murdered lady which is said to haunt the church, for which she loved to labor in her lifetime. The famous trial and conviction of the Rev. Mr. Pettit last November for his crime in the summer of 1889 are still fresh in mind, and it is only since the jury's verdict that these ghostly visitations in the church have been begun by a spirit whose body lies buried far off in New York state.

These ghost stories did not gain general currency till about the middle of December. Since a number of prominent citizens have seen the ghost, however, another aspect is given the affair, although there are still a few who scoff. The "ghost walk" is between the parsonage and the church, a distance of several hundred yards, along an unfrequented and private path first made by the Rev. Pettit during his pastorate there. The ghost is never seen in the parsonage or about the yard, but usually from about halfway to the church until it glides through the front door, which though always locked, seems to readily open to the ghost. The apparition is never seen to leave the edifice, and always, shortly after its entrance the organ can be heard giving forth the hymns which were dearest to Mrs. Pettit during her lifetime.

Jonathan Meharry [his name was actually David], father of Mrs. Whitehead, thus narrates his experience with the unearthly visitor:

"It was on one of those moonlit Wednesday nights in February, about 11 o'clock, that I approached the Shawnee church on my way home from Wingate. I was tired, and, I expect, was dozing a little on my seat, when directly in front of the church my horse stopped still, with a snort that thoroughly aroused me. I looked at him and saw that he was trembling in every limb; his ears were thrust forward and he seemed paralyzed with fear of some approaching danger. I raised my eyes and saw that which gave me as great a turn as it did old Bird. Coming directly down Fred Pettit's path to my right and about one hundred yards from the church, was what looked to me for all the world like Mrs. Pettit, wearing the same traveling dress from which she returned from South Bend just before her death. My emotions were strange and indefinite, and after having passed my hand over my eyes as if to remove the illusion I became quiet through a fascination whose power I was unable to shake off, but which rendered my mind wonderfully clear and susceptible to an impression of what I saw. I had heard of the ghost from others, and though no spiritualist, I was wholly unprepared for any such manifestation as I beheld.

"The ghost came on down the path directly toward me, and I had a remarkably good view of the features by the light of the moon. A more troubled face I never saw, and the lips moved constantly as though in prayer, just as I had often observed her pray silently in services during her lifetime.

"Arrived at the corner of the church the spirit turned and proceeded directly to the door. Reaching the threshold she paused, raised her arms toward heaven and wrung her hands in a supplicating manner. The position was retained for several seconds, when she pushed open the door, which yielded noiselessly and so closed after her. Almost immediately the air was filled with the strains of 'Rock of Ages.' The music was from the organ but it was unearthly and grewsome. The first selection was followed by another unfamiliar, yet ineffably sweet, which died away in the strain that filled the soul with religious rapture. How long I sat there after the music ceased I cannot say, but I was aroused from my lethargy by old Bird breaking into a trot which soon left the church behind."

The experience of Mr. Meharry has been that of several others, and no one can account for the appearance save by conjectures, which are numerous and varied.

Logansport [IN] Journal 9 July 1891: p. 3 INDIANA

NOTE: The Rev. W.[illiam] Fred Pettit was the popular and energetic minister of the Methodist church in Shawnee Mound. His wife was a woman devoted to her church, home, and child. Pettit's intimacy with the wealthy and widowed

Mrs. Elma C. Whitehead was noted and he was asked to resign his ministry. He then took up law (he later returned to the ministry) and very kindly drew up a will for Mrs. Whitehead's father, Mr. Meharry. The papers pointed out that the minister had a good idea of Mrs. Whitehead's expectations, adding, "The most liberal men would hesitate to call her attractive, and it is difficult to assign a reason for Mr. Pettit's devotion to her, unless it was some power hidden from the casual eye." Whatever her fascinations, they were enough to tempt the former minister to buy strychnine and give several doses to his wife, who told her doctor that there was poison in the cup of tea her husband had given her. The doctor originally certified death by "acute malarial poisoning," not wishing to upset the family with his "suspicions." Mrs. Whitehead was indicted as well, but upon being released on bail, fled the state until the trial was over, so she would not have to testify. She was painted in the press either as a designing woman or the victim of an unscrupulous murderer. She died in 1899. Pettit had extracted a promise from her to marry him once his wife was dead. One wonders what her life expectancy would have been had Pettit gotten away with his wife's murder.

FURTHER READING: For an admirably extensive compendium of 19th-century murder, see Robert Wilhelm's Murder by Gaslight site: http://www.murderbygaslight.com/. Two excellent books on (primarily) 19th-century murder (sans ghosts) are *Victorian Studies in Scarlet*, Richard Altick and *The Enjoyment of Murder*, William Roughead.

11.

The Wild Man of Stamford

Forgotten Fortean Mysteries

I am a collector of notes upon subjects that have diversity — such as
deviations from concentricity in the lunar crater Copernicus, and a sudden
appearance of purple Englishmen — stationary meteor-radiants, and a
reported growth of hair on the bald head of a mummy — and 'Did the girl
swallow the octopus?'

-Charles Fort-

One of the more enjoyable features of studying 19th-century newspapers is discovering fantastical Fortean tales. If not simply fictional, they probably have logical explanations, but they are so wonderfully pointless and they amuse rather than educate or elevate. Big snake (or snaix, as they were jocularly known) stories were a perennial favorite. This snake story, as they say, caps the climax.

UP AGAINST IT.
What A Farmer Says He Saw.
A Snake of Fire Thirty Feet Long Confronts Him
It Cavorts in the Atmosphere, Encircles the Barn.
Then Rises Into Space, Bursts and Dissolves.
A Dog in the Barn Dies and Turns to Stone
While the Horses Are Riveted To the Floor in Their Stalls.
The Farmer Either Electrified By Paralysis or Paralyzed By
Electricity, But He Talks.

Delphi, Ind., February 24. The home of Mark Weston, situated near Alexandria, a small town south-east of this city, is now the center of attraction for hundreds of curious people, drawn by one of the most remarkable phenomenon ever recorded in this section. The people who have visited the scene gaze in awe upon the startling work wrought by some indescribable power. The story was graphically told by Mr. Weston to your correspondent to-day, and is verified by witnesses.

He says: "Just after dark night before last I had occasion to go out to the barn to look after the horses. A public highway passes within 200 yards of my house, and the barn is built about twenty rods from the house due south and somewhat nearer the road. I started from the house in the direction of the barn and had gone perhaps half the distance when I noticed something playing along the ground that looked like a tremendous fiery snake. The object crossed my path, and as it did so I felt the air grow much colder, and

A PECULIAR, MOANING SOUND

Arose, like the sighing of the wind through the trees, only it was loud enough to drown a man's voice when he would shout. Then I felt something come over me like electricity, and I became motionless, as though I had grown fast to the ground.

"I was terribly scared, but I never lost the use of my hands or legs through fear, though there was something peculiar in the air that simply paralyzed me. When the thing had got perhaps fifty feet from me going west it turned and came back, and as it did so the moaning sound changed to a shrill whistle, something like a locomotive would make, and when it got just in front of me it took a course directly away from me and toward the barn. It traveled very rapidly and looked like a large, ragged streak of fire, perhaps thirty feet long and eighteen inches in diameter. The thing reached the barn, and in almost an instant ran directly up the front of the building and onto the roof. I expected every moment to see the barn

BURST INTO FLAMES

But it did not. The great fiery snake ran with great rapidity all over the building, in almost every direction, up and down, cross-wise and every way, I suppose, a thousand times. The thing came to the front of the building and elevated itself until it stood straight on its tail fully thirty feet in the air. I was perfectly conscious all the time, but try as I would I could not move from the spot. After the thing had remained in an upright position for, I presume, three or four minutes, there was a sudden explosion like the discharge of a cannon, and the thing disappeared entirely. With the disappearance of the strange phenomenon I felt a shock like the first one I had felt and at the same time I gained control of my limbs. I hastened to the house, told my wife what I had seen and she thought I was crazy, but upon my insisting she consented to accompany me to investigate the matter at daylight.

"You can imagine our surprise upon reaching the barn to find it covered with

A REMARKABLE NET-WORK

Resembling large ropes of ice. They appeared to pass around the building in exactly the way the fiery monster had passed. It was not ice, however, but seemed to be more of a crystal, for it would not melt even when we held a flame to it, and when struck with a hatchet it simply gave a dull-like sound and did not break. Upon entering the barn we were amazed as two good horses stood in their stall immovable. They were alive, but neither could move a muscle. They seemed to be paralyzed and stood there more like statues than anything else. They were warm and breathed all right, but aside from this you could not tell they were alive. I applied the whip and they never flinched. A dog that sleeps in the barn

WAS DEAD

And appeared completely petrified. He was lying on the ground with his head on his paws just like he was sleeping. When I left home this afternoon everything was just as I have described it to you." Mr. Weston says that the house has been visited by hundreds of people and that the entire community are marveling at the strange and weird visitation. He has taken his wife and family to a neighboring farm house and says he will not return till every evidence of the strange phenomenon has disappeared.

Cincinnati [OH] Enquirer 25 February 1893: p. 9 INDIANA

NOTE: This marvelously bizarre story nevertheless tells of some features that are consistent with lightning strikes or ball lightning. Some lightning-struck corpses appear completely rigid with rigor mortis—petrified does not necessarily mean turned to stone. The horses, with a larger body mass and standing further off the ground, might have been merely paralyzed instead of killed. Depending on whether the roof of the barn was slate or tin, lightning could have crystallized or drawn something out of the material, causing the strange ice-like network. Those diverting speculations aside, Alexandria is about 70 miles and several counties away from Delphi and Mark Weston does not appear in the census or grave reports. I have noticed that the *Cincinnati Enquirer*, while often a sober and respectable chronicler of the day's news, seems to have gone a bit giddy when reporting stories from the neighboring state of Indiana.

This next story has the appearance of being a candid look at what started out as a journalistic hoax about a wild man. In a classic case of ostension, the wild man suddenly sprang from legend into vivid, real-life accounts. (Or was it a local conspiracy of pranksters?) A plausible explanation is then given, long after the fact, which does not quite explain all sightings of the creature. It must also be noted that this alleged history of the wild man was printed 50 years after the original "scare" and written by a "principal in its exploitation." However, the articles that follow it are from the 1860s and '70s and may corroborate some of the sightings in this story.

THE STAMFORD WILD MAN
A BERKSHIRE SCARE OF 1861
THE MYSTERY STILL UNSOLVED
Though a Principal in Its Exploitation Here Gives
Some Explanation.

[Written by William H. Phillips for *The Sunday Republican*.]
There are yet living in North Adams and in the northern towns of Berkshire County and in the extreme southern tier of towns of Vermont a few persons who have a memory of what was known in the summer of 1861 as the "Stamford wild man." It is now over 50 years since this mysterious character, whose real personality will ever remain a myth, threw the citizens of all this region into genuine paroxysms of fright, from which it took several months to recover.

The public origin of the Stamford wild man, whatever might have been his personal right to existence, was due to a scarcity of local news on one rainy day in 1861, just after the first northern Berkshire troops had gone to the front in the civil war. *The North Adams Transcript*, after having just been combined with the *Hoosac Valley News* by W.H. Phillips, was printed in the North Adams house block, now the site of the Wilson house. Its editor, note-book in hand, had just canvassed the then village for a customary weekly batch of items, and found its places of business and citizens full of gloom and inactivity over the perilous state of affairs in the nation, with more than a Sunday stillness pervading every locality. Sitting down in his sanctum, he ran his hands wildly through his hair and tried to think up some subject for an editorial, or for local mention, but in vain, when suddenly [he found] a scrap of loose paper on which was penciled that "a queer old chap, clothed in rags, with long hair and unkempt beard had been recently seen in Stamford." This was enough; something must be had to fill the columns of the paper, and some great excitement was needed to break up the general gloom and monotony which had spread over the locality like a pall of darkness, and this was the opportunity. Then the editor, with this slight building material in hand, and a heavy draft upon his imagination, proceeded to paint a picture of what he called the "wild man of Stamford" which was fairly terrifying. Such was the depressed state of the public mind over national events and prostrated business that the majority of the editor's readers swallowed the temptingly baited announcement with greedy avidity, but a very few wiseacres feebly protested if at all.

The article, which came like a clap of thunder out of a clear sky, was extensively copied and credited to the *Transcript* by the daily and weekly newspapers in the northern states, the only doubt as to its veracity being courteously made by the *Troy Daily Times*, which placed a pound of interrogation points (which no one but editors understood), and the end of an item referring to this wild man, while Editor Ben Cook of the *Bennington Banner* advised the *Transcript* editor "to throw aside the pen and types and take up the profession of a portrait painter." This accouchement of the Stamford wild man was the first and last imaginative pen work of this editor, the eyes and imagination of the public doing all the work for him afterward, while he jovially acted as its amanuensis. Before his next week's issue, July 25, 1861, Stephen B. Willard and several prominent gentlemen from Stamford called at the *Transcript* office and reported that they had had a glimpse of this mysterious creature, while it was reported that Burlingame & Ray of North Adams were entirely out of locks, padlocks and window fasteners, this dearth having been caused by the citizens of Stamford, who previous to this time in their peaceful security had never thought of locking up their houses either by day or night. Besides, in this issue of the *Transcript* appeared this article, the facts therein being communicated by the parties mentioned therein: Last week, while Curtis Wilbor of Stamford was hunting on the mountains east of Wilmarth's Tavern, he came upon what he supposed was a large animal digging roots. He took aim and shot, but his gun hanging fire, thereupon said animal straightened up to the size and stature of a seven-foot man, covered with hair from head to foot, and with an unearthly yell, started off into the dense woods with the fleetness of a deer, while Wilbor, overcome by this strange appearance, made his feet fly as fast as possible in the direction of home. A body of armed citizens at once urged Wilbor to retrace his steps in the attempt to capture this creature, but such was his fear that he could not be persuaded to visit the scene of his encounter. This inflamed the citizens to a high pitch of excitement, several of them affirming that they had heard the cries of this strange being in the nighttime. The next day a pursuing party discovered the footprints, or resemblance to feet of a monster human being, by the side of the mountain road, which Wilbor insisted the strange being crossed, and halloing loudly, they affirmed that the creature answered back with prolonged howls.

Many See the Wild Man.

By this time quite a crowd of reliable men in Stamford and Clarksburg, had reported that they had caught a glimpse of what they termed a "wild man," or had heard his shrieks in the forests adjoining their farm-houses and nearly all the population of North Adams as well, believed that some lunatic, entirely destitute of clothing, was wandering about in the woods, and there was a loud call for a formidable posse of citizens having firearms, to turn out and hunt him down. Besides, it was in the height of the berry-picking season, and the women and children having entirely deserted their usual harvest fields, the price of all small wild fruits were quadrupled and the general scarceness seemed to inaugurate a berry famine. Besides there was no need of a curfew bell; as children as well as men and women were very careful to hide beneath the family roof-tree for the night, as soon as the sun dropped behind the western mountains. Then, too, the evidence had become so strong that some wild and mysterious wanderer was skulking among the foothills of the Green and Hoosac Mountain fastnesses, clothed only in garments alone provided by the invisible looms and shuttles of Nature, that hardly a single doubting Thomas remained in the field.

Described by the Pierce Boys.

Then this item appeared in the columns of the *Transcript*, under the date of August 1, 1861:

Two brothers named Pierce of Stamford, having been attracted by the noise of strange howlings in the woods near their homes, courageously concluded to hunt out the object of these outcries. Placing double charges in their guns, they cautiously ascended the East mountain side, when they suddenly came in sight of a creature, which they describe as being six feet in hight [sic] bearing great resemblance to the human form, the body being covered with long, coarse, black hair, with a luxuriant mass of the same crowning the head and face. With a fierce howl the creature rushed upon the Pierce boys, one of whom leveled his gun and fired upon it, but was so frightened that he missed his aim and his bullet fell far wide of its mark. Dropping his powder flask in his terror, both he and his brother came tearing down the steep mountainside at a breakneck speed, and the mystery still remaining unsolved, the community was thrown into a still greater panic than ever, and no one in the town pretended to step out beyond the threshold of the house after nightfall.

Then came a perfect whirlwind of reports of the appearance and pranks of this mysterious creature who seems to have been left to amuse himself as full master of the situation. A man named Sitterly of Stamford was awakened at midnight by loud thumpings on the door and sides of his house. Crawling out of bed, he went to a window and caught sight of the creature and called out to know what was wanted, when, with an unearthly shriek it fled from the yard.

A party who were picking berries just north of the Beaver Mill suddenly sighted this strange creature who approached them with swinging arms and uttering a wild gibberish, which drove them from the field in reckless haste, leaving their pails and baskets behind them. One of this party was certain that the creature bore resemblance to a chimpanzee or African baboon, which gave rise to a report that it was an animal that had escaped from some traveling menagerie. Quite a number of farmers were also certain that it had killed and eaten sheep in their mountain pasture, while some asserted that it had milked their cows in their yards after nightfall. Another report that gained much credence was that a small cave had been discovered in Stamford, which was evidently one of the creature's retreats and bones found at its mouth were said to have been sent to Amherst and Williams College authorities for examination.

The Flames Fanned Again.

Then there appeared in the *Transcript's* issue of August 8, 1861, an article which again raised public curiosity to the highest pitch and which read as follows:

Dexter Smith and William Hoale of this village, while riding past a piece of woods north of the Noble Smith farm, in Stamford one day last week, observed a hideous-looking object, covered with rags and hair, with a long beard. As it suddenly emerged from the skirt of the woods, it uttered a shriek, making horrid grimaces at them, and repeatedly thrust out its tongue. They judged that the creature was about six feet in height and declared that is appearance was enough to startle the nervous organization of anyone up to a high degree of tension. At any rate they vamoosed the locality as soon as possible. In the same issue was noted the fact that while two young men were blue-berrying on the Pine Cone to the north of Blackinton on the previous Monday, a creature answering most of the previous descriptions of the Stamford wild man made its appearance on the rocks at the summit of the pinnacle, and after a number of hideous contortions of body and face, with an unearthly yell made off into the woods. Whereupon the boys made the best of time in a flight homeward, where they arrived in a thoroughly frightened condition. A party of Blackinton hunters started out at once in pursuit of the creature, but it successfully eluded them.

All through the month of August 1861, the wild man seemed to be fairly ubiquitous in the manner and places of his appearance. He was next seen in Florida, where several persons were badly frightened, and evidently descended the mountain from this locality into South Adams, where he put to panic flight a score of juveniles who were berrying in Bowen's woods. A few days after he was seen in the woods in the same vicinity by a lad named Marsh and a colored boy, both of whom fled for home in great affright, leaving their berry baskets behind them; as also on the next day by a valiant crowd of women berry pickers, who then and there gave up that industry for the season. The next Sunday a grand hunt was instituted by the village hunters, who fell upon the trail of the creature, but which finally evaded them by lunging into a dense swamp, into which they dared not follow.

Williams Students Interested.

It was at this juncture that a number of Williams College students thought to have a little fun over this wild man and the citizens of North Adams and Stamford who were on the keen lookout for him. Thereupon they made a huge scarecrow in the shape of half-man and half-beast, and hiring a shed of L. Jaquith on Holden Street set it up therein, a huge chain confining the image to a stout post. They then conveyed the image thereto under the cover of night and placarded the village with the announcement that the wild man of Stamford had been captured and confined, noting the place of his imprisonment, and stating that he could be seen free of charge. All one forenoon Holden Street was thronged with the curious from all the region roundabout to see this creature, and the memory of their being so grossly humbugged was never an enjoyable one.

The final appearance of the supposed Stamford wild man in that staid old Vermont town and near the villages in extreme northern Berkshire was so thoroughly convincing that this character was not a myth or a fable, that if anyone doubted if such a character really existed except in vivid imaginations, he kept it to himself, for fear of general ridicule. In the *Transcript* issue of September 1, 1861, appeared this article:

Daniel Workman, the veteran ambrotypist and photographist of this village, whose gallery is in the third story of the North Adams house, and directly above the office of the *Transcript*, relates to us a strange experience, which he passed through with a friend near the summit of the high mountain directly north of this village. Last Friday afternoon in company with his dear friend, Rev. Mr. Torrey, a noted New York Universalist minister, he ascended the North Mountain to avail himself of an outlook over northern Berkshire and southern Vermont, a beautiful scenic view of natural beauty and wildness only to be seen from this grand eminence. They had made no change in their costumes for this mountain ascension and therefore their garments were their Sunday best. They had spent a full hour on the lovely mountain top and side and a feeling of thoroughly gratified sense and quiet had stolen over them, when out of the bushes jumped the Stamford wild man, at once recognized from the printed descriptions which had been previously given in the *Transcript* of this strange creature, and of whose real existence Workman confessed himself to have been skeptical, a state of mind which he said he no longer enjoyed. Covered with hair and tatterdemalion rags, with a huge pole or club in one of his hands, in the wink of an eye the creature planted himself directly in front of them. As every nerve in their bodies was trembling with fear, he wildly looked down upon them from his high raised head, being fully six feet in height. Then, to their astonishment, he offered his hand as it were in friendship, whereupon, though being far from bold, but always being held to be polite, Workman shook hands with him with all the courage he could master, his friend being very pale and very much alarmed for fear he would do them bodily injury, as they were both unarmed even to a walking stick. Trying to appear careless, Workman asked the creature a few questions, and gained not a syllable in reply. Finally with a vacant stare the creature placed one hand upon his breast, and swinging his club in the other with strange murmurings made a few outlandish motions and disappeared into the bushes as suddenly as he had appeared. It was a fact that they descended the mountain without taking into account wood roads, paths or trails, their garments bearing distinct marks of their struggles through thickets and undergrowth, having seen enough of the untamed beauties and mysteries of Nature for a single day.

The next appearance of this creature was a week later in North Pownal, where it put to flight a bevy of berry pickers in a high pasture fronted by a precipice. A few days later, bearing the same description as first given of it in Stamford, it followed a school-teacher in Pownal with maniacal gestures, contortions of countenance and screams until she was nearly frightened out of her senses. Soon after an armed party of 16 men got on its track and pursued it. One of these is said to have overtaken it and was so overcome by its appearance that he dared not fire or lay hands on it. It was thus that the Stamford wild man passed out of range of the *Transcript's* correspondents, but it was soon heard of in another field, while its pranks and sudden appearances were carefully chronicled for several weeks by Editor Ben Cook of the *Bennington Banner*, who even up to the appearance of the creature in Pownal had had the temerity to doubt that there was such a character. Thus the *Banner* authenticated the creature's appearance in Woodford, North Bennington and on the old Bennington battlefield in a number of its weekly editions, his pen portraits being about the same as those which had been given in the *Transcript*.

Then this mysterious creature suddenly disappeared from Vermont, upon which the editor of the *Banner* facetiously asked the editor of the *Transcript* in his local columns what had become of the "Stamford wild man," to which the editor of the *Transcript* as facetiously replied "that the last that he knew of the Stamford wild man was that he was publishing a newspaper called the *Bennington Banner*."

Editorial Amenities

A half-dozen copies of the *Transcript* were mailed to subscribers in Bennington every week, and a few lovers of humor, who had their place of gathering in a store in the old Adams block in that town, gathered together the copies containing this laughable retort on the home editor, and organized a squad to take a copy one by one up three flights of stairs in that building and point out the squib to the editor and to inquire "if he had seen it." These jokers so wrought upon the somewhat hot temper of the editor that before the newspapers were all worn out by rough handling he himself was fairly wild. Finally this sport was brought to an abrupt termination by the jokers persuading an innocent old farmer named Page, who was going up to the editorial sanctum to pay his subscription, to hand the editor the *Transcript* and ask him the regular stereotyped question "if he had seen it."

This harmless old agriculturalist trudged into the sanctum with the paper in his hand, and so angered became the editor at the oft-repeated and exasperating sight that he snatched up the first thing which came to his hand, which proved to be his well-filled inkstand, and hurled it at Page, with the result that both men were terribly bespattered, as well as was the sanctum itself. Just as the irate old farmer was about to administer a well-merited pummeling to the irate scribe, the latter bust out in a loud laugh, realizing that a gang of village jokers had made their scheme a howling success, and explaining the situation to Farmer Page, calmed him down by presenting him with a $5 old Stark bank bill and a receipt for the *Banner* for one year, at the same time making him take an oath to keep the affair secret. Then he piloted him down the rear stairs, that he might escape the notice of Steve Bingham and his fun-loving crowd. But they had their eyes too keenly fixed on the situation, and before the old gentleman had gone a block away overhauled him and secured a full account of the escapade, in which they were abetted by Mrs. Page, who demanded of him the cause of his bespattered garments, looking, as she said, as though he had "been bathing in the Black Sea, or sleeping on the top of Stephen Evans's huge grapevine arbor."

However, much of the truth or private or public imagination, there might have been in the tales about the Stamford wild man and his exploits, it was always a subject of keen satisfaction to the editor of the *Transcript* that this character came so prominently to the front as thoroughly to absorb public attention at a time when the clouds of gloom caused by the outbreak of the civil war and the departure of the male members of so many families to the front in patriotic response to the call of Abraham Lincoln for troops to save the country, as for a time fairly to stagnate all channels of business and so completely to discourage all classes of the people as, it might be said, to render them incompetent to perform the duties due not only to themselves, but to those who had gone forth to do battle for the perpetuity of the republic. At any rate, the pranks of the Stamford wild man so locally broke in upon this mental and physical torpor at this time that the curiosity and fright which they engendered for a short but trying period of time fairly drove our national troubles to the wall.

Amusement for the Campfire.

Besides this, quite a number of *Transcripts* were mailed each week to members of Co. B, 10th Massachusetts regiment in their camp at Fair Oaks, Va., and other localities in which the regiment was located in the early years of the war. It was afterward learned that the company faithfully watched for this appearance of the home paper, reading its every column, advertisements and all, with the greatest interest, discussing the local items appearing therein around the mess table and while lying or sitting around their campfires. When the *Transcript* first arrived those off duty after dark chose their best reader in the several tent groups, seated him on a barrel, with a torchbearer on each side, and silently listened to the good and bad news from Berkshire.

Returning members of Co. B. afterward affirmed that these *Transcripts* were then passed over to members of the other companies in the regiment, and in turn by them to the soldiers in other northern regiments for perusal until the sheets were worn to tatters. They also reported that the account of the pranks of the Stamford wild man afforded all one of the greatest treats they had in the first year of the war, and that on the receipt of the paper this news was the first that the "barrel-reader" was called upon to look up. The guessing as to what this creature might be, the character and eccentricities of those who were reported to have caught sight of it, and the history and appearance of the localities in which it presented itself were themes of thrilling interest, and reclaimed many an hour on the part of these Western Massachusetts troops from sadness, homesickness and gloomy doubts and forebodings.

Still a Mystery.

In conclusion it can be stated that in 1866 a company of gentleman holding a session in the *Transcript* sanctum in the old North Adams house, on a certain evening, at which was present the editor, three prominent pastors of the then village, two members of the legal profession and physicians, were agreeably interrupted by the entrance of Daniel Workman, the veteran photographer. Much to the nervousness and chagrin of the editor, the physician began to question Mr. Workman in regard to the appearance of the wild man seen by Rev. Mr. Torrey and himself on the North Mountain in September, 1861. The general appearance of this character Mr. Workman faithfully described, it being about the same as already given in this article. But when he spoke of the stare the creature gave him and his strange mutterings as he swept off under cover of the bushes, the doctor exclaimed: "I thought it was a humbug invention of a mischievous editor from the first, for the creature you saw and which scared you out of your boots was no other than old Pollard's idiot. I have long been the physician of the Pollard family, who live in a little clearing on the north side of that mountain. They have a grown-up son who is a hopeless idiot, who in the warmer months they allow to roam at will into the North Mountain woods, as he is perfectly harmless." Much to the disquiet of the editor and of Mr. Workman, one of the mysterious later appearances of the supposed Stamford wild man was thus thoroughly accounted for. Yet the mystery of the original Stamford wild man and his long list of appearances in Stamford and other localities has never been satisfactorily explained. He may have been a pioneer member of the great tramp family of today, a mischievous maniac, a veritable wild hermit of the woodlands, or a disguised mountain marauder subsisting on wild berries and on milk and meat supplies seized from hillside farms and homesteads. As the first general and unwelcome disturber of the peace and quiet of dwellers outside the village settlements in the vicinage of the Green and Hoosac mountains at any rate he was the first and last successful specimen of his kind known among the northern Berkshire and southern Vermont hills.

The Springfield [MA] Sunday Republican 9 November 1913: p. 16
MASSACHUSETTS and VERMONT

NOTE: While the preceding article purports to be a late look back at the Stamford Wildman story, what follows are several 19th-century pieces connected with the story. I have found few articles on the wild man from the 1860s. Do we reluctantly conclude that the preceding article is another item created "due to a scarcity of local news on one rainy day" in 1913?

BIG HUMBUG

It is believed that there is a wild man in the woods between North Adams and Stamford. He has been seen several times, and his shrieks at night have been heard. There was a report in North Adams last Monday that the wild man had been captured, and hundreds wended their way to a place where the strange man was said to be confined. Crowds entered the shed and gazed upon the strange being, who was chained and immoveable in the corner, with a long beard and glassy eyes. Men went so far as to shut up their stores and discontinue business to take a peep at this celebrated individual, while crinoline from the factories and dwellings crowded the highway in eager haste. After a large number had been humbugged by an image which was got up for the frolicsome students of Williamstown, the hoax leaked out.

Pittsfield Berkshire [MA] County Eagle 15 August 1861: p. 2
MASSACHUSETTS

The "wild man" who has terrified the women and children of Adams and Clarksburg and several towns in that vicinity, for two summers past, has been caught and thrashed gloriously, and is therefore in a fair way to recover from his wildness. His name is Ed. Johnson.

Pittsfield Berkshire [MA] County Eagle 2 July 1863: p. 2
MASSACHUSETTS

NOTE: As you see, Ed Johnson was not mentioned in the 1913 article, although the Williamstown student "humbug" was.

This 1879 report of an "enraged maniac" is again ambiguous as to the creature's species.

TWO TERRIFIED HUNTERS
Chased Out of the Berkshire Hills by an Enraged Maniac on Whom They Fired.

From the New York *Sun.*

Pittsfield, Mass., Oct. 16. Two Vermont hunters, John Simmons and William Shegan, aver that they met with a strange adventure a day or two since on "Pine Scrabble" Peak, just east of Blackinton Village, four miles north of North Adams. This pine-capped peak was, some years ago, the resort of wild animals, and of late it has been seldom visited. The story of the hunters is that, while hunting in the vicinity of this mountain, they heard a slight noise near a rugged cliff, and saw a huge, hairy object, apparently half man and half beast, spring from behind the cliff and start for the woods, running with the speed of the wind. Mistaking it for a wild animal, one of the hunters fired at it. The shot appeared to take effect in the arm, for, with a scream of pain, the creature halted, tapped the wound, and, turning, charged its pursuers, who, with empty guns in hand, dared not measure strength with such a foe. Dropping their guns both sought safety in flight and stopped only when compelled to do so for lack of ability to run further. The men say that they are positive that the creature resembled a man in its general appearance. It was wild-eyed, and very fierce in its disposition, judging from the short time they saw it.

The hunters' story revives a long forgotten, but now distinctly re-called yarn to the effect that many years ago a lunatic, then a young man, escaped from his keepers from somewhere near the New York State line, and gained the mountain fastnesses, where he evaded pursuit, and, it is thought, subsisted on berries and the flesh of animals killed through some means best known to himself. Several years later a strange creature, answering the description of the being recently seen, with the exception of the grizzly beard, was discovered by a party of children where were berry-ing on the mountain, and it is thought that this may be the same.

The hunters say that they are positive that it was no optical illusion, but a genuine wild man, and a very fierce one at that. The creature's arms, they say, were long and hairy, and it looked very much like a full-grown gorilla. They aver that it ran with remarkable swiftness, all the time ut-tering loud cries, as though in pain and enraged. They declare that it was only by their utmost exertion that they escaped their pursuer, and they say that there is not money enough in Massachusetts to hire them to again venture across its path.

There is talk of organizing an armed force in Williamstown to go in search of the creature.

Daily Inter Ocean [Chicago, IL] 24 October 1879: p. 10
MASSACHUSETTS and VERMONT

NOTE: A search of the 19th-century Springfield, Massachusetts papers revealed over 900 stories about "wildmen," nearly all of them from other states.

There were a shocking number of "wild man" stories in the papers in general, from the earliest times and they are written using language ("bestial" "hairy" "maniac") that makes it difficult to tell whether a hermit, a lunatic, or a non-human animal is involved. A particular epidemic of wild men stories in the 1870s may reflect a high incidence of mental illness among Civil War veterans.

This next curious little story from the Great War received scant newspaper coverage and there seems to have been no resolution to the story. The *Jackson Citizen Patriot* is the source for many a Fortean tale. It is difficult to know if this was an editorial policy—when a certain Warren G. Harding was editor of the *Marion Star*, for example, he never met a ghost yarn or a big snake story he didn't like—or if the *Patriot* had some inventive writers on staff. The people mentioned in this article, however, are real enough. I may not be casting my newspaper net wide enough, but why is the main source for this Texas story a Michigan paper?

If a genuine record of events, was this a psychokinetic event set in motion by the worries of a mother with two soldier sons? Was it random bug paths interpreted as a map of Europe? It is certainly possible that the "specialist in making maps" altered the image, perhaps subconsciously, to create a more "accurate" image of Europe. There is always the notion that it was merely a simulacrum like the face of Dean Vaughan seen in mold on the wall of Llandaff Cathedral or the Virgin Mary in a tree stump. There is also the obvious answer: it was a hoax inspired by a dirty ceiling to relieve the monotony of small-town life.

"GHOST MAP" APPEARS ON COTTAGE WALL; UNSEEN HANDS OUTLINE WAR ZONE
Little Texas Town Agog Over Weird Tracery That Limns Europe's Battleground

By Marie Barnett

Dallas, Tex., March 11. One of the most mysterious cases of "handwriting on the wall" since Daniel's time has set agog the flourishing little town of Gainesville and the country for a hundred miles around.

At the home of Mr. and Mrs. Nathaniel Vice, 205 Broadway on the morning of Jan. 18, there appeared in the natural gas soot which had collected on the ceiling of the front room a mysterious white streak, which during the weeks that followed, gradually assumed well-defined shape.

When complete, it was identified by soldiers returning from Europe as a perfect map of the war zone. On one side of the map was a serpent, scaley and coiled; on the other side was the head of a man.

Clyde Denton, a Gainesville citizen who is a specialist in making maps, made a sketch of the unique outlines and found that he had a map identical in shape with the European countries that took part in the war.

"The entire battle line was pictured," Denton declared. "Little dots marked off the advancing armies, just as countless newspaper maps in America had pictured from day to day the movements of the troops."

Identified by Soldier.

An army officer, Lieut. Pierce, of Whitesboro, made a trip to Gainesville to see the mysterious map. He pointed out the place where he had landed in Europe, and the location of the battles in which he had fought.

Mrs. Elinor Hancock, who lives in Dallas, returned home from a visit to Gainesville and told friends about the strange affair.

"The old country is clearly outlined," she said. "At one side of the map there is a snake. On the other side is a head which was thought by some to be President Wilson, and by others to be Taft or Roosevelt. I couldn't decide whose features they were."

How the pictures got there no one knows, except that it was not the work of human hands. Perhaps an insect crawling through the thin coating of soot left the strange tracery, or possibly it was steam from the tea kettle that caused the lines to form and dots to appear, just as little pathways trickle across the window of a warm room on a cold day.

But many persons tinged with the instinctive mysticism of humanity, insist that ghostly fingers fashioned in the night an outline of the nations at war, these nations whose dead are numberless.

The home is humble and they who live there are plain and simple. Mrs. Vice keeps boarders. When Oklahoma natural gas replaced Texas gas in Gainesville, Mrs. Vice says, her stoves smoked considerably until readjusted. Thus a fine black powder coated the paper on ceiling and walls.

"On the morning of Jan. 18, when I woke up," she says, "I noticed a white streak a foot or so long, glaring conspicuously in the soot, very much as though white twice had been pasted there.

Busy with her morning meal and subsequent cleaning up, Mrs. Vice dismissed the strange occurrence. But the next morning she found the line had lengthened and was beginning to take shape.

During the next few weeks the work of formation went on, precise and mysterious. Finally, one of the boarders, an Irishman, called attention to the definite forms the lines were taking. The snake had appeared by now, and the human face.

Said the man from the Land of the Banshee.

"It's the doing of the spirits."

And so the word went out that strange things were going on in the little home on Broadway.

The first modern "Daniel" who interpreted the map was a soldier just returned from France. He pointed out the numerous dots as the battle line. He traced the boundaries of Belgium and France and Germany.

Crowds, first from Gainesville and later from miles around, began flocking to the little home, watching the gradual growth of the map from day to day as it spread with uncanny accuracy, across the ceiling and down the wall.

Visitors so completely upset Mrs. Vice's work that she had to get a neighbor to receive the callers. The map specialist begged permission to reproduce the drawing.

Showman's Offer Refused

An amusement promoter wanted to purchase exhibition rights and charge admission to the house. But Mrs. Vice said that if there were anything supernatural to the things it was not for her to make folks pay to see.

The Vices, however, have become the most important persons of their community. Strangers getting off the train learn, before reaching their hotel, about the "ghost map." Every child in town can direct the way to the celebrated cottage. It is the most frequent and most electrifying topic of conversation, the greatest sensation since Ballard Pike came home with a German helmet.

Mrs. Vice is somewhat reticent about publicity.

"Suppose the boys should see our names and pictures in the paper," she says. "What would they think?"

Her "boys" are A.J. Vice, in France, and Robert Vice at Camp Cody.

But Mr. Vice retorts, "Well, Ma, we don't care what the boys say. When a lady reporter comes all the way over from Dallas to get your photograph, I reckon you ought to give it to her. Give her the one on the postal card that's got us both."

Jackson [MI] Citizen Patriot 11 March 1919: p. 14 TEXAS

SPOOK BEES IN A GROVE.

While Their Buzzing Is Heard Plainly No Man Has Ever Seen Them.

Away back in the 50s there was a Shawnee Indian village on the South Canadian River about 85 miles west of South McAlester, but the old village has long since disappeared. On the spot where the young Shawnee buck sung his kiowala [kiowa—love song flute?] to his dusky maiden, and courted his best girl by the light of the moon, only an occasional rock hearth and a few graves are left to indicate the former hunting ground of the red man.

Near the old village site now lives a white man. Just on the border of this man's farm is a spot which seems to have been the thickest settled part of the Shawnee village, and here is a grove of black oak trees. In this grove are two very large post oak trees, one in the south and one in the north end of the grove. In the grove can be heard most any day the buzzing of a swarm of bees so plainly that the noise has fooled many old bee-hunters, but all their search has never revealed a single bee.

Now comes the most peculiar part of this peculiar tale. The large post oak tree standing at the north end of the grove is the curiosity of the bunch, for not long ago a young man, hearing of the bees, went to the spot and proceeded to look carefully up each tree in the grove until he came to the north oak. He was within two feet of this tree looking up when he heard a noise just like a carpenter at work nailing boards, and the noise seemed to come from the tree. He went around it several times trying to locate the hammering, but it still seemed to come from the tree; the hammering continued until he happened to touch the tree with his hand, when it suddenly stopped. The man went away amazed. A day or so after this the man had occasion to again pass that way. He slipped up to the tree and listened for the hammering, and sure enough it was as plain as ever. He touched the tree with the end of his finger and as before the noise stopped. This man and several others have tried touching the tree several times since with the same results. They say that the humming of bees and the curious hammering can be heard any day, but no one has been able to explain the mysteries of this enchanted grove. Galveston News.

Logansport [IN] Pharos 30 August 1898: p. 7 OKLAHOMA

NOTE: This is an unusual tale from the "mystery hum" category, blended with the hammering of the phantom coffin-maker. (See Further Reading in Chapter 2 on tokens of death.)

Reincarnation was not a common subject in the popular press, unless the article was about Theosophy, history, or eastern religions. However, this next odd story is about none of those subjects, making it seem all the more out-of-place.

GIRL'S SPIRIT IN A PARTRIDGE
Bird's Queer Action Excites Awe in All.

New York Journal

The sleepy old town of Strafford, lying far back in the New Hampshire hills, remote from railroads and rarely visited by the stranger from the outside world except in summer time, when the vacationist seeks the tonic of its wind-swept hills, has a sensation in a supposed spirit manifestation of the strangest kind that ever disturbed the peace of superstitious man.

A simple bird, a wood partridge, by its phenomenal actions has led half the people for miles around to believe that it is ruled by the spirit of the dead and the other half to shake their heads in wonder at that which they cannot understand.

The bird appears only in the vicinity of a lonely burying ground, the tiny private cemetery of the family on whose ancestral farm it is located and where a beautiful girl was laid to rest a few months ago. Those of the neighbors who speak their thoughts openly declare that her soul has been transmigrated to the humble body of the bird that she may come back to earth and be near her loved ones.

Vina Garland, the young woman whose sad death is so much talked about to-day, was of a character distinctly apart from that of the ordinary country girl. She was the daughter of Charles Garland, a well-to-do farmer, and though she was physically somewhat frail, she developed a tender beauty that increased as she advanced in years toward womanhood.

But it was her intellectual attainments that made her most remarkable. From the days when a little tot, she followed her father to his work in the fields, she showed a tendency to observation and study that surprised her elders, and when, later on, she took her books to the little country school of her district, she early made such progress, as to set her far ahead of her schoolmates.

At the age when other girls were plodding through the intermediate grades she was teaching, and at the age of 18 she was made an assistant in the staid old Northwood Seminary, of which Professor Loren G. Williams is principal.

Alas, the career that began with such promise was but short. The duties of the position so far beyond her years proved too arduous for the young teacher, and her health, never robust, gradually declined. She was taken ill and was brought back to the old home, never to leave it again in life.

All the countryside turned out to her funeral, and many eyes were wet with tears as they looked for the last time on the sweet face that rested so peacefully in the flower-lined casket. She was buried, as her fathers had been before her for generations, back in the little walled-in yard that lay with its mossy headstones and overhanging trees on the hill above her childhood's home.

Several weeks had passed after the young teacher's death when the mysterious bird made its appearance. Farmer Garland was at work one day plying with his team between the farmhouse and a field that lay a short distance above the cemetery, when he was astonished, as he was passing the spot where his daughter was buried, to see a full-grown partridge suddenly appear in front of his horses.

At first Mr. Garland thought it was a mother bird defending her young and, remembering how fond his lost daughter was of the wild birds that lived about her home he tried to scare it away from its dangerous proximity to the horses' hoofs. But the partridge seemed utterly devoid of fear and when the driver sprang to the ground it stopped with a strangely appealing air, as if waiting for him to come to it. It even allowed him to push it bodily from the path.

Wondering at its strange actions, of which the farmer, in his long experience in woodcraft and in country life, had never heard the like, he mounted his cart and proceeded on to the field. The bird followed along beside his team like a dog, and when he started to return it still kept beside his horses. But when it arrived back near the burying ground it left him as suddenly as it had first appeared.

Mr. Garland returned shortly with a second load and again the bird appeared and accompanied him to the field and back as before. All day it followed him to and fro, and when night came the farmer, who had been impressed to the point of nervousness by the bird's strange actions, went back alone to the spot where it had shown itself.

Instantly it appeared and the farmer, seating himself on the grass, called softly to it. As readily as if it had always known his voice, the bird responded, and walking to his side, hopped to his knee.

On the instant the man felt a strange thrill shoot over him—a peculiar feeling such as he had never known before. It was not a faintness, but it seemed as if some mystical influence was holding him in a spell. He threw out one hand to support himself, and had just strength to raise the other and say "Come."

Unhesitatingly the bird stepped on his hand, and brushing its beak softly on his wrist uttered a low note that sounded to his strained senses like a wail of suffering.

Putting the bird from him with trembling hands the farmer hastily arose and returned to his home.

The strange story soon spread about the neighborhood and created a profound sensation. In this section the partridge is one of the shyest of birds, and a tame partridge was before unheard of. No one would believe the facts until they had seen the partridge for themselves and had seen Mr. Garland fondle it as he would a kitten.

Ever since the day when it first appeared the bird has been a part of the farmer's daily life. He has visited it constantly and has never tired of showing it to visitors. No matter how busy he may be, when a stranger calls and asks about the mysterious bird he will lay everything else aside and lead the viewer to the spot where it is always found.

The presence of strangers never seems to have any effect on the partridge. It regards them with apparent indifference, but with any member of the Garland family it displays an affection that is unmistakable.

The theory of a supernatural agency spread rapidly from the first. While many of the staid country folk were reluctant to admit their own belief, they whispered the suggestion to others, and it needed but a touch of confidence for many to express their downright conviction. It was the more readily accepted because the cemetery on the Garland place had once before been reputed to be haunted.

That Vina Garland's spirit is striving to communicate with the loved ones left behind is believed by many. They say that the young teacher had some message for her parents before she died, but was taken away so quickly that she did not deliver it and is endeavoring through the bird, in some way not understood, to make it known.

Many believe that her spirit actually inhabits the bird and with superstitious fear refuse to touch it or approach it closely.

"It is Vina Garland," they say, "and it brings no good to meddle with the dead."

St. Louis [MO] Republic 7 November 1900: p. 6 NEW HAMPSHIRE

NOTE: The transmigration of souls in rural 1900 New Hampshire? Theosophy, with its Eastern doctrines, had undoubtedly made inroads into public consciousness. However, the Transcendentalists were equally keen on Eastern religion and philosophy. A significant quote from Ralph Waldo Emerson, c. 1870: "It is the secret of the world that all things subsist and do not die, but only retire a little from sight and afterwards return again.... Nothing is dead: men feign themselves dead, and endure mock funerals and mournful obituaries, and there they stand looking out of the window, sound and well, in some new and strange disguise . . ."

Another possibility is that the partridge was young and imprinted on Garland, as newly-hatched goslings do.

A Mysterious Apparition

On the evening of the 25th, ult., a harmless dog was shot by William Richardson, while passing through his premises accompanying some children to a writing school. On Friday night, the 4th inst., the apparition of said mastiff made his appearance at the gate of Mr. R. about 11 o'clock at night. Mr. R. being aroused from his sleep by the voice of howling, mourning, and wailing with ferocious scratching at intervals, sprang from his bed and rushed to the front door, and on opening it his own dog ran into his house and took refuge under the bed. Mr. R. tried in vain to hiss his dog, but could not get him out of the house. He started out himself in the direction, from whence the voice came, put his hands upon the fence in the act of jumping over, which brought him in immediate contact with a large black dog, poised on his hind legs, eyes dilated and mouth open, having every appearance of a ferocious mad dog. Mr. R's bravery suddenly left him; he was then taken with a retrograde movement, bounded into the house, and in a few moments returned to the scene with a loaded gun. He took deliberate aim and fired at the black object, but a few yards from him, when lo and behold! the dog or apparition immediately vanished in the smoke of the gun.

A short time after the above occurrence, Mr. S.M. Frogge, living near Mr. Richardson's, was aroused from his slumbers by a singular noise outside. Running in haste to ascertain the cause he stumbled over this same rabid animal. He gave one prolonged scream, calling on his wife that he had been bitten by a mad dog. A young man boarding with the family was awakened by the screams of Mr. F. and others of the household. On learning the cause of the confusion, he immediately seized several sticks of stove wood, and hurled them in quick succession at the phantom ghost. To increase his fright the object moved not. At this juncture the young man bounded into the house and into bed, leaving the family to take care of themselves.

Soon after this the family of J. Lake was awakened by an incessant scratching at the door. Mr. L. arose and opened the door. What a frightened scene met his gaze. There stood the same dog monster, poised on his hind feet, fore paws elevated, and with mouth open, ready to pounce upon his victim. Mr. L. shrank back with a terrific yell, seized his gun, and discharged the weapon immediately in the face of the ferocious looking object. A terrible shriek rent the air as of someone in terrible agony. Mr. L. shut the door to exclude the terrible noise outside. Shortly after, the wife went to the door and looked out. The apparition had disappeared and everything was quiet.

Early on the following morning Mr. J.R. Frogge went to his barnyard to feed his stock, and, on going to the corn crib, what did he observe but the ghost dog with his head projecting out from the corn crib door as if ready to jump upon his prey. Mr. F. went back to the house and procured an ax, with the determination to exterminate the brute, and had advanced to within a few paces of the dog, to find him perfectly lifeless.

This dog is known to have been dead for the last two weeks. How the poor cur managed to carry his lifeless carcass around and make so many frightful visits is the mystery.

The Freeborn County Standard [Albert Lea, MN] 30 March 1876: p. 1
MINNESOTA

NOTE: Is this a tale of a zombie animal? "Hissing" a dog was to tell him to "shoo." The men's terror of mad dogs was justifiable; at this time there was no treatment for rabies or hydrophobia as it was called. The papers frequently printed stories of the awful deaths of those afflicted; they were true horror stories.

A Coffin on a Roof of a House

Wheeling, March 30. On a prominent street of this city, daily passed by hundreds of persons, there stands a two-story brick building, around which clings an air of mystery which renders it an object of curiosity to the entire neighborhood. The building is an old one, having been erected some forty years ago, and is at present occupied by a German laborer and his family. The roof of their house is an old style peaked one, and upon the side facing the street there may be seen, faintly when the weather is dry, but very distinctly when rain is falling, the outlines of a full-sized coffin, with its foot toward the eve of the roof and its head to the comb or apex. From the opposite sidewalk on sunny, bright days the figure assumes a somewhat reddish tinge, and in heavy storms it stands forth as prominently as though printed in jet black ink upon virgin paper. For many years this unpleasant object has been visible, no one being able to solve the mystery with which it is surrounded. Once the owner of the premises caused the shingles of the roof to be removed and replaced with new ones, in the hope of thus getting rid of the coffin. For a time he seemed to have been successful, but one day, during a heavy rain, a passing pedestrian familiar with the story glanced at the roof, and there, faint yet perfect, was the old coffin. Since that time the impression has gradually become more distinct, until it is now as bright as before.

Newark [OH] Daily Advocate 30 March 1886: p. 1 WEST VIRGINIA

A Ghost in the Form of a Baby

We have something on the summit of the Welsh Mountain, midway between Morgantown and Waynesburg, and about one-fourth a mile from the main road. For the past two weeks the cries of a child could be heard by persons passing along the road, and on a Sunday night as Robert Gorman, residing north of Downingtown, in company with another gentleman and two ladies, were passing the point, the cries became heartrending, and they thought someone was treating a child shamefully. After walking a short distance one of the ladies, a Miss Ellie Parker, who resides near Paoli, stopped suddenly, and told the party to look up at the top of a large tree just in front of them, and there was seen a baby seated in a small basket, swinging back and forth, with but faint cries.

The ladies became frightened at the sight and begged one of the gentlemen to try and get up the tree and bring the child down. The distance up to the first limb was some twenty feet, and the gentlemen found it was impossible to get up. While the conversation was going on as to how the child could be brought down the child gave one scream, and as if by magic the basket fell half the distance to the ground, causing the ladies to scream, and the entire party to be more or less frightened. In less time than it takes to write this the basket and its contents were back to their place again, the child crying all the time.

This movement struck terror into the party. They watched the movement of the basket, and saw the baby plainly for five minutes afterward, and all at once the basket and its contents disappeared. The ladies state that the child was alive, for they saw it move when it fell down toward them.

On Monday evening a party numbering some twenty repaired to the place, and all saw the same thing. Mr. S. J. Peters, residing south of Lancaster City, was one of the party on Monday night, and he says he saw the baby in the basket, saw it move, and saw the falling and the disappearing.

Reading Eagle

Lewistown [PA] Gazette 8 September 1875: p. 1 PENNSYLVANIA

NOTE: I don't really know what to make of this story, which seems to suggest that the apparition was on some kind of visionary tape-loop, replaying the basket's fall over and over. It may possibly be related to those repetitive ghosts who are said to walk on the anniversary of some tragedy, but on a tighter schedule.

Researchers of poltergeist activity such as Nandor Fodor and Dr. William Roll have discussed the psychological component to the chaotic phenomena that accompany a poltergeist infestation. Fodor, in particular, was a great believer in the symbolic content of manifestations. What can we deduce from the following story of a "haunted" Catholic rectory?

"HAUNTED" PRIEST TELLS OF GHOSTS
Father Donohue Explains Why He Fled from His Parish House.
MANY AWFUL SIGHTS.

Brockton, Mass., Aug. 3. Descendants of the witches of Salem town—or perhaps more sportive ghosts—have stirred the town of South Hanover to its depths and driven from the parish house of the Church of the Sacred Heart the Rev. Charles F. Donohue and his household.

Father Donohue, who is one of the best known priests in the archdiocese, and his entire household vouch for the statement that clocks and furniture have been lifted by unseen hands and dashed to pieces in broad daylight and in dead of night. Seeing heavy furniture topple over, hearing an alarm clock thrown heavily and shattering against the wall, and beholding a hat tree move all around the front hall on its own wooden legs proved altogether too much for the nerves of the priest and his household, they explain. Even a squad of men who volunteered to watch the house fled, telling of furniture that fell apart; dishes that danced on a table and pictures that moved on a wall before their eyes.

The manifestations, it is said, began a week ago. Members of a committee that had charge of a picnic to be held by the parish were seated in the upper part of the house, when knockings were heard. Later dishes were heard to fall and break. A close examination failed to reveal any source from which such knocks could have sprung.

Bedclothes are Ripped.

During one of the most terrifying scenes bedclothes were said to have been snatched from their places and ripped before the eyes of Miss Margaret O'Connell, the housekeeper, and James Hoben, a friend of Father Donohue, who had ridiculed the first story and had gone to see for himself.

"I cannot account for it at all," said Father Donohue. "I realize how it sounds, but it is true, nevertheless that I have seen pieces of furniture dashed to the floor and broken with no possible explanation at hand. It is all very mystifying.

"Why, a few nights ago I was compelled to sleep on a cot just outside the room where Miss O'Connell and Mrs. A.E. Hoben and her daughter were sleeping, because they had been terrified by their furniture being dashed about the room in the dead of night.

"My housekeeper was in the sitting room and I was busy in my study when suddenly the dishes in the pantry rattled to the floor. We made an examination, but aside from finding the dishes on the floor, we could see nothing wrong. Then everything was quiet, but suddenly the noises were heard again and this time a table in the kitchen was overturned, the legs were broken and several things in the room were moved as if by invisible hands.

Organ Stool Broken.

"In the front hall was a small cabinet organ, in front of which stood a stool. The organ remained intact, but the stool was broken, the screws loosened and thrown about the room and one of the iron braces bent.

I had placed my alarm clock near the head of my bed, and about 11 o'clock was awakened by strange noises and saw the clock fly across the room and hit the wall. I arose and picked it up, placing it at the head of the bed again. It was unbroken and continued to tick. I was unable to get to sleep again, and in a short time I heard another crash and the clock had gone from the head of the bed, down a flight of stairs leading to the upper story. This time it was smashed to pieces, and the only thing left was the glass front, which was not injured in the slightest. The remainder of the clock was a wreck."

Several parishioners are on guard, but the strange conditions continue, it is asserted. The priest is in a state of nervous breakdown. He is staying temporarily with neighbors.

The house was owned and occupied for many years by Francis Marion Munroe, a well-known character of the town, who died six years ago. Mr. Munroe was a member of no church, inclined to agnosticism.

Fort Wayne [IN] Sentinel 3 August 1912: p. 14 MASSACHUSETTS

Another account adds: "We all went to downstairs rooms to finish the night. The next morning, we found the beds upstairs torn apart and the bed clothes torn and ripped." *Lima [OH] News* 24 July 1912: p. 13

NOTE: Housekeepers for Roman Catholic priests were required by Canon Law to be either elderly or related to the priest, so that there could be no appearance of sexual impropriety. There seem to have been quite a few women either living or visiting at this rectory. Since poltergeist activity is often symbolic, the ripping up of the bedclothes is significant. I wonder, too, at the "state of nervous breakdown" of the unfortunate Father Donohue. Was it triggered by guilt or by terror? Poltergeist activity was not well-understood and might have been thought to be a diabolic attack. There also seems to be a hint that the former, agnostic owner, had come back to wreak havoc.

To finish the chapter and take us into the next chapter on the deadly Women in Black, a story of a ghastly Woman in Black, in a lunatic asylum:

A Spook Among Lunatics.
Kings County Insane Asylum Has a Ghost Draped in Black.

The Kings County Insane Asylum in Flatbush is now the scene of the nightly visits of a ghost, clad in black, and with an annoying habit of swishing suddenly upon unwary attendants in a certain corridor after the usual hours of midnight. The attendants are wrought up over it, and the doctors even say something, they can't tell just what has happened. All agree that a rustling, swishing noise, like that made by trailing skirts, is heard in that corridor at times in the night, and no one has been able to tell what causes it.

The other night one of the nurses, Mrs. Mary Geary, had occasion to go through that corridor. Suddenly she heard that dreadful, unaccountable noise behind her. She was petrified by fear. The next moment the ghost was upon her, whirled as quick as a flash and peered into her face.

Mrs. Geary gave one shriek and fell fainting on the floor. She has not yet recovered from her fright sufficiently to be about her duties. She is positive that she saw the ghost, and as the days go by and she gets calmer she is able to give more intelligent accounts of its appearance. It is very tall and skeleton-like, draped in black, and gives out a sensation of cold. Except for the matter of color, this corresponds very well with the accepted accounts of the appearance of these visitors.

The asylum people became so wrought up over the matter that Dr. O'Hanlon and Mrs. Mollie Clay sat up one night and watched for the ghost. They had a club and revolver with them, and would have made it very warm for any spook. The visitor did not appear that night. The mysterious rustlings, however, continue, and that basement corridor is avoided as much as possible after nightfall.

The New York Times 28 November 1892 NEW YORK

NOTE: The Flatbush Insane Asylum was notorious for its overcrowding and patient abuse, which triggered multiple investigations over the course of the century. Patients were scalded to death and beaten by nurses who also urged patients to beat the weaker inmates. If the Woman in Black was an omen of death, she was in the right place.

12.

Daughters of Darkness
The Women in Black

Shadow, ever at our side!
Veiled spectre, journeying with us stride for stride.

-Victor Hugo-

Every era has its paranormal obsessions and its panics. The 17th century feared witches. The 18th century went in terror of Scratching Fanny, the Cock Lane Ghost. The 19th century brought a wealth of passions and panics: The Hammersmith Ghost, Spring-heeled Jack and Jack the Ripper, the Rochester Rappings, the Phantom Airships, and the kissing bug. The lax, post-Freud world of the 20th century was fascinated by flying saucer flaps, alien abductions, and Satanic Ritual Abuse. Some of these preoccupations were nine-day wonders. Several were the foundation for religions still practiced. Some continue to mystify today.

One of the panics, little remembered, was that of the Women in Black who descended like carrion crows on the eastern coast of the United States beginning in the 1860s. These veiled creatures emerged from the twilight of mourning after the carnage of the Civil War and for several decades, roughly between 1870 and 1910, ghostly female figures in widows' weeds caused panic wherever they appeared. Like the contagious UFO flaps of the 1960s, their dark influence spread quickly from town to town with panics widening like a pool of spilt ink across the country.

As a supernatural entity, the Woman in Black has a long and distinguished history: The *Erinyes*, the avenging Greek goddesses of the netherworld wore the long, black robes of mourners. Black-clad Celtic battle furies and prophetesses were described by the Roman historian Tacitus. Victorian murderesses and the Vamps of the '20s seduced in black satin. Banshees, witches, the Grim Reaper, and black widows: all wear the fabric of darkness.

This chapter cannot be a comprehensive study of the Women in Black—they need a book to do them justice. Articles on these ghosts were quite numerous and space allows the inclusion of only a few representative examples, which, while widely separated geographically, are strikingly similar in their details. You'll find a special focus on the Pennsylvania coal country apparitions.

There are common motifs in the Women in Black panics: the specters almost always appear out of doors. They move noiselessly. They do not speak. They are often described as tall and skeletal. They are usually heavily veiled. They are often believed to be men dressed as women. They flit through alleys and backyards and vanish when cornered. They are too solid to walk through; too insubstantial to catch. They are not quite ghosts, but fall into that twilight place between reality and nightmare, that world where we are pursued, but cannot run.

As we observed in Chapter 9, there is a particular category of road ghost, often female, that is seen always from behind. No matter how much the pursuer (inevitably a single man) runs or lashes his horse, he cannot catch up to the creature and does not see her face. The Women in Black behave much like this archetype: they walk the roads, paths, sidewalks and alleys in the dark and escape inexplicably. Only rarely can their faces be seen, unless, of course, one deliberately raises her veil to reveal some horror beneath, as in this story:

A Weeping Specter

(Houston (Texas) Cor. *Globe-Democrat*)

The community is much exercised over a ghost which has been seen frequently of late in the northern suburbs of our city. It is apparently the spook of an old woman, who walks toward the close of day down Young Avenue weeping audibly, though in a low voice, and wringing her hands. On her first appearance, about ten days ago, she was accosted by Officer John Burklin, who inquired of her if she was in trouble, and, receiving no reply, allowed her to proceed; but on her passing him the next night, still evincing the same distress and disinclination to reply, he endeavored to halt her. Having no idea but that she was some person demented, he put out his hand to touch her on the shoulder, but was instantly nearly paralyzed by a blast of air so icy as to seem to really congeal the blood in his veins. He fell back as if from a blow, and for some minutes was unable to command himself sufficiently to explain the cause of his condition to friends who came to his assistance.

The specter in the meanwhile continued her way down the avenue without once lifting her head, which was closely swathed in a black shawl, well drawn up over it. As nearly as can be seen in the dim light of the evening hour she chooses for her perambulation, the rest of her dress is that of a person in humble circumstances, scant and ill-fitting, while her bent figure and slow, painful gait show her to be advanced in years. She was lain in wait for the following evening, when it was seen that she came from the direction of the Houston and Texas Central machine shops, and reaching Washington Street paused, appearing to glance uncertainly down it, then beginning her low moaning and wringing of the hands, turned off into the avenue and disappeared at its end among the trees growing on Buffalo Bayou. She was accosted repeated by different persons, but made no sign that she heard them, never ceasing her weeping for a moment. The phantom has been seen frequently since, though she will sometimes miss a night, but after thus failing to appear will, the following evening, seem to hurry along, as if trying to make up for lost time.

Speaking of the ghost, George Griffin, who owns a small grocery store on Young's Avenue, says: "I waited for her one evening near the place where she is usually first seen, and, growing impatient, had turned my face toward home, when just in front of me I saw her limping along. Now, I am positive she did not pass me, and the moment before I had glanced down the sidewalk and seen that there was no one in sight, but a child playing some dozen yards ahead; so how that old woman got there, puzzles me, unless she was spun out of thin air. The child saw her, too, and running up, seemed to catch her by the skirt, when I saw it tumbling over, and by the time I reached it, it was lying on the pavement kicking in a fit, with the old woman going on as if she was deaf, dumb and blind. The mother of the child came running and I took after the ghost, catching it just as it got to the corner of Washington Street where it stops every time it walks. I stopped too, when it did so—within four or five feet of it—and, as I am a living man, I saw a skeleton's bony face peeping out of that black thing it wears over its head as it looked down the street. That is, it was a skeleton's face, all except the eyes; they were there, burning like two coals of fire. I can tell you it was an awful sight."

The only explanation that can be found for the ghost's appearing is the fact that about the time it was first seen a quantity of human bones were disinterred near the end of Young's Avenue by the men employed in laying a new curbing, and which were somewhat unthoughtedly [sic] thrown into the bayou.

Cincinnati [OH] Enquirer 18 January 1891: p. 6 TEXAS

NOTE: This weeping Texan ghost may be identified with the Hispanic specter *La Llorona*, the weeping woman, said to be the ghost of a woman who murdered her children.

Just as the Victorians codified the palette of grief: the dead black crepe of first mourning through the lilacs and pearl greys of half-mourning, so was there a gradation of the Women in Black, shading through the ghostly, the ghastly, the mad, the malevolent, and the mischief-maker.

Speculation about the motives of the mysterious Women in Black was rife. When the specters first appeared they were seen as an omen of death, a harbinger of evil, a ghost, or a banshee. Starting in the 1890s, the visitations were subject to various interpretations: madwoman, man in disguise, or burglar in drag. Further into the 20th century, there is a journalistic tendency to explain away all Women in Black sightings as wandering lunatics, stalkers or peepers, retiring widows, or men disguised for criminal purposes, including transvestism. But the Women in Black still remained a mystery, as expressed in this excerpt from a 1912 article:

> The "women in black" are definite, tangible, entities, but who shall solve the mystery of their appearance and behavior, and the uncanny feeling that attaches to their appearance, in the minds of so many men?
>
> Is the "woman in black" somber and unknown, a real harbinger of evil, or is it merely a disordered fancy that plays us so many pranks, that leads us so often to imagine the connection between her presence and our misfortune?"
> *Colorado Springs [CO] Gazette* 7 April 1912: p. 4

Do the participants in such panics truly just "imagine" the connection between "her presence and our misfortune?" For example, an article about a New Orleans Woman in Black was widely circulated at the end of 1877. In the spring of 1878, one of the deadliest Yellow Fever epidemics in New Orleans history broke out, killing nearly 5,000. The apparition was said to have been an omen of the horror to come. The Woman in Black was also linked to mine disasters and other types of epidemics and accidents as we will see below. While the term "banshee" was never used in Women in Black coverage, those who feared her identified her with that wailing harbinger of doom.

Parallels also can be drawn between Women in Black visitations and the Hammersmith Ghost and later 19th-century ghost panics or with the panics surrounding that fearsome entity Spring-heeled Jack and his more lethal namesake Jack the Ripper. The 19th century produced a surprising quantity of other panic-inducing Jacks such as Jack the Ink-Splasher (New York City), Jack the Slasher, Jack the Kisser, and Jack the Hugger, all found across the United States.

The Woman in Black was the female equivalent of a "Jack,"—a Jack in widow's clothing, if you will. However, unlike the Jacks, the Woman in Black was rarely found in a large city like New York or Chicago, but terrorized the populace in small- to medium-sized towns, very often county seats.

ALBIA'S GHOST.
The "Woman in Black" Continues to Haunt That Town.
SHE CANNOT BE CAPTURED,
Although Repeated Efforts Have Been Made by Men and Boys on Several Occasions.

Albia's "Woman in Black"

Albia, Aug. 9. The mystery of the "Woman in Black," who still haunts our quiet little city, is not as yet cleared up. Night after night her ghostly form is seen prowling through the streets and alleys, striking terror to the unfortunate being who falls in her path. All efforts to clear up the mystery or to prove her identity are fruitless. Scores of men and boys are constantly on the alert to capture her but she evades all pursuit. Several say they have fired at her, but without effect. Several children returning home from town a few evenings ago were chased and frightened almost to death. She was seen on the top of a residence in the east part of the city, but disappeared in the twinkling of an eye. She has a special aversion to ladies, chasing them at every opportunity. Excitement runs high, and it is the principal subject of nearly all conversations. Ladies dare not leave their homes after dark for fear of the dreadful monster. There seems to be no explanation as to why it is here or where it came from. Various descriptions of its appearance are to be had, but all agree that it is the form of a woman dressed in black, with a long flowing veil. Some say she is six or seven feet tall, while others claim she is small.

The Cedar Rapids [IA] Evening Gazette 9 August 1892: p. 2 IOWA

NOTE: There was a large dust explosion at the Chicago and Iowa coal mine three miles outside of Albia, at Cedar, 14 February 1893. One man was beheaded; some 20 others were badly burned and others received lesser wounds. It is probable that some in Albia looked back at the previous summer's dark apparition as an omen.

A typical "black ghost" arrived in Alma, Nebraska in 1902.

See it? A black ghost? It haunts the town of Alma. No need of a curfew there? Little boys keep indoors at night and their fathers also have a strangely growing preference for home in the evening. The ghost has singled out no special hours for its assaults. Any time between night and morning will do and the lone man on the street need not be surprised to see suddenly ahead of him the wan figure of a woman clad in garments of the darkest shades, a long veil of mourning flowing down from her pallid features. Noiselessly and without apparent movement she steals along the way. If you run she pursues you. If you charge upon her she retreats, invisibly gaining headway. None has yet succeeded in catching her, but she has terrorized a multitude. It is thought she is some woman who died in great agony; nobody has suggested whom. Incantations that may drive her away are advertised for.

The Courier [Lincoln, NE] 1 March 1902: p. 9 NEBRASKA

The *Courier* article was the first report on the Alma Woman in Black. This article from a Montana newspaper gave much more detail about some local celebrity witnesses and speculated that the apparition was the Centerville ghost found in the chapter on Men in Black.

MAY BE SAME OLD GHOST
A Black-Robed Specter Has Bobbed Up in Nebraska
In the Guise of a Woman
Possible That She is the One That Made Consternation and Fear Run Rampant in Centerville Last Year.

The Centerville black ghost disappeared some months ago and no word has come to Butte regarding it, or he, or she, since. The last time an expedition of brave men went up to the railroad cut to visit the black mystery several shots were fired into the place where its body ought to have been, but no blood marked the trail of vanishing specter, and no blood or bone or rag or hair has been seen since to indicate that the two brave newspaper reporters hit anything but the broad side of the railroad cut.

However, withal, nevertheless, but, a black ghost has made its appearance in Alma, Neb., and perhaps investigation will show to the inquiring public that this ghost is the same one that created so much furor and scare here last year. But the Nebraska ghost is a woman, a little woman garbed in the black robes of night. She has flirted with Congressman Shallenberger, Editor Wetherald of the Alma (Neb.) *Journal*, Frank Grissby, a carriage dealer, and other prominent men, and they have all failed to kiss the hand of the receding, yet unexpectedly present dame.

Black ghosts are unusual, and Butte gave the first real, genuine, portable, all round, good black ghost to the world. Now that it has disappeared and a black ghost has bobbed up in Nebraska, there is a possible chance for the argument that after all Butte's ghost was a woman who had taken unto herself the invisible wings and gone hence to the land of Bryan.

The specter first made its appearance in Alma three weeks ago. Mr. Wetherald was sitting at his office window working in the evening. The air outside was balmy and the window was up a few inches.

Without warning his kerosene lamp was blown out. He looked up and saw standing just outside the tall figure of a woman in black.

With western gallantry he raised the window. Mr. Wetherald kept his eye fixed upon the woman's form, but no sooner had he thrown the window up than she disappeared—melted away.

Suspecting a trick, he said nothing. A few evenings later, just as he stepped out of his office, the woman passed him, evidently in a great hurry. She had not gone more than thirty feet when—whisk! She disappeared in thin air.

Mr. Weatherald confided his experiences to none until a day or two later when he met Congressman Shallenberger, who had made a flying trip home to look after private business. Shallenberger, in the course of the conversation, made some cautious inquiries about a strange woman in black. Then they made mutual confession.

The congressman said he had finished his work at the bank about 10 p.m. and had started home. As he passed the first alley crossing he felt a sudden rush of air.

The next moment a black-garbed figure, that of a woman, heavily veiled, darted out of the alley, passed him with a long, swinging stride, and ten paces ahead of him vanished completely from sight. The street was only dimly lighted, but the vanishing occurred in plain sight of the banker.

Within a week the black ghost, as it is now known, had been seen by a dozen different men and ghost-layers began the task of trapping the specter. It was at first suspected that it was a trick played by his wife upon one of the first men to see the apparition.

The man had been twice married. He promised his first wife on her deathbed that he would not marry again. She told him she would haunt him if he did. He forgot both promise and threat inside of 18 months.

His second venture was not a happy one, and some of the townsfolk thought No. 2 might be trying to get even with him by living up to No. 1's threat. But the woman was absolved from suspicion by convincing evidence within three nights. The ghost was seen by three young men at a time when the woman was known to be within doors at home.

Some of the scoffers have sought to catch the figure, but the most rapid pursuit fails. She vanishes before any one can come within 30 feet of her.

Wiley Shultz, a deacon in the Methodist Church, was one of those who pooh-poohed the stories. Last Thursday night he was pursued by the woman.

The favorite pastime of the ghost seems to be to rush past lone pedestrians, homeward bound at unusual hours, and to vanish after going a dozen paces. The figure is described as unmistakably that of a woman. The face is evidently veiled.

Anaconda [MT] Standard 23 March 1902: p. 9 NEBRASKA

NOTE: See Chapter 5 for the story of the Centerville black ghost, which seemed to be male. The "land of Bryan" refers to William Jennings Bryan, Nebraska's favorite son and Democratic senator. This story also makes the point that "black ghosts are rare." Certainly while the history of ghosts is full of Women in White and Grey Ladies, the Women in Black seem to be a uniquely late Victorian phenomenon.

SHE FADED IN AIR
The Strange Thing Witnessed by Three Prominent Citizens of Tipton

Tipton, Ind., November 20. A few days since, while Johnson Storer, a saloonist, was sitting at his place of business, in conversation with two citizens, the door opened, and glancing toward the door the men saw a woman enter. She was dressed in black and wore a heavy veil. Mr. Storer, thinking the lady had called on a matter of business, arose from his chair and advanced to meet her, but she suddenly faded away, vanishing in the very atmosphere.

At the time of the appearance of the strange apparition the men were talking politics, and their thoughts were entirely foreign to anything supernatural; hence, they are satisfied it was not imagination. They heard the woman's footsteps, saw her haggard face and pale, bony fingers. Neither of the men can explain the strange phenomenon.

Cincinnati [OH] Enquirer 21 November 1891: p. 1 INDIANA

NOTE: This well-witnessed apparition is one of the few Women in Black seen indoors and unveiled.

While most Women in Black simply glided about peaceably, some were more aggressive.

People of an Illinois Town Wrought Up over a Mystery

During the last week citizens of the north and west portions of this city have been considerably excited over the mysterious actions of a woman dressed in black and heavily veiled, who appears upon the streets after dark. Several of our citizens have met this strange individual, who moves quietly about never uttering a sound. Wednesday evening about 9 o'clock one citizen and his wife were on their way home in the West Side. Near the schoolhouse the "woman in black" suddenly confronted them, and, without making the slightest sound, except the rustling of skirts, struck the wife a sharp blow on her cheek.

The lady assailed, almost fainted from the blow, which came so unexpectedly, and before her husband had time to look for the assailant the mysterious person had disappeared.

Friday evening she was seen by three parties in the shadow of the Walker mansion, on North Tenth Street. She appears to be nearly six feet tall. Her gown is solid black, with a heavy veil reaching almost to the bottom of her skirts. Her step is noiseless, and she invariably strikes a blow with her hand as she peers into the face of anyone she meets. She has never been seen to enter or come out of a house and is never seen before 7 o'clock in the evening and not later than 11 o'clock.

Cincinnati [OH] Enquirer 29 December 1898: p. 4 ILLINOIS

WOMAN IN BLACK APPEARED THURSDAY
Romaldo Reyes Says Apparition Grabbed at Him.
Citizens of West Side Have Placed Crosses on Their Doors—
One Man Wards Off Apparition With Picture of Devil

It would require a new system of computation to ascertain exactly how high up in the air the Mexican population of San Antonio ascended Thursday. The Woman In Black was seen Wednesday night and Thursday morning. Notwithstanding the ban placed upon the matter by the Catholic clergy many of the Mexicans employed the sign of the cross as an exorcism against the apparition which set the west side agog Wednesday night. At 403 South Concho Street two uncomical devils were painted on the door. No visit by the Woman In Black was reported at this place and the occupants have assumed that this was as effective as the symbol which was recommended by Don Pedro.

Romaldo Reyes, a Mexican peddler living on South Concho Street says that about 5 o'clock Thursday morning he started out to purchase his stock of vegetables. He was one of the skeptics who the night before had failed to place the sign of the cross upon his door. As he opened his portal he saw the Woman In Black waiting for him, he says. As he stepped out of his door she made a grab for him. He called for his daughter and as the latter came promptly the Woman In Black faded away. The Woman In Black has become very real to some of the residents on the west side and the sign of the cross adorns the majority of the residences on that side of the city.

San Antonio [TX] Express 5 May 1905: p. 5 TEXAS

NOTE: Don Pedro was Don Pedro Jaramillo [d. 1907], a famous *curandero* known as "The Healer of Los Olmos." I have not been able to identify the symbol he recommended, unless it is the cross.

The San Antonio Woman in Black continued her visitations into the next year, where she is called the "Phantasma" and takes on *bruja*-like characteristics.

STARTLED BY WOMAN IN BLACK

San Antonio, Tex., Feb. 1. All the trans-San Pedro section of San Antonio...is in a turmoil of excitement and distress over the second visitation of the "Phantasma." The "Phantasma" is a woman in black. None but the Mexican residents across the San Pedro have seen her; but they have, and they say her existence is real. Most of their houses have crosses in many places, and the gates are almost all adorned with crosses marked rudely in chalk. For the "Phantasma" is a horrible thing to have enter the house. Her coming brings death unless she be placated by presents. Last spring the "Phantasma" visited the Mexican settlement of San Antonio. Notice of her coming reached the town a few days before she arrived. On the appointed date the woman, accompanied by a child, stopped in front of a Mexican home on Laredo Street. There was a cross on the door. She passed to the next house and entered, asking for supper. The request was denied and the next day the sick child in the house died. So confident are the Mexicans who have seen the woman in black that such an apparition has appeared that the city police department has accepted their story as true. But the police are not superstitious, and they are now looking for the woman in black—whom they think is not a phantom at all, but a designing person who works upon the credulity of the ignorant Mexicans.

Evening News [San Jose, CA] 1 February 1906: p. 7 TEXAS

NOTE: The Women in Black are not usually associated with witchcraft so this "Phantasma," who must be placated by the terrified citizens is something of an anomalous anomaly. Is she merely the death omen or actually responsible for the death? Like the weeping ghost from Houston, her victim was a child.

The town notable for being the site of the "Mad Gasser of Mattoon" panic of the mid-1940s, also had a Woman in Black episode.

MATTOON'S WOMAN IN BLACK.
Ghastly Apparition Keeping the People of that Town Home Nights.

Mattoon, Ills., Jan 22. This city possesses a ghost and hundreds of residents refuse to leave their homes after nightfall for fear of encountering the visitor. Three weeks ago a "woman in black" first made her appearance near the Hawthorne School, flitting to different residences, peering into windows and nearly frightening the inmates into hysterics. Chief of Police Lyons and a posse laid in wait for the supposed spirit, and although they say they saw it, it always eluded pursuit and was bullet proof. When organized parties hunted for the ghost in one section of the city it would appear in other sections.

Friday night while the apparition was gliding among the trees near the South Side School a band of men heavily armed rushed upon it. Fifty shots failed to bring it low. Clubs aimed at it cleared empty space. The pursuers solemnly aver that the woman floated through the air and passed through a door into the school building.
Waterloo [IA] Daily Courier 22 January 1901: p. 2 ILLINOIS

NOTE: For a thorough account of the Mattoon Gasser, see *Mysterious America*, Loren Coleman, 2007.

The dark pall of the Women in Black fell particularly heavily on mining communities in Pennsylvania. Life there, as in all "coal patch" towns, was harsh. Miners and their families were essentially owned by the coal companies, tied to dangerous, low-paying jobs and cheated at every turn by corrupt overseers and company stores. If a miner was injured, he got nothing from the coal company and was evicted from his company house if he could not work, as was his widow, if he was killed. The hazards were many: methane and coal dust explosions, fires, runaway coal cars, black lung, and rock falls. There were also clashes between the different ethnic groups of immigrants, financial panics, labor strikes, and riots. Conditions were right, according to our modern social scientists, for an outbreak of "mass hysteria." Judge for yourself from the following accounts if that is a plausible explanation.

This story marked one of the opening salvos of the Pennsylvania Women in Black panics.

THE WOMAN IN BLACK.

For more than a week timid and superstitious people throughout Scranton, Pa., have been kept in a constant state of trepidation by the appearance, in various places and at unseasonable hours, of an uncanny figure that is now quite generally spoken of as "The Woman in Black." The weird visitor first made her appearance in the Pine Brook portion of the city, and was seen by two young women who were on their way home from a Saturday night "hop." At a short distance from their homes, where the street is spanned by the Delaware and Hudson Canal Company's track, the young women were stopped by the woman in black, who said nothing, but assumed a menacing attitude toward them. The girls were terrified and started to run, but the woman in black overtook one of them and hugged her until she almost fainted. The other girl returned with help just in time, and the specter then disappeared like a flash. Since then the woman in black has made her appearance in various parts of the city— mostly in the outskirts and in the early hours of evening. Some of those who have seen her declare that she fired at them, and this having been reported to the police they are keeping a sharp lookout for the nocturnal disturber.

A few evenings ago a workman employed near the Lackawanna Iron and Coal Company's blast furnace ran up to a group of his fellow-workmen and reported to them with bated breath and bulging eyes that he had just seen the woman in black, and that she was at that moment hiding in a lumber pile a short way from the bank of Roaring Brook. Immediately there was a rush in that direction, and although it was rather dark several declared that they saw a female figure dressed in black emerging from the lumber pile and running toward the river. Thinking they would be able to capture it some of the men followed in close pursuit, but when they were near the river bank the woman in black sprang over a precipice and disappeared in the cave of an abandoned mine. Then lamps were procured and some of the men ventured into the cave and made diligent search, but could not find anybody hiding there. While this exciting chase was going on a large crowd of persons assembled on the bridge which crosses Roaring Brook at that point, and the pursuers of the woman in black were urged not to desist until they had hunted down their game.

The girls employed in the silk mill have, it is said, been frequently frightened within the past few days by this twilight visitor, whose queer antics have produced something like a panic in some portions of the city. It is believed by some that the woman in black is a crazy individual at large, who is taking this method of indulging a wild fancy, while the more superstitious are of the opinion that it is a veritable ghost. There are yet others who suppose that the "woman in black" is some evil-minded man who is masquerading in female attire for the purpose of frightening timid persons. Some men whose friends have been frightened by the specter are looking for the woman in black with revolvers, and will not hesitate to shoot in case they see anything like the apparition that has been described to them. A mischievous young man named Farber tried to frighten a few of his friends in an alley in the Hyde Park portion of the city the other night by personating the woman in black, but he was promptly arrested by the police and held to bail for appearance at court. He confessed that it was his first appearance in the character, but he is rather fortunate that the police were first to find him, or he might have been the principal character in a funeral.

The woman in black was seen again on Sunday night near the silk mill by a number of girls, who were chased for some distance by her. Whether the figure be a myth or a reality, it has caused a genuine sensation throughout the city, and there are hundreds of persons who fear to venture out of their homes after dark lest they should meet the woman in black.

Columbus [GA] Daily Enquirer 12 November 1886: p. 5 PENNSYLVANIA

NOTE: A specter who hugged a girl until she almost fainted and then makes a spectacular leap: that is the behavior of a "Jack." This story makes the standard suggestions that the creature is an insane woman or a man. In the mischievous Farber, we see the usual ghost impersonator who is caught and confesses. Yet the confession solved nothing. The attacks continued and spread. As an article from the *New York Times* wrote:

For several weeks past the towns and villages of the Lackawanna and Wyoming Valleys have been terrorized by a myth called the Woman in Black....Its antics at that time were briefly reported in *The Times* as a novelty to demonstrate the effect of a craze, but since then the Woman in Black hallucination has taken possession of the entire region, and every town and hamlet has its own special edition of the uncanny visitor.

To judge by the squibs in the various papers, it was a matter of civic pride for a community to have a Woman in Black. The *Times* goes on to show the far-reaching nature of the sightings.

After doing all the suburbs of Scranton the spectre betook itself to Archbald, a mining town about nine miles north of this city. There it appeared with great regularity for a week or more, and then proceeded to Carbondale, some seven miles further on....[where] the Woman in Black...was credited with having appeared in a dozen places at once. While the hair of such of Carbondale's reputable citizens as are not bald was fairly on end with fear of the sable terror, some enterprising resident of Pittston suddenly saw the Woman in Black on the Depot Bridge. She was going in the direction of West Pittston and her eyes were brighter than the electric lights. The news of her presence soon spread, and a night or two later, she was encountered at the Junction, at Sebastopol, at Cork-lane, Frogtown, and other aristocratic suburbs of the town.... [W]hile the excitement was at its height the apparition suddenly appeared in Wilkesbarre...

The people living on the outskirts of the place were soon thrown into a state of terror from which they have not yet recovered, although the Woman in Black has recently been seen in Kingston, Nanticoke, and Plymouth—across the river. Of late she has not contented herself with simply "appearing," but has assaulted a number of persons, and in some instances has committed robbery. Thus the hallucination which was at first harmless has become serious by affording unscrupulous and criminally disposed persons an opportunity to do their wicked work under the mask of the Woman in Black.

The citizens of the Second Ward of Wilkesbarre have resolved on not letting the thing pass as a hoax. Several girls were frightened in that neighborhood a few evenings ago by the spectre, and their friends have offered a reward of $50 for the arrest of the individual who masqueraded as the Woman in Black on that occasion. A bartender at Nanticoke was set upon the other night by some one personating the terrible female, and who tried to rob him. Various assaults of a similar nature are reported from other parts of the valley, and what was at first merely a source of terror to the superstitious has become a grim reality in several towns....
New York Times 7 January 1887 PENNSYLVANIA

NOTE: In this story we see reports of the use of the Woman in Black persona as cover for robbery, assault, and other criminal activities. It must have been tempting for a criminal to take advantage of the fear the Women in Black aroused.

This next account was reprinted in newspapers far from Pennsylvania and it remains a classic account of the Woman in Black as a death omen.

A BLACK GHOST
The Apparition of a Woman Dressed in Black Has Been Seen in Carbondale, Pa.
People Have Chased the Ghost, But She Disappears Suddenly and Mysteriously.
Superstitious People Regard it as the Harbinger of a Mine Disaster.
A Ghostly Visitor.

Carbondale, Pa., Feb. 11. Superstitious people in this city and neighborhood—and there are many among the large mining population—are greatly disturbed over the appearance in this city of what they call a black ghost. This mysterious apparition has been seen three times within the past fortnight, each time just after midnight, and in different parts of the town. It is in the form of a woman dressed in black from head to foot. A "caller" in the employ of the Erie Railroad Company, whose duty it was to awaken their men who go out on the trains, was the first to see it. The woman in black was standing in the street near the railway depot. The caller approached her and she moved slowly away toward the city. The caller and another railroad man wondering what could have brought a woman alone to that part of the town at such an unusual hour, followed her. She seemed to be moving slowly along the street, but although the men walked as rapidly as they could, and then broke into a run, they could not overtake the figure in black, she keeping a few yards in advance with the same apparent slow movement, and finally suddenly disappearing from sight entirely. A few nights later the woman in black appeared again in another part of the city, led two citizens a similarly weird chase and then disappeared in the same uncanny way. Early on Friday morning she was seen and disappeared under the same mysterious circumstances, near the old Coal Brook Mine entrance. Miners say that a short time before the disastrous cave-in at the Delaware and Hudson Canal Company's old No. 1 mine in this city, fifty years ago, a black ghost, just like the one that is prowling about the town now appeared under the same circumstances three times. Twenty-eight years ago this winter, the same woman in black, or one with the same habits, appeared three times, just as this one has done, and the memorable plague of black fever, which carried away scores of men, women and children in Carbondale and vicinity, followed her appearance. Superstitious people hereabouts are greatly disturbed over the reappearance of this black ghost. *Bismarck [ND] Daily Tribune* 12 February 1892: p. 1 PENNSYLVANIA

NOTE: The "black fever" of 1864 is reported here:

MALIGNANT DISEASE

A very fatal disease, called by some black fever, is prevailing in Luzerne and Wayne Counties.... The disease closely resembles a very malignant type of scarlet fever, and...its ravages are confined almost entirely to children, and...only to those who have not previously had the scarlet fever... The victim is seized with an intense pain in some part of the body—generally the head—and in most cases if not at once relieved, dies in from one to twenty hours. After death the body becomes more or less black, a circumstance which has given rise to the name of the disease....The disease has assumed an alarming aspect in Scranton, and quite a number of deaths have also occurred at Carbondale. [400 deaths out of a population of 6,000. Source: *A Text-book of the Theory and Practice of Medicine, Volume 1*, William Pepper, 1893]
Plain Dealer [Cleveland, OH] 22 January 1864: p. 2

In this Carbondale account, we again find the road ghost whom no one can overtake (see Chapter 9). The cave-in at the Delaware and Hudson Canal Company's No. 1 Mine occurred 12 January 1846. Fourteen men were killed. Additionally, there were a number of dire events in 1892. At the time of this article Plymouth, about 40 miles away, was experiencing a lethal diphtheria epidemic. Cholera was decimating Europe and the Pittsburg papers reported that immigrants who sailed to the United States in the "plague ship" *Missilia* had dispersed to Carbondale and Hazelton, another coal town about 60 miles away, also visited by Women in Black. In addition, a Carbondale mine caught fire, although not the Coal Brook Mine where the Woman in Black disappeared. "Fire has again broken out in the abandoned workings of the No. 2 mine at Carbondale, after several weeks of flooding which it was believed had extinguished the flames. The workings extend under a large surface area between that city and Jermyn, and unless soon suppressed will work incalculable damage to the town of Mayfield, which is built over them." [*The Evening Bulletin* [Maysville, KY] 13 August 1892: p. 1]

Carbondale and the surrounding area was first settled by English, Scottish, and a large number of Welsh immigrants, many of whom worked in the mines. A second wave of immigration brought the Irish. Some of these immigrants imported their beliefs in banshees and *Gwrach-y-Rhibyn*, as the Welsh banshees were called, but the dark robes of the banshee were supplanted by the widow's veil. Widows were hardly a rare sight. Why should a figure in mourning arouse such terror? And why, given a wealth of miners' superstitions, were the Women in Black, those harbingers of death, never actually reported down in the mines?

The tongue-in-cheek answer is that even ghostly women in the workings were bad luck. But I have another, tentative theory. Nineteenth-century fiction and nonfiction alike offer an unrelentingly grim commentary about the misery of the working-class widow. In the coal towns, communities poised on the edge of a precipice of death and poverty, where no one knew if a husband or father would return home that night, the widow was no merry symbol of sexual or financial freedom, but a terrifying reminder of mortality and economic instability. Perhaps this is why the Woman in Black did not appear in the mines, but remained above, in the land of the wives and children, haunting the women who waited there and who mourned.

In a rare variation, the Scranton-area Woman in Black was associated with a Man in Black, who, although seen on the streets, looked like a traditional Knocker, a malevolent mine spirit.

The Factoryville Man in Black

I notice that the ghost story which originated in Scranton ten years ago bids fair to go on forever. In the fall of '86 a yarn was started to the ef-

THE "MAN IN BLACK."

fect that a mysterious woman clad in black garments had been seen near the air shaft of one of the abandoned mines of the iron company. Upon being approached the "woman in black" suddenly disappeared down the shaft. According to reports this awful wraith soon began to evince a disposition to chase persons at nightfall, and though many brave young men endeavored to catch the "woman in black" they never succeeded. The story of the "woman in black" soon spread over the country and in a few weeks the town that could not boast of a sable spectre did not amount to much. The late Adam Motchman, a waggish cigar-maker of upper Lackawanna Avenue, claimed to have been the originator of the

Scranton "woman in black" hoax and used to take great delight in relating the manner in which he fooled the innocent residents in the vicinity of the old rolling mill. Although the Scranton "woman in black" no longer troubles the timid youths and maidens at night, the residents of other towns and cities still seem to have faith in the sable spectres. Factoryville is one of the latest to report a dark wanderer. The Factoryville ghost, however, is a man, and is even more terrible in appearance than the Scranton spectre of ten years ago. It is thought that close inspection would reveal the fact that he is of flesh and blood, but no one dare venture near. As will be seen by the accompanying sketch, the Factoryville mystery is an individual of sinister appearance and a man who should be given a wide berth. From all accounts it is evident that Factoryville is the stamping ground of a most uncanny spirit or else there is need of temperance work in that beautiful little village.

The Scranton [PA] Tribune 16 January 1897: p. 4 PENNSYLVANIA

NOTE: You'll find the Knocker-like Factoryville Man in Black in Chapter 5, with the other Men in Black.

Despite Motchman's "confession," sightings continued. Then a Woman in Black assailant was captured in Scranton, leading to an explanation that explained nothing.

MYSTERIOUS WOMAN CAUGHT
Known as the "Woman in Black" on the West Side.

A woman alleged to be "the woman in black" who has frightened many timid West Side people, has been arrested. She is Mrs. Thomas Kennedy. Her arrest was caused by Mrs. John Riley who had a warrant issued by Alderman Millar on the strength of an affidavit that Mrs. Kennedy had purposely frightened her.

The case will be heard before Alderman Millar this evening. It promises to be interesting. Ten witnesses for Mrs. Riley have been subpoenaed to corroborate her charge.

Mrs. Riley says that "the woman in black" has been terrifying pedestrians, especially women and children, on Merrifield Avenue. The mysterious person's usual plan of action was to step from behind a tree, shrubbery or gate post and, with her head and features concealed in the folds of a black shawl, frighten unsuspecting passersby nearly to death.

Mrs. Riley says the "woman in black" appeared in front of her last Monday night and caused her to fall in a swoon. The black-robed figure was chased by some men and caught and proved to be Mrs. Kennedy, Mrs. Riley alleges.

The Scranton [PA] Tribune 9 September 1898: p. 7 PENNSYLVANIA

NOTE: It is possible that Mrs. Kennedy was behind a localized Woman in Black flap, but reports are too widespread for her to have been behind all of them.

In the 1880s, a fresh wave of immigrants from Eastern and Southern Europe arrived in Pennsylvania. This is reflected in the next story, which is an oddity in the Women in Black canon as it is the only time a Pennsylvania Woman in Black is explicitly called a vampire. This might have been due to the influence of Hungarian miners who brought their vampire traditions with them.

Tyrone's "Woman in Black."

Tyrone is having the "woman in black" scare just now. This lady has a habit of wandering from town to town, frightening inoffensive men, and, it is said, carrying off children who are out at night. Just who she is, is unknown, but she is thought to be a vampire, dead and inhabiting the grave by day, and alive and coming out at night to feast on the blood of men and children. This Tyrone vampire, if such the "woman in black" is, avoids women. An ancient prescription says that the only certain method of preventing the vampire's attack, which is always at the victim's throat, which the vampire pierces during the victim's sleep, and from which the victim's blood is sucked, is to make a wreath of garlic leaves and wear it about the neck.

Vampires live until their hearts are pierced by one that loves them best, wandering about the earth at night, but returning to the grave by day. If a vampire is not killed during the life of those who loved it before it died, humanly speaking, or before it became a vampire, it lives forever and there is but slight chance for the selected victim to escape its attacks. The worst danger of the vampire is that whoever is attacked by one becomes a vampire after death, and seeks to gain possession of those she or he (for they are of both sexes) loved most in life. They travel thousands of miles in a single night, but if they should be caught out of the grave by the rising sun they are harmless, and powerless to enter until night, and if their grave be covered with garlic they can never again enter, and can no longer

do anyone injury, becoming merely inoffensive, shivering and suffering ghosts. *Huntingdon Journal*
Tyrone [PA] Herald 5 March 1903: p. 5 PENNSYLVANIA

NOTE: It is surprising to find only one Woman in Black described as a vampire. While the concept would have been understood by Eastern Europeans and New Englanders, to the general public, the term more usually had the connotation of "homewrecker" or "seducer." A vampire—male or female—lured spouses away from their happy homes. However, much of the information in this article is taken directly from Bram Stoker's *Dracula*, first published in 1897.

The next squib is the first I have seen linking the double panic of a "Jack" and a Woman in Black.

Bellefonte and Mt. Carmel each have a bugbear. The former a "woman in black" and the latter a "Jack the hugger." Both are having a wholesome effect on the young, inasmuch as they are afraid to go out after dark. A person of this sort might effect a great good in Bloomsburg, in the way of eliminating the nocturnal parade element in the girls of tender years, who walk the streets at an hour when they had ought to be at home in bed. *The Columbian* [Bloomsburg, PA] 2 April 1903: p. 5 PENNSYLVANIA

NOTE: Many of the Women in Black (and the "Jack") stories mention the salutary influence of such panics on the youth of the community, who no longer roam the streets. The date of this story may make it suspect, but in a story reported on 14 August 1903 about "street ogres" from Belleville, Illinois, a mysterious Woman in Black and a "Jack the Kisser" are also linked.

Bill Ellis, who has studied Pennsylvania folklore and panics extensively, told of a singular Hazleton apparition.

Strange as it may seem, the woman in black, who has figured so extensively throughout the coal region towns, has now made her appearance in the Third Ward [i.e., in downtown Hazleton], and has already stricken terror to the young men who reside in that ward. She was first encountered by Allen Weir, brother-in-law to Letter Carrier Edward Hughes, on Monday morning about 12:30 o'clock, but the story did not leak out until yesterday.

Weir was on his way home after spending the evening with friends. He was jogging leisurely along Hazle Street and when he reached the corner of Mine Street, he was startled to be confronted by the woman in black.

She commanded him to halt, and the next moment she pointed a revolver at him. By this time beads of sweat were coursing over Weir's body, he believing that his last hour had come.

The woman looked Weir over carefully and after she was through she told him that he might move on, as he was not the one she was looking for. Weir promptly obeyed the command, in fact he was in such a hurry that he took to his heels and was soon out of sight. 14 March 1907 "Hazleton paper" quoted in *Aliens, Ghosts and Cults: Legends We Live,* Bill Ellis (Jackson, MS: University Press of Mississippi, 2001) p. 111. PENNSYLVANIA

Intriguingly, Ellis says "The Hazleton lady in black, though, really is a woman [as opposed to a murderous man in disguise] and a Wilkes-Barre informant remembered one popular explanation: the lady in black was the widow of a miner killed by the terrorist labor group the Molly Maguires. Perpetually in mourning, she devoted her life to looking for her husband's murderers. The man encountered 'was not the one she was looking for'; presumably when she found what looked like the right man, she would revenge her dead husband." [*Ibid.*, p. 111]

Ellis brings us up to date with the Woman in Black by telling of contemporary Polish "Women in Black," who behave like vanishing hitchhikers, but are identified as the Black Virgin and of traditions of a ghostly, faceless nun in a black habit in the Hazleton area, who hitches rides along the Stockton Mountain Road. He quotes a Hazleton couple who said that they encountered a "lady all in black" standing by a lilac bush. The woman glared at the couple with eyes "as big as saucers," like the supernatural Black Dogs of the British Isles. Ellis discusses several possibilities for the Women in Black traditions in this area, including mass hysteria.

There has been much talk by distinguished academics about "mass hysteria" and "memes" and "viral" panics. These theories beg the question: If the power of suggestion leads to mass hysteria, what is the *physical mechanism* that causes people to panic and see similar visions? It has been said that tensions in Puerto Rico over United States statehood brought to life the *Chupacabras*. In a similar vein, did the stresses of life and death in the coal-mining country of Pennsylvania create the Woman in Black panics, which followed the popular "meme" concept, spreading rapidly from village to village?

Yet, why a widow? Why not a giant ghost or a fiery devil? Why not the Grim Reaper or a traditional banshee who wailed when men were to die? There is also the fact that the same entity was reported from many other states. If social pressures can create visions of veiled apparitions or cause people to find dead animals torn apart by what they claim is a blood-drinking monster, then perhaps we ought to study what material mechanism is at work, brought to life by these social pressures.

By the 1920s, the Women in Black had dwindled to a mere shadow of themselves, and then disappeared from American streets, becoming, instead, a staple of stage, screen, fiction, and criminal scandal. Part of this may have had to do with the mourning veil going the way of the horse-drawn buggy. Or perhaps it had to do with better street lighting or wider education, which swept away old-fashioned superstition and credulity.

What was the Woman in Black? A New World banshee? A blackdamp elemental? Simply a hallucination born of fear? Think of the Russians with snow on their boots whom countless people swore that they saw on British soil in 1914. The Soviet submarines "spotted" in Swedish waters during the Cold War era. Phantom Social Workers and Killer Clowns. The images shift with the times, but the fear of the unknown lingers.

The Woman in Black still walks. She is everything we fear: the darkness, poverty, pain, and loss.

She is Death. And she waits, just around some dark corner, for us all.

FURTHER READING: There is a chapter on Ohio's Women in Black in *The Face in the Window: Haunting Ohio Tales,* Chris Woodyard, Kestrel Publications, 2013. You'll also find the story of the Woman in Black panic of Massillon, Ohio in two parts at http://hauntedohiobooks.com/news/the-woman-in-black-death-stalks-plum-street and http://hauntedohiobooks.com/news/the-woman-in-black-of-massillon-ohio-part-2/. For Victorian ghost panics see "Ghost Mobs," Roger Clarke, *Fortean Times* 296, February 2013, pp. 42-45 and "Spurious Spirits," Jacob Middleton, *Fortean Times* 297, March 2013, pp. 32-37.

Bibliography

The Anomalist, http://www.anomalist.com

Dr. Beachcombing's Bizarre History Blog http://www.strangehistory.net

Citro, Joseph A., *Green Mountain Ghosts, Ghouls & Unsolved Mysteries*, Mariner Books, 2012

_____*The Vermont Monster Guide*, UPNE, 2000 (with Stephen R. Bissette)

Clark, Jerome, *Unnatural Phenomena: A Guide to the Bizarre Wonders of North America*, ABC-CLIO, 2005

Coleman, Loren, *Mysterious America*, Pocket Books, 2007

Davies, Owen, *The Haunted: A Social History of Ghosts*, New York: Palgrave Macmillan, 2007

Ellis, Bill, *Aliens, Ghosts and Cults: Legends We Live*, Jackson, MS: University Press of Mississippi, 2001

Evans, Hilary, *Seeing Ghosts: Experiences of the Paranormal*, London: John Murray, 2002

_____*Visions, Apparitions, Alien Visitors: A Comparative Study of the Entity Enigma*, Wellingborough, Northamptonshire: The Aquarian Press, 1984

Fort, Charles, Jim Steinmeyer, intro., *The Book of the Damned: The Collected Works of Charles Fort. Four Complete Volumes: The Book of the Damned, New Lands, Lo!, and Wild Talents*, Tarcher, 2008

Fortean Times http://www.forteantimes.com

LeCouteux, Claude, *The Secret History of Poltergeists and Haunted Houses*, Rochester, VT: Inner Traditions, 2007

Maxwell-Stuart, P.G., *Ghosts: A History of Phantoms, Ghouls & Other Spirits of the Dead*, Stroud, Gloucestershire: Tempus Publishing Ltd., 2006

Woodyard, Chris, *The Face in the Window: Haunting Ohio Tales*, Beavercreek, OH: Kestrel Publications, 2013

_____*The Headless Horror: Strange and Ghostly Ohio Tales*, Beavercreek, OH: Kestrel Publications, 2013

_____*The Victorian Book of Death*, Beavercreek, OH: Kestrel Publications, 2014

_____*When the Banshee Howls: Tales of the Uncanny*, Beavercreek, OH: Kestrel Publications, 2014

General Index

Index by State

NOTE: It is a puzzle to me why there are clusters of stories from Indiana and Pennsylvania. I used a variety of newspapers, but a good story always won out over a less gripping one and I paid very little attention to location until the index was compiled. The Women in Black of the Pennsylvania coal country may have skewed the Pennsylvania statistics, but I cannot account for Indiana.

Find copies of this and other books
by Chris Woodyard at your local bookstore or library.

Also available at Amazon or Barnes & Noble and
personally autographed copies may be purchased at:

www.hauntedohiobooks.com

Please join us on Facebook at
Haunted Ohio by Chris Woodyard
And Twitter @ hauntedohiobook

Chris writes two blogs: www.hauntedohiobooks.com,
which covers international Fortean topics.

And www.mrsdaffodildigresses.wordpress.com, about
costume, history, and ephemera.